THE QUEENS OF
ANIMATION

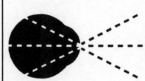

This Large Print Book carries the
Seal of Approval of N.A.V.H.

THE QUEENS OF
ANIMATION

THE UNTOLD STORY OF THE WOMEN WHO TRANSFORMED THE WORLD OF DISNEY AND MADE CINEMATIC HISTORY

NATHALIA HOLT

THORNDIKE PRESS
A part of Gale, a Cengage Company

LIBRARY OF CONGRESS CIP DATA ON FILE.
CATALOGUING IN PUBLICATION FOR THIS BOOK
IS AVAILABLE FROM THE LIBRARY OF CONGRESS

ISBN-13: 978-1-4328-7617-3 (hardcover alk. paper)

Published in 2020 by arrangement with Little, Brown and Company, a division of Hachette Book Group

Printed in Mexico
Print Number: 01   Print Year: 2020

For my happily ever after:
Larkin, Eleanor, and Philippa

CONTENTS

The connections between and among women are the most feared, the most problematic, and the most potentially transforming force on the planet.

— Adrienne Rich, *On Lies, Secrets, and Silence: Selected Prose*

The flower that blooms in adversity is the most rare and beautiful of all.

— *Mulan*

PREFACE

When you are six years old and Cinderella arrives at the ball, you might put on a tutu and a tiara. You might dress up your baby sister in elbow-length satin gloves, their feathered ends frayed from constant use, grab her hands, slippery now that they're encased in the flimsy pink material, and twirl around the room. You won't keep time with the music but instead wade in a childhood bliss seemingly designed for moments such as this one. At least that's what it was like at my house while I was researching this book.

There is a scene in Walt Disney's 1950 animated classic where a long, blue curtain opens, the prince sees Cinderella, and the two begin waltzing under the stars. It is the dance my daughters yearn for, accompanied by a song as familiar as any lullaby, in a film that has become part of the very DNA of their childhood.

11

A passion for *Cinderella* is not something I expected from or even sought out for them. I would never have thought a movie made more than fifty years before my children were born would provide such entertainment. Perhaps this is because I have never been a Disney fanatic. Until I began writing this book, I viewed the Disney princesses, with their fluffy dresses and vulnerable demeanors, warily, suspicious that they had been dropped into my life by unknown misogynistic forces that were bent on turning my daughters into boy-crazy women.

Princesses were mostly absent from my childhood. When I was a kid, my dad and I would walk from our apartment on Eighty-Sixth Street and Broadway in Manhattan to the Thalia Theater, a straight shot all the way up to West Ninety-Fifth Street. Every step of that walk was pure delight to me. My toes felt so light, it was as though they were flying over the pavement. Not so with my dad. As a jazz trombonist he had often worked late the night before and so he would stumble, half awake, my hand dragging him as I urged, "Walk faster, Daddy." The entrance to the theater was shadowed by the buildings surrounding it, with the name Thalia, all lowercase, prominent above its marquee. I knew nothing about Greek muses, and it would be years before a teacher explained to me the lighthearted appeal of Thalia, the goddess of comedy. Yet as the word formed a portion of my own name, it seemed that the theater was a part of me.

The moment you walked in under swelling art moderne arches, you could feel the dark, cool air surround you like a cocoon. We never sat up front in the aging building but instead headed toward the back. Because of the theater's odd dipping floor, a reverse parabolic design, my dad said the view was better there. As the room became dark and the projector hummed its happy working song, I could feel the excitement building in me. In the summers, the Thalia Theater played cartoon marathons, hours of Walter Lantz, Ub Iwerks, Tex Avery, and Chuck Jones, Friz Freleng's Warner Brothers classics, Mickey Mouse and Silly Symphony shorts, and even some silent black-and-white Felix the Cat shorts from the 1920s.

They were all made many decades before I or even my dad was born. Yet I never considered their age, as the humor they contained was timeless. All I knew was that I loved Bugs Bunny, Daffy Duck, Porky Pig, and, especially, my dad, who occasionally would doze off next to me, his chest rising and falling in an easy, slow rhythm as the antics of Wile E. Coyote continued on-screen. I might not have loved princesses when I was little or sung along with Ariel, Belle, or Pocahontas, but cartoons meant the world to me.

My dad and I always stayed for the credits. It was a point of pride for him, a refusal to be rushed and a simple act of acknowledgment to the artists who made the movies. For those early cartoons, the credits were brief, so I happily watched the names scroll down the screen. One point quickly became clear: men, and men alone, made the cartoons I loved. I hunted for feminine-sounding names, but they were completely absent.

Years later, while I was researching one of my books, a woman I interviewed told me about a place she used to work in the 1930s and 1940s. The environment, she said, was electric. The artists there cared little for money or fame. Instead they wanted to create something beautiful, something the world had never seen before. The place she was referring to was the Walt Disney Studios. In her memories of this exciting time, I noted one strange fact — there were many women in her stories.

When historians talk about the early contributions of women at the Walt Disney Studios, they often cite the employees of the Ink and Paint department. This female-led group traced the animators' sketches in ink directly onto sheets of plastic that were destined for the camera lens and then colored them in with bright hues. The position required an inherent artistry, and it wasn't the only role women occupied at the famed studio. Before my interview in 2013, I'd had no idea that women were responsible for so many of the classic Walt Disney films I love or that their influence had been largely forgotten.

I wanted to learn more and so I turned to one of the numerous biographies of Walt Disney that have been written over the years. In my eagerness, I tore through the pages, waiting for the names that I had so recently learned — Bianca, Grace, Sylvia, Retta, and Mary — to show up. They didn't. I turned to another biography in which two of these women's names were briefly mentioned, but their accomplishments were not. Worse, the women were referred to in patronizing terms. A famed artist who worked as an art director at the studio for decades was introduced merely in the

15

context of her husband, as "his wife, Mary." There was no indication of the magnitude of her influence at the studio. I kept hunting for traces of these artists, but despite the multitude of official histories that document the rise of Walt Disney, the contributions of the women he worked with remained unacknowledged. Dejected, I began searching out the women themselves, eager to hear firsthand the experiences that so many biographies had failed to capture.

By 2015, I worried that I had started my search too late. While I had found a few artists who could remember in sparkling detail their lives at the studio, the vast majority of the women I sought had passed away. Had the stories of their experiences and accomplishments died along with them? As I began to pack my notebooks and research materials away, I considered who holds on to our memories after we leave this earth. The answer was suddenly clear: If I wanted answers about these women, I would have to find those they had loved. Tracking down their families and friends was sometimes easier than I expected and sometimes quite challenging, but almost all of those I contacted generously shared with me tender memories, whispered over the phone or in person, along with letters, diaries, love notes, and photographs. The histories I documented represent just a small fraction of the total number of women who worked for the Walt Disney Studios, and yet, because their memories were preserved, I was able to reconstruct their narratives in detail. At last, a story began to take shape, one far more enchanting and yet more heartrending than I had ever expected.

Now when my daughters dance blissfully to the song "So This Is Love," I can tell them how its sweet refrain and the lush imagery on the screen came to be and how many female artists, though left out of the on-screen credits, worked to create the magical scene they adore. The artistry contained within this classic piece of cinema has lived on for decades and will continue to be passed from one generation to the next, but the stories of the women responsible for it, and their profound struggles, are only now revealed.

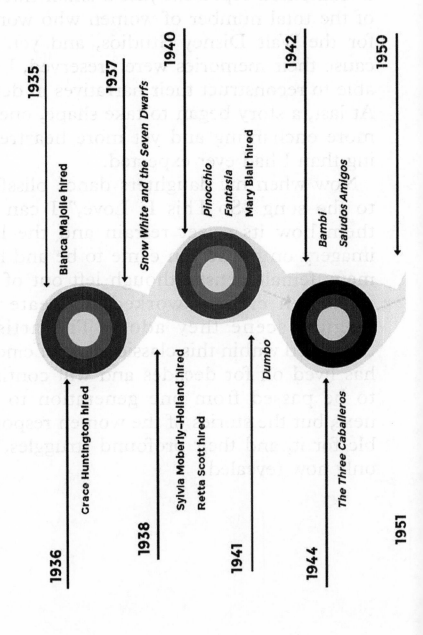

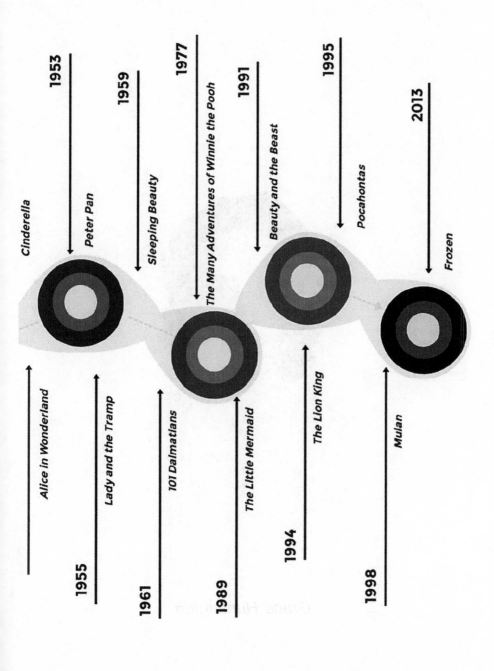

Cinderella — 1953

Peter Pan — 1959

Sleeping Beauty

The Many Adventures of Winnie the Pooh — 1977

Beauty and the Beast — 1991

Pocahontas — 1995

Frozen — 2013

Alice in Wonderland — 1955

Lady and the Tramp

101 Dalmatians — 1961

The Little Mermaid — 1989

The Lion King — 1994

Mulan — 1998

Grace Huntington

Retta Scott

Sylvia Holland

Bianca Majolie

Mary Blair

CHAPTER 1
ONE DAY WHEN
WE WERE YOUNG

When Bianca Majolie stood up at the front of the room, the blood immediately drained from her face, her palms started to sweat, and she could feel her heart pounding. Bianca took a deep breath and opened her mouth to speak, but no sound came out. Her mouth felt dry and gritty, as if her saliva had given up and left to hide in the pit of her stomach. It was January 25, 1937, and Bianca wished she could hide too. She had worked for the Walt Disney Studios for two years and she dreaded nothing more than the story department meetings where the writers pitched their ideas in front of the group. It was not due to a lack of talent on her part. Bianca's characters and lively plots were destined for the silver screen. Nor was it her shy personality. When necessary, her soft-spoken tone gave way to the loud, booming voice of one passionate about her work. The problem stemmed from the fact that she was born a woman in a world that wanted men.

She skipped as many of the meetings as she could, her excuses ranging from mundane claims of illness to fantastic tales of car accidents complete with shattered glass sprinkled across the highway and the smell of burned rubber. Her alibis were mostly unnecessary — there was no obligation to attend a meeting unless you were the one pitching. When it was her turn to share her ideas with the group, she approached the matter as she would swimming in the chilly Pacific Ocean: better to just get it over with, plunge into the waves headfirst, and let the cold water numb your body.

On this January day, however, the room felt colder than the Arctic. Everyone knew that *Snow White* was Walt's darling, and the hapless writer who suggested changes to one of its scenes, even if necessary, was certain to incur the wrath of the room. As Bianca stood there in silence, she could hear lighthearted laughter outside the windows, and for a moment, she imagined she was one of the women on the other side of the glass, relaxing on the lawn without a care in the world. *I could be like them,* she thought. *All I have to do is leave.*

At the Walt Disney Studios, it was not

enough to simply have an idea or even write a script. In the story department, you had to stand up in front of your colleagues and act it out. As much as Bianca hated dramatizing her ideas at the meeting, she loved watching the other writers perform their material. Dick Lundy could mimic the voice of Donald Duck flawlessly as he pretended to walk across the street, then slip and fall right in front of her seat, his body twisting in contortions worthy of the Three Stooges, before he tittered in Minnie Mouse's falsetto: "Oh, Donald, have a nice trip? Tee-hee-hee." The room would roar with laughter, Bianca joining in until tears ran down her face. Sometimes they would don costumes; once, the men applied rouge and lipstick and performed an elaborate cancan, kicking their knobby-kneed legs as high as they could while they belted out tunes. The atmosphere could be boisterous, full of pure joy and childish antics, and it made Bianca proud to be one of them.

But other times it could be terrible. The men would yell obscenities and throw wads of balled-up paper at the presenter when they considered an idea unworthy of development. At these moments, Bianca could feel her colleagues' aggression, the room becoming a pressure cooker for the unlucky person whose only crime was sharing his or her work. Too often, it seemed that the ugliest responses, the ones that could shake the confidence of even the most talented writers, were directed at her. At these moments, Bianca wished she had some special ability to distract her colleagues from her flaws. If only she were a great beauty or could sing or dance or even, more humbly, mimic the happy squeak of Mickey Mouse. Sometimes what she wanted most was to be a man, if only for the few hours a week she spent at story meetings.

Bianca thought about this now as she stood trembling before her peers and resolved to appear confident. With a deep breath, she shoved her natural shyness aside and placed her storyboards — corkboards filled with artwork pinned in sequence — on the wooden easels facing the group. Her sketches showed dancing flowers and animals. Voices of dissent started rising almost immediately and Bianca found herself shouting, trying to get her ideas heard, but her soft voice was drowned out. In the midst of the fray, Walt Disney quietly walked up to the easels and yanked Bianca's sketches from the corkboards, sending pushpins flying. With hardly a word, he ripped the papers in half. The room went silent as the scraps of Bianca's work fell to the floor, a smiling flower peeking out from under one page.

The moment represented Bianca's worst fears realized, and like Snow White scrambling through the forest to escape the huntsman, she instantly fled. She could hear the group of men running after her, the pounding of their feet growing louder as they continued to taunt her. She had never been so thankful to have a private office. She ran into it, turned the lock, then covered her face with her hands and let the tears of embarrassment and shame she had been holding back flow. As she caught her breath she could hear shouts on the other side of the door and then her colleagues' insistent knocking. The voice of one of the men, "Big Roy" Williams, a firebrand with a famously short temper, suddenly rose clearly from the crowd as he yelled, "This won't do!" The rapping seemed suddenly to grow angrier. Bianca cowered in the corner, her heart beating wildly, and her panicky gasps for air becoming high-pitched. She felt helpless. It wasn't enough to have her work rejected by Walt, whom she respected and who was frequently her champion. She knew that the team wanted her to be thoroughly humiliated. Her tears fueled their cruelty.

The wooden door frame began bending now, the plywood and nails no match for the pressure of so many men on the other side. With a loud *craack,* the wood splintered, the door gave way, and a crowd of men tumbled into Bianca's sanctuary. She buried her head in her arms, covering her ears to try to block their shouts, but it was no use. She would have to take it like a man. "This is why we can't use women," Walt said of the incident, "they can't take a little criticism."

Bianca was an awkward seventeen-year-old when she first met Walter Elias Disney. They both attended McKinley High School in Chicago, Illinois. When she saw Walt dressed in the drab fatigues of the American Red Cross ambulance service, she shyly approached and handed him her yearbook. Walt was sixteen but pretending to be seventeen in order to join the war effort; he'd even lied about his birth date on the Red Cross application. He desperately wanted to be like his three older brothers, who would come home on leave looking handsome in their navy uniforms, their sailor caps jauntily tilted on their heads.

(Instead, he would find himself in the last days of World War I driving an ambulance through Europe, occasionally doodling on the vehicle's canvas flaps.) But that day in high school, he scribbled cartoons in Bianca's yearbook, smiled, and walked away. It was a moment that meant little to either of them at the time, being but the briefest of encounters, yet the memory of the interaction would linger, destined to sway both of their futures.

Bianca was born Bianca Maggioli in Rome on September 13, 1900, and immigrated to Chicago with her family in 1914. Her high-school French teacher soon Americanized her name to Blanche Majolie. She never felt like a Blanche, though. It was the name of a stranger, and it was Walt who, two decades later, ultimately insisted she shake it off.

Bianca studied composition, anatomy, and painting at the Chicago Academy of Fine Arts, then moved to New York City to take further classes in drawing and sculpture; after that, she pursued fashion assignments throughout Europe. She lived in Rome and Paris, but the glamorous life of fashion did little to pay the bills, and in 1929, disappointed in her hopes and a little lonely, she moved back to New York City and took a job as an art director and brochure designer

31

for the J. C. Penney catalog.

Bianca found the heat oppressive that first summer as she rode the streetcar lines that cut Manhattan Island into rectangles, as you would slice a sheet cake. With her bobbed hair and shift dresses, she was the epitome of the stylish flapper and she fit in perfectly with her new, fashionable friends at the department store's offices. Yet Bianca, like nearly everyone else, was hardly prepared for where the country was headed.

She was sitting at her desk, sketching women in dropped-waist dresses for Penney's brochure, on October 29, 1929, when she heard a woman shout, "The stock market's collapsed! Everyone's in the street!" Bianca rushed to the window overlooking Sixth Avenue and Fifty-Second Street, but there was nothing out of the ordinary below, merely the usual cars and people out walking at that hour. "No, not here," said one of the women who worked with her. "All the men are at Wall Street, trying to get their money back." Bianca looked around and realized that, sure enough, their workplace was currently composed entirely of women. For the past week, news of the stock market's impending collapse had been on everyone's lips. The tense atmosphere made Bianca nervous, even though she didn't own any stocks herself and couldn't imagine that her family in Chicago would be affected by the events in a city nearly eight hundred miles away. A few days earlier, one of the men she worked with had quieted her nerves by telling her things were sure to improve and that the bankers were optimistic about the market's recovery. Yet even with her incomplete knowledge of the financial system, she could tell, on this day that came to be known as Black Tuesday, that things were different.

In the midst of the largest financial crisis the world had ever seen, a small number of entrepreneurs were able to climb out of the muck and find success. In 1929, one of them was Bianca's former classmate Walt Disney. The year before, the character Mickey Mouse had made a smash hit in an eight-minute cartoon called *Steamboat Willie,* the first Mickey Mouse animated short to synchronize movement with sound. In other hands, accompanying the adventures of a hand-drawn mouse with music and sound effects might have been a clumsy endeavor, neither lifelike nor humorous, but Walt had an innate sense of how to integrate the soundtrack with the story. As Mickey and Minnie made music by cranking the tail of a goat, yanking the tails of nursing piglets, and tapping the teeth of a cow, the synchronized sound brought the scenes to life in a way that audiences had never experienced before.

The cartoon was Thomas Edison's dream realized. In the late 1800s, Edison had imagined integrating the sound of his phonograph with the moving pictures captured by his camera, but the technology eluded him. At the end of his life he would see it finally come to fruition with the advent of the talkies. Yet he was not as impressed with the results as one might expect. "I don't think the talking moving picture will ever be successful in the United States," Edison said to the newspaper *Film Daily* in 1927. "Americans prefer silent drama." While silent pictures still dominated the box office, the world of movies was on the precipice of monumental change.

The transformation began with the microphone. Before microphones made their appearance, at the end of the nineteenth century, the waves created by sound could travel only as far as a person could shout or an instrument could blare. The energy within those sound waves quickly dissipated. By using a magnetic field, the microphone took the energy created by sound and turned it into something more powerful: an electric current. Now that energy, instead of being lost, could be recorded and stored forever. By the 1920s, an innovative technique to store that energy was to record it on film. The electric current created by the microphone was boosted by an amplifier and then run through a light valve. The valve consisted of a thin piece of metal sitting between the lamp of a camera and a strip of film. The electricity caused the valve to vibrate according to the tempo and volume of the original sound, deflecting the light through the opening and thus converting sound into light. The light was then photographed onto the narrow edge of a filmstrip, giving permanence to what was once fleeting. When Walt Disney gave Mickey Mouse his high falsetto voice, speaking into an RCA 77 microphone in a recording studio in New York City, the sound was transformed into wiggly lines on film.

While Walt had no trouble matching his voice to the action of his troublemaking mouse, the sixteen-piece orchestra hired for *Steamboat Willie* couldn't keep up with the pace of the animation. To fix this for Walt, audio engineers developed the click track, a technique to keep the sound and effects timed to the film. Small holes were punched directly into the edge of the film, creating a tiny bouncing ball. The ball bounced to the tempo of the cartoon and served as a metronome that the conductor used to keep the orchestra synchronized with the action. It wasn't easy to make thousands of hand-punched holes, but the perforations ensured that the music and pictures were coupled as closely as possible. The technique became known as Mickey-Mousing.

Using the sound technology on *Steamboat Willie,* developed by a company called Powers Cinephone, took all of Walt's savings and more. To come up with the $4,986.69 it cost, Walt had to mortgage his studio and his home, then sell his car, a 1926 Moon Roadster. The gamble, however, paid off. By the end of 1929, Walt was bringing in five hundred dollars a week and had officially formed Walt Disney Productions Ltd.

Much of the success of Mickey Mouse lay in the character's optimistic message during a time of despair. In a March 10, 1935, article titled "Mickey Mouse Emerges as an Economist" in the *New York Times Magazine,* the writer L. H. Robbins declared, "The fresh cheering is for Mickey the Big Business Man, the world's super-salesman. He finds work for jobless folk. He lifts corporations out of bankruptcy. Wherever he scampers, here or overseas, the sun of prosperity breaks through the clouds."

One late afternoon in February 1934, Bianca walked along Seventh Avenue, the low winter sun illuminating the street so brightly that it made the Manhattan tenements as dark as silhouettes. As fortunate as she had felt over the past five years, especially when she considered how few people had steady paychecks, she was unsatisfied in her career and in her life. She was supposed to meet friends that evening, but she felt a sudden need for solitude. She ducked into a movie house and sat down to watch the newsreels.

When they ended, people moved in and out of their seats as a cartoon started up. Bianca barely noticed what she was watching until she heard the roar of laughter. It struck her that it had been a while since she had heard an audience laugh with such abandon — certainly the news of the day didn't inspire merriment. Then she saw a familiar name on the screen: *A Walt Disney Comic.* She had known about his success, of course, but sitting in the darkened theater, she was filled with awe at what he had created. Admiration and jealousy running together, she felt an urge to bring her own animated character into the world and imagined what it would be like to see her art on the screen, worshipped by millions. She went home and started sketching a comic strip about a young girl named Stella who was constantly on the hunt for a job. Thwarted by the Great Depression, a theme that it seemed no one could escape in either fantasy or reality, Stella found that something always went wrong in her search. Bianca printed the dialogue in speech bubbles, relying heavily on jokes made at Stella's expense. Underlying the humor, Stella's struggles had a theme, echoing Bianca's own need, of finding somewhere to belong in a world gone adrift.

On April 1, 1934, Bianca sent a letter to Walt Disney asking him to visit her in New York, telling him about her comic strip, and joking, "I'm five feet tall and don't bite." Although she doubted he would remember her and was not sure exactly what sort of guidance she expected from him, she couldn't help but count the days before she might hear back. It took ten days for the letter to reach him in Hollywood and three more before he wrote a response. His answer was worth waiting for. It would change the course of her life.

In his playful manner, Walt expressed regret that Bianca didn't bite and then invited her to send him her comic strips so he could assist her.

A correspondence began between them, and Bianca was touched by his warm, generous personality, even when his attempts to help her comic strip did not pan out. On New Year's Day 1935, she made a resolution that she would leave Penney's. She wanted to be an artist again, to rediscover the young, optimistic student she had once been. To spark her creativity, she planned a trip through China, Korea, and Japan, squirreling away her earnings, every dollar representing days of her freedom. By February, though, she had set those plans aside to travel to Los Angeles. She met Walt at one of his favorite spots, the Tam O'Shanter, which sat just outside Hollywood in a Tudor-style building. With its pitched roof, iron chandeliers, and stone fireplace, it looked more like a movie set than a restaurant.

In this atmospheric location, Walt launched into the story of Snow White. He described the wicked queen, the loyal dwarfs, and the handsome prince vividly. The fairy tale was familiar, at least in the blurry way of half-forgotten childhood memories, but his narration was fresh. Walt loved telling the story of Snow White and repeated it often to almost anyone who would listen. Soon, though, he brought the conversation back to what Bianca had traveled across the country for: her art career.

Bianca gingerly placed her portfolio on the table. Neatly organized inside were her sketches and story ideas. In anticipation of Walt's seeing them, she had rearranged them countless times. She needn't have worried — when he cracked open the oversize binder, he was instantly overwhelmed by her talent. Her delicate lines forming softly colored flowers were unlike anything he had seen come out of his studio. She had never studied cartooning and had no desire to be an animator, but her story ideas were remarkable. Although his story artists were all men, he believed so strongly in her skill that he offered her a six-month apprenticeship in the story department.

Bianca hesitated. She hadn't been expecting her life to change so quickly, yet it was what she desperately wanted: to work for her passion, not just for money, and see the result of her hard work reflected in the smiling faces of an audience. She said she'd think about it. The next day was Valentine's Day, and she decided not to wait any longer to give Walt her answer. She wrote to him in a playful manner, referencing an inside joke between them: "You are everything and much more than I visualized, and the really amazing thing is that you haven't changed, in spite of the terrifying eyebrow lift, that succeeds only in arousing my merriment." She accepted his offer and said she would start as soon as possible.

Their letters reveal a mutual respect and a lighthearted friendship but not a romance. In 1925, Walt had married a woman named Lillian Bounds who worked for him in the Ink and Paint department. In her letters, Bianca congratulated him on finding a spouse and laughed at herself for being an old maid at the age of thirty-five. She had no interest in marriage. She wanted the freedom to work, and Walt viewed her independence as an asset.

With no prior experience in entertainment, Bianca had had only a basic understanding of the inner workings of a Hollywood production before she started at Walt Disney Studios. She was surprised when she saw the Ink and Paint department packed with women, roughly a hundred of them hunched over their desks. Most were under the age of twenty-five. After the animators sketched each scene of the movie, every second of film requiring twenty to thirty drawings, the women of Ink and Paint traced their lines using india ink on transparent sheets of cellulose, or cels. After the ink dried, they flipped each delicate sheet over and colored inside the lines, using every paint tint imaginable. In the studio, the Ink and Paint women were focused, but during their breaks, they often sprawled companionably across the grass under the palm trees that stood outside the small complex of one- and two-story buildings. They seemed so young and carefree to Bianca. The story department where she worked had a very different atmosphere. There, she had the distinct feeling that her coworkers were looking for any weakness they could find.

The story department was located in a timeworn L-shaped building on Hyperion Avenue in Hollywood, and the quarters were cramped. Before she received her private office, a mark of seniority, Bianca had been penned in next to Joseph Roy Williams, known as "Big Roy," and Walter Kelly, two men with big personalities who delighted in teasing their new female coworker and passing a football in front of her nose as she tried to concentrate on her sketches. Although the three had similar responsibilities, Bianca was paid far less than her male counterparts. She started at eighteen dollars a week while most of the men around her made seventy-five to eighty-five dollars a week. Some employees earned even more. Art Babbitt, a young animator who joined Disney in 1932, took home a lavish $288 a week.

For a time, Babbitt held drawing sessions in his bachelor pad, hiring women to model nude for the Disney animators to sketch. When Walt found out, he insisted they transfer the extracurricular activity to the studio, initiating what would become an enduring tradition: the Disney life-drawing class. Bianca loved the classes. They were reminiscent of her days at art school in Chicago. As she sketched models in all the glory of their naked forms, she was reminded that at its heart, this business was about putting pencil to paper.

Bianca had arrived at an auspicious moment in the studio's history. In February 1936, after numerous delays, the animators at Disney had finally begun working on the first full-length animated movie: *Snow White.* The movie had burst into their lives at the end of a workday back in February 1934; Walt had stopped all of his most trusted staff members as they left for home, gave them each fifty cents to buy dinner, and told them to hurry back. When the team of artists and animators returned at seven thirty, they found the soundstage dark except for a single spotlight. None of them were quite sure what to expect, so they sat down nervously, speculating about what their boss was up to this time. Walt took the stage and not only told the story of Snow White but also acted it out. His voice became as high-pitched as a child's as he pranced in front of them playing the princess, then turned deep and rumbling as he emulated the witch's evil laugh. At the end of his performance, the audience members were mesmerized. They had seen their future and it would be the story of a young princess.

Walt's performance became legendary at the studios. For decades, the animators present that night would recount how he had captivated them with the tale of Snow White. Bianca had not yet joined the studio on that magical evening, but she too had felt entranced by Walt's tale during their meeting at the Tam O'Shanter, and she got there just as work on the feature had begun in earnest.

Less romantic than the film's origin, however, was the day-to-day work on the movie. The meetings of the story department were long and intense, with every detail of the script being revised and debated. Just a single scene of the proposed film, in which frogs jumped into a pair of shoes and chased Dopey the dwarf, prompted five long meetings over the course of three weeks, only to be cut in the end. Some of the script changes Bianca participated in were large, conceptual shifts, such as Walt's idea of making the woods come alive around Snow White in a terrifying frenzy. The branches transform into hands that grab at the princess as she runs through the forest, while the wind blows her to and fro, giving the unsettling sensation that the natural world has turned against her. Other times, the writers argued over minute details; for instance, going over and over Dopey's precise movements as he runs down a flight of stairs.

As the team worked on *Snow White,* Bianca learned about a brand-new technique called storyboarding. Ted Sears, the head of the story department, had helped invent it. Bianca mostly liked Ted, who had occupied his supervisor position since 1931. He was one of the best gagmen at the studio, perfectly suited to writing jokes and sketching comedy routines, although he couldn't draw to save his life. But with Bianca's respect, there was also fear; Ted could be brutal in his criticism, and she often heard his jeers rise loudly above the crowd at meetings.

Ted's voice reached peak intensity at one particular story meeting in which the staff debated what clothes Snow White should wear. It was just one of twenty-five story meetings the staff held to discuss her dress. These were frequently held in the evenings, around seven o'clock, and on this occasion the room was packed with writers and animators, everyone jumping in with ideas while Walt sat quietly on the side. Animator Myron "Grim" Natwick tacked a few sketches of the princess on the corkboard. Under his pencil, Snow White had grown long, dark eyelashes; she held up her dress to reveal a shapely calf, and her lips formed a deep red pout. From the beginning, Walt had said he envisioned Snow White as an innocent child, so to see her depicted as a sexy, sophisticated woman was jarring. The staffers yelled about her provocative pose until poor Natwick took the sketches down. Eventually they would decide to make one of her outfits a peasant dress, patches visible near the hem, paired with simple brown clogs. By giving her modest clothing and a demure demeanor, they had made Snow White the epitome of wholesomeness.

At Walt Disney Studios, as at other cartoon studios of the era, writers developed the story ideas while working closely with animators creating preliminary sketches. Many writers, like Bianca, found a background in art essential as they made the first rough drafts of the characters and scenes. Once the story began to gain traction, the writers and animators would produce an explosion of sketches to capture all their ideas for the project, the bad along with the good. The sheer amount of paper frustrated Ted; it was impossible to assess the flow of the action when there were so many sketches floating around. Working on the animated short *Three Little Pigs* in 1933, Ted couldn't keep the characters and their developing personalities straight. One of the story men, Webb Smith, grabbed a handful of pushpins and started to tack the scenes and dialogue in order on the wall. When he was finished, they could view the progression of the entire cartoon. This made it far easier to shuffle the scenes and assess what needed to be cut or added. With *Snow White,* storyboards became crucial, as the artists were working with thousands of sketches.

Bianca relished the organization of the storyboards and devoted a great deal of time to rearranging her scenes. For this process, the environment in the story department was intense but collegial, the men spending long hours together. Bianca's presence was like a rainstorm moving in at the end of a hot and sticky summer day, breaking the humidity and leaving the atmosphere clean and cool. While comedy gags and slapstick action often dominated the meetings, Bianca's work was new and fresh, using story lines that reflected the complexity of human relationships with a mix of sensitivity and playfulness.

One of her first projects was a short released in March 1936 called *Elmer Elephant.* In the cartoon, a young elephant is teased and mocked by the other animal children before finally using his trunk to save the day and gain approval. As Bianca wrote the script and rough-sketched the round, cheerful ears and face of Elmer, she considered how difficult it was for her to fit into the masculine environment at the studio. She hoped to find a happy ending like Elmer's, her artistic talents acting as the elephant's trunk had.

While Bianca struggled to fit into the male

world of animation, the studio was discouraging other women from joining her. The standard rejection letter sent by Walt Disney Studios to all women applying made this clear: "Women do not do any of the creative work in connection with preparing the cartoons for the screen, as that task is performed entirely by young men." The letter went on to describe the work available to women in the studio's Ink and Paint department, yet it also warned women not to get their hopes up about even this lesser role, noting, "It would not be advisable to come to Hollywood. . . . There are really few openings in comparison with the number of girls who apply."

Fortunately, one of these letters didn't make its way to 419 Lorraine Boulevard in Los Angeles, a stately white colonial home with a sweeping driveway lined with bowing oak trees. The outside of the home exuded wealth, but the inside revealed the crumbling façade of the family's fortunes. Although the Huntingtons had once been very wealthy, they, like most Americans, had lost their savings in the stock market crash of '29 and were struggling to pay the bills. Mr. and Mrs. Harwood Huntington had three children, Charles, Harriet, and Grace. In 1936, Grace Huntington was twenty-three and had her head in the clouds. Grace loved airplanes and longed to experience the thrill of piloting. She also dreamed of finding a job in which she could apply her passion for writing and drawing, perhaps earning enough money to buy her own plane, or at least pay for flight lessons. Her parents, however, just wanted her to get married.

Grace's days were spent navigating the social scene as her family dictated, but her nights were for writing. Grace would head to the Vista Theater, watch a cartoon and catch an early movie, then stop to drink coffee on the way home. With the vigor of youth, she would stay up writing until seven in the morning, filling notebooks with her stories. Her goal was to get a job at Walt Disney Studios, a mere five miles from her house.

Although she never felt her stories were quite finished, she reached the point where she could go no further with her editing and so decided it was time to submit something. She took her best work and, through a friend, managed to have it read by Ted Sears, the man Bianca both feared and admired. When Grace learned she had a job interview, she felt as light and nimble as Wendy Darling flying over London in one of her favorite books, *Peter and Wendy* by

J. M. Barrie. In her naïveté, Grace figured she would learn immediately whether her dreams of working for Disney would come true, unaware that she was hoping to enter a department that was more akin to a secret society than a business. While Sears could recommend Grace, the story department was Walt's crown jewel and no one could enter unless invited by him personally.

When Grace met with Walt the next week, the minutes seemed to fly by although the interview lasted an hour and a half. They spoke at length about her stories, discussing her different ideas for material. Soon, though, Walt said the words she had been dreading. "You know I don't like to hire a woman in the story department," he began. "In the first place, it takes years to train a good story man. Then if the story man turns out to be a story girl, the chances are ten to one that she will marry and leave the studio high and dry, with all the money that had been spent on her training gone to waste and there will be nothing to show for it."

Grace could only nod as she thought of all the married women she knew. Her mother, her friends, her neighbors — they were all housewives. Not a single one had both a husband and a career. When she realized this, her face flushed with resentment, and she suddenly felt determined to get this job, the first she had ever applied for. As Walt described it, this might be the only chance she would ever have to work.

Walt seemed to recognize her frustration as he explained, the edge gone from his voice, that if a girl could write, perhaps she could work at home after she married so that she could continue to contribute her ideas. For Walt, these words were not an empty promise — he would soon prove that he meant them.

There was still one huge hurdle for Grace to leap. She would be the second woman joining the exclusive club, but that did not mean that the chauvinistic atmosphere of the department would alter. "It's difficult for a woman to fit in this work," Walt told her. "The men will resent you. They swear a lot. That is their relaxation. They have to relax in order to produce good gags and you can't interfere with that relaxation. If you are easily shocked or hurt, it's just going to be too bad."

Walt watched her face carefully as he told her this, waiting for her eyes to pop. This moment was a test, his way of determining her resiliency in a workplace that alternated between creative amusement and obnoxious yelling. What Walt didn't realize was that these words were practically music to Grace's ears. She had spent much of her young life annoyed by the limitations of her gender, wishing that she had been born a man every time she was told that something she wanted to do was not ladylike — or simply too difficult for a woman. Here was Walt Disney himself offering her a chance to dive headfirst into the world of men and leave behind the cultural constraints of womanhood. It seemed the job would be the perfect antidote to her prim upbringing.

When she entered the story department just a week later, she could feel every eye on her. She had never attracted so much attention in her life; the curious and wary gazes of the men made her feel like an alien. She fought back her anxiety. *Let them look,* she thought. She had decided that no matter what happened or what anyone did or said, she was going to hold on to this job. As Bianca traded glances with the new hire across the room, she smiled, wishing she could adequately warn her about what lay ahead. Unfortunately she knew from personal experience that nothing could prepare you for the horror of your first writers' meeting at Walt Disney Studios.

CHAPTER 2
WHISTLE WHILE YOU WORK

Under her desk was a pig. Grace stared unbelievingly at the real live farm animal rooting its dusty pink snout in a heap of crumpled paper, the garbage can beside it overturned. She glanced around the room looking for some explanation for the animal's appearance, but nothing else in the office was amiss. The men of the story department sat at their desks, seemingly oblivious to their barnyard intruder. Grace put her hands on her hips and called out to the room, "Hello? What's going on here? There's a pig at my desk!"

The men turned their heads toward her, their faces bland and expressionless at first, but then the quiet room exploded. All around her, the story men and animators erupted with laughter, clapping madly, as if they were watching the final act of a star-studded performance. Grace looked around, astounded, before smiling and giggling nervously, trying to pretend that she didn't mind being the object of persistent jokes. *This must be what Walt meant when he said that I couldn't be too sensitive,* she thought as she stared into the pig's brown eyes, her smile now frozen in place.

Grace was struggling to fit in at the studios at 2719 Hyperion Avenue in a neighborhood known as Silver Lake, just east of Hollywood. From the outside, the Walt Disney Studios looked homey and un-intimidating. There was a small cluster of white stucco buildings with red-clay roof tiles surrounded by a whitewashed brick wall. At the top of the main building hung a cheerful hand-painted sign: WALT DISNEY STUDIOS, MICKEY MOUSE AND SILLY SYM-PHONY SOUND CARTOONS. A cartoon Mickey Mouse stood at its peak, his hand raised in welcome. Despite the fame of Mickey Mouse, the "mouse studio" con-fused local residents, and quite a few stray cats were tossed over the fence by well-meaning neighbors. The kittens found their new home far more comfortable than Grace did at first. They spent their days napping in the grass and were doted on by the studio staff; even Walt would stoop to stroke them.

The feline population wasn't the only aspect of the studio that was growing. In

1936, the company took out an ad in *Popular Mechanics* that read "Walt Disney Wants Artists" in bold type; this was followed by "Walt Disney, creator of Mickey Mouse and Silly Symphonies, offers exceptional opportunities to trained male artists. Write for particulars, giving age and occupation."

The advertisement itself was not new — the company had put out similar ones over the past few years — but its placement in the prominent magazine brought in a flood of young men, all of them starting work at the same time as Grace. Establishing a career in animation was an arduous slog. The atmosphere was jovial on the surface, but the competition was cutthroat. Animators were hired at a fast pace. They were employed as apprentices and stuffed in a rear building known as the annex, and the new hires knew that the majority of them would last mere months. If they wanted to stay, they had to prove themselves, and quickly. While the ability to steadily churn out drawings was one requirement of the job, artistry in creating the characters was the true necessity. Whether an animator could breathe life into his drawings determined if he would ultimately last at the studio. With this pressure, the atmosphere in the annex turned aggressive, even among those with permanent jobs. Practical jokes became a way to release tension, and the young staff was relentless. The long hours spent together formed a rushed intimacy among them all even as they tortured one another at story meetings. While Walt often held smaller meetings with his writers, large story meetings also took place that were attended by members of both the animation and story departments.

Grace's first story meeting was as painful as Bianca had feared it would be. As Grace approached the soundstage building where the regular meetings were held, a security guard blocked her path.

"Sorry, ma'am, this is a story meeting. Restricted entry."

"I'm a writer here and I'm supposed to attend these meetings," Grace explained, puzzled.

"Women aren't admitted to the story meetings. It's men only," the guard said gruffly, then turned his head from her.

"No, no, you're mistaken. I'm a new hire, and I should be in there." She gestured to the door. "And anyway there's another woman in the story department!"

"Nope, all the women work in Ink and Paint." The guard pointed to the building across the unkempt, weed-filled lot. "No women in here. I'm afraid I can't let you in."

Grace could feel the anger bubbling up as she fought to keep her voice calm. "I'm going in now. The meeting is starting and I need to be a part of it." She stomped by the security guard, who was too stunned by her boldness to restrain her.

Her cheeks flushed from the encounter, she made her way through the double doors and down the aisle. She was early, despite her delayed entry, but inside, fifty men already filled the room. As she searched for a seat, the men began calling and whistling, trying to attract her notice as if she were a shapely woman passing a particularly crass crowd of high-school boys. The whistles rattled her, heightening her insecurities and forming an invisible barrier of exclusion somewhat stronger than the one imposed by the security guard outside. Ignoring their pursed lips and open mouths, she spotted a seat in the middle of an empty row and sat, her muscles tense even as the room continued to fill with more writers and animators. She waited for another woman to come in so she could point out how mistaken the security guard had been. Yet none appeared; all the rows around her became crammed with men, seventy-five staff members ulti-

Grace sometimes felt she needed armor to attend story meetings, as shown in one of her sketches.
(Courtesy Berkeley Brandt)

mately packing in, until every seat in the auditorium appeared to be filled except for two — the ones on either side of Grace.

While Grace sank into the embarrassment of isolation, Bianca reveled in her solitude. She skipped as many story meetings as she could, her attendance becoming infrequent not entirely due to her pride or her fear but simply because she felt her time was better spent elsewhere.

She sometimes retreated to odd places. One day Bianca got a call she had long been anticipating: A new baby was coming into the world. Walt had arranged for the staff at the San Diego Zoo to call Bianca when a pregnant deer went into labor, a process that typically lasted twelve hours or more, and now the time had come. Bianca dropped what she was doing and drove the two and a half hours south. She arrived at the zoo to see a white-tailed deer lying in the grass with a small pair of hooves beginning to emerge from her womb. She immediately got out her sketch pad and pencils and began drawing the doe, tracing the long curve of the animal's neck. Her grip on her pencils faltered, however, when the fawn made its first appearance in the world. Bianca watched, mesmerized, as the doe stood and licked her newborn, its sticky brown coat dappled with white spots as it lay trembling in a heap.

Within ten minutes, the baby was already testing out its new legs, standing up and wobbling uncontrollably before falling down again. Bianca laughed as she watched the animal's persistence. She wasn't expecting to find comedy here, yet it was just the sort she reveled in, the tenderness of the fawn's birth mingling with the silly spectacle of its first steps. She recognized that the sweetness of the situation enhanced its humor. She drew the wobbly legs of the newborn over and over, making copious notes as she observed the first meeting between mother and child. She could feel in her gut that here, in this moment, was a critical scene in their next project, and she wanted to be sure to capture it completely.

Even as the studio's staff labored over *Snow White,* having no idea whether their first foray into feature films would be a huge success or merely a long cartoon few would bother to sit through, Walt was looking to the future. Bianca was at the forefront of that endeavor. The studio was interested in adapting Felix Salten's novel *Bambi: A Life in the Woods,* first published in serialized form in a Viennese newspaper in 1923. While Walt was working on obtaining the rights, which had already been optioned by another filmmaker, Bianca began to explore the possibilities of the story. There was beauty in the book, a description of the woods such as she had never read before, and it made her feel incomparably tranquil — that is, until the humans showed up.

The human ability to destroy what is beautiful and precious was growing in 1936. As Bianca was finding artistic inspiration in

Salten's novel, other copies of it were being thrown into bonfires in Nazi-controlled Germany. The book was banned not only because of the author's Jewish heritage but also for its metaphors about anti-Semitism. At one point in the story, the deer ponder peaceful integration with the human world, asking each other, "Will they ever stop persecuting us?"

Many readers understood the book as an allegory about the Jewish experience of oppression in Europe. The experience of marginalization is repeated throughout the book; even the butterflies of Salten's novel experience a diaspora not unlike that of Jewish communities. Bambi describes the winged creatures as "beautiful losers [who are] always searching farther and farther because all the good places have already been taken."

The book's message of peace made the project dear to Bianca. She had come to the studio seeking purpose in her life, and in many ways the cartoon shorts that were the primary output of Walt Disney Studios were failing to provide it. Sometimes she felt she had little to add to the crass jokes, crude stereotypes, and predictable gags. Her story ideas for the shorts, which she poured hours into developing, were often passed over.

Despite the stinging unhappiness of her work life and her feelings of inadequacy, however, her career at the studios was taking off. Her *Elmer Elephant* Silly Symphony short was proving exceptionally popular in theaters. Walt showed Bianca a report from Kay Kamen, the studio's merchandising executive, saying that the character had "taken hold" and that it would be "a good idea if we could have another *Elmer Elephant* picture."

The elephant who tried to fit in, endured rejection, then found strength in his perceived physical flaws was a surprising success. *Elmer Elephant* was different from the other Silly Symphony shorts. Bianca had infused the story with anguish and longing in a way that had not been attempted by Walt Disney Studios before. The slapstick comedy, though still present, was diminished, and the story department found a lesson for their own work: that sadness transforms comedy, tingeing its edges with emotion and thus delivering fewer laughs but more real humor. Despite the importance of this message, it wasn't at all clear whether Walt would make more shorts like Bianca's.

After an awkward first few months for

Grace, her isolation at the studio was ebbing. She had friends, her confidence was growing, and she found herself able to make significant contributions at story meetings for both the shorts they were developing and the one project that absorbed more energy than any other: *Snow White.*

Perhaps the success of Grace and Bianca encouraged Walt to hire more women. In the summer of 1936, he brought a woman named Dorothy Ann Blank into the story department. Right away people realized she was an unusual hire, unable to sketch or draw, a talent that most of the writers used in shaping their plots. What she lacked in ability in the visual arts, however, she made up for in her adroit prose. Dorothy was a journalist who had worked for *College Humor* and *Redbook* before being hired by a publicist named Hal Horne. Horne published the *Mickey Mouse Magazine,* a children's periodical that had so little success that by 1936, Walt and his brother Roy, feeling pity for the man, let him produce it on a royalty-free basis.

Horne's offices on Fifth Avenue in New York City looked like a hoarder's paradise. Several rooms were filled with boxes of three-by-five-inch index cards; they lined the walls and occupied every inch of available space. These cards were his "gag file," a collection of six million jokes that Horne sometimes rented to comedians or comic-strip artists. The cards were the comedic contents of his skull, although they were not particularly amusing. Along with stale, uninspired one-liners, the files were crammed with jokes organized into categories such as "Dumb Dames" and "Laziness." Perhaps to compensate Horne for his failed enterprise and the loss of much of his personal fortune, over fifty thousand dollars, Walt agreed to purchase the gag file for a substantial sum: twenty thousand dollars. Walt had become accustomed to paying for laughs. In the story department, he regularly handed out five dollars per gag in the hopes of encouraging better comedy than his writers' regular salaries could command.

The collection of white cards made its way from New York to Los Angeles, but it did not travel alone. Accompanying the gag file to its new home was Dorothy Ann Blank, who, although Walt didn't realize it yet, would become far more valuable to the studio than the vast joke collection. The index cards were soon organized by Dorothy and one of the studio's librarians, Lillian Grainger, in a card-catalog format, neatly arranged in pullout drawers and housed in an area that became known as "the room of a million jokes."

Horne's comedy was wooden and artificial, so the story department promptly dismissed the jokes on the index cards, but Dorothy could not be so easily ignored. Women were no longer a complete oddity in the story department, and it was quite clear that Dorothy could hold her own with the writers. She exuded confidence with the effortlessness of a person who knows her worth, and she dived into *Snow White* without hesitation. By the end of 1936 she was exerting significant influence on the scene cards for *Snow White and the Seven Dwarfs,* rewriting the summaries in her own succinct style. Most important, she was writing story treatments, the outlines that shape the script of the entire film.

Dorothy realized that Walt was obsessed with every aspect of *Snow White.* At story meetings he would delve into each scene in detail. Yet he was concealing an issue that threatened all their livelihoods: The studio was completely out of money. Walt and Roy had spent a million dollars on it so far, a substantial sum for a film at the time, and they needed more. Around town, some called the movie "Disney's Folly," believing the big-budget cartoon was destined for failure. Walt hoped that making a feature film would end the financial woes of the studio, and he and Roy quietly met with their banker and desperately tried to convince the man that they were a worthy investment.

Unaware of the troubles of her employer, Dorothy became consumed with whittling away at the scenes, keeping only what was essential. At Walt's direction, she was paring down the script so that not a word was wasted. Dorothy also wrote the title cards, the filmed, printed text that accompanies the scenes. Near the end of the film, as the seasons pass while the seven dwarfs wait for Snow White to awaken from her slumber, Dorothy wrote, "So beautiful, even in death, that the dwarfs could not find it in their hearts to bury her." And as snow falls: "They fashioned a coffin of glass and gold, and kept eternal vigil by her side." Her sentences advanced the story in as few words as possible. It was Walt himself who rewrote the last title card of the film, editing Dorothy's words to read simply, "The Prince, who had searched far and wide, heard of the maiden who slept in the glass coffin."

The fact that Dorothy could not draw made her unusual in the story department.

While most of the artists there sat at their desks sketching with paper and pencil, Dorothy was frequently at her typewriter. The clanging of the carriage return, loud as it was, could barely be heard above the persistent din of the department, which was frequently filled with the animated chatter of the artists as they sketched. Many of the writers couldn't type; Grace could only peck at the machine with two fingers. Dorothy's typewriter did give her the advantage of space, however. Most writers did not have the luxury of an office and so worked crammed together, their elbows occasionally bumping as they drew mouse ears or princess dresses. Dorothy and her typewriter had a prime corner location, and from this vantage point she could survey the room, her eyes meandering across the faces of her colleagues as she searched the air for ideas.

Dorothy noticed that one of the story men was often looking back at her. Joe Grant had been working for Walt for three years. Originally hired as a caricaturist, he had made his way into the story department not so much because of his gift for words but because of his art, from which emerged complex plots and refined dialogue. Yet it now seemed that Joe had become obsessed with Dorothy's image. She frequently saw him sketching her from a perch nearby, periodically staring at her before returning to the page.

Most new hires would have shied from his gaze, afraid to disturb the dynamics of the story department and possibly become the target of pranks, but Dorothy was rarely afraid of anyone. "What are you doing?" she asked him bluntly when she noticed him watching her.

"You are an inspiration," Joe replied with a smile, but Dorothy was not so easily mollified.

"But why are you sketching me?" she demanded.

"I'm modeling your face for one of our characters in *Snow White.*"

"Which one?"

"The evil queen," Joe replied curtly.

Dorothy burst out laughing — his answer had been so unexpected — and soon Joe was laughing too. At last Dorothy said, "At least I'm not the old hag!"

Thanks to Joe, it was not merely Dorothy's words that would find a permanent home in the film but her face as well: her arched eyebrows, her almond-shaped eyes, and her long, straight nose were all reflected in the face of the beautiful but vain and wicked stepmother.

In their own department, the animators frequently propped up mirrors on their desks so that they could capture their facial expressions and infuse realism into their animation. They would take their rough sketches, hand them over to be photographed, then bring the film to a Moviola, an early device used by film editors to view individual shots and check whether the movements they had created were true to life. Meanwhile, the story department went over the plot for *Snow White* again and again, mercilessly cutting scenes in order to bring the story into crisp focus and working with the composers to weave the musical score into the story. Yet no matter what they did, the art the animators created was flat. There was no dimension, no depth.

In the mid-1930s, most animation was produced by hand-drawing the characters on cels and then placing the cels, one panel at a time, on top of a painted background. The animation camera would take a picture of the combined artwork from above, each shot but one frame of the movie. With every frame, the background shifted ever so slightly backward, so that when viewing the sequence on film, the observer got the impression of forward movement. Compared to the walking, talking characters, however, the background offered little variety. It was typically painted onto a long roll of paper that was dragged behind the characters. There was no sense of perspective and little detail. If the camera zoomed in, the images would become severely distorted, making the scene even less realistic. It was an undeniable problem for the studio.

The solution lay in a trick taken from live theater: adapt the set to let the characters move through the scenery, not merely on top of it. Just as cutouts and objects are placed at different points up- and downstage from the actors, the animators needed to create depth between the elements of their backgrounds. In early 1937, this became possible thanks to a relatively new invention in the art of animation: the multiplane camera. The camera stood just over eleven feet tall and incorporated horizontal beams over long metal cradles designed to hold massive glass frames.

Instead of photographing a flat two-dimensional background, the multiplane camera separated each element of the scene: the foreground, the middle ground, and the background. Each part of the backdrop was painted on a long pane of glass and then placed in a cradle that moved independently of the others, up and down and from side to side. At the very top, positioned to look down through the panes of glass, were the eyes of the structure: a Victor 16 mm movie camera. Some of the pieces of glass were hand-painted in oils; the immovable glass closest to the floor was often tinted the color of the sky. Those panes closest to the camera were kept clear so that cels with the artists' animation could be gently laid on top. With the camera shooting from above, the con-traption gave depth and realism to the scene, transforming the flat panes of painted glass and plastic into a three-dimensional world.

Bill Garity and a team of engineers were testing the limits of this new technology in the studio's motion picture laboratory, improving on the design as he tweaked the camera's motion and timing. As innovative as the equipment was, though, it was hardly the first of its kind.

Charlotte "Lotte" Reiniger, a German filmmaker, is widely recognized for develop-ing the first multiplane camera for her 1926 animated feature *The Adventures of Prince Achmed*. Reiniger's features were filmed in silhouette. To create her characters, she would deftly cut out of black cardboard the shapes of people, flowers, animals, and fairies. She placed the silhouettes, exquisite in their detail, onto vertical planes of glass hung in front of the movie camera. The resulting scenes were so rich that her fairytale films drew viewers deep into misty forests, took them on a flight through the clouds on a magical horse, and plunged them beneath the surface of a meadow pond.

Reiniger's innovations were finding fresh application in California. Even before Walt began testing the multiplane camera, his competitor and sometime friend Ub Iwerks was building his own. Iwerks and Walt had met in Kansas City, Missouri, in 1919, where Ub animated Mickey Mouse and Silly Symphony shorts and played a critical role in shaping Walt's characters. By 1930, he'd left Walt to start his own studio, and by 1933, he had built a multiplane camera from an old Chevrolet chassis. Its structure was horizontal, unlike Reiniger's vertical mechanism, but otherwise operated similarly. Yet despite his prowess at bringing depth into his cartoon shorts, Iwerks couldn't match the success of Mickey Mouse, and his studio closed its doors in 1936.

Walt saw the potential of the multiplane camera to bring realism to *Snow White*. But before Walt Disney Studios could use the system for a feature film, they had to assess the technique. Their testing ground was an animated short titled *The Old Mill*. Released in 1937, the cartoon had neither a defined plot nor any central characters, but it was a veritable workshop for the many improvements Walt wanted to bring to *Snow White*. In addition to their first use of the multiplane camera, the team toyed with complex lighting and water effects, realistic portrayal of animals, and heightened mood and suspense. The outcome was stunning. The cartoon would go on to win two Academy Awards, one for best short and one for technical achievement. The company filed a patent for the multiplane technology and set to work filming *Snow White* with the nimble new machinery.

By the winter of 1937, the pressure on Walt Disney Studios was mounting and its precarious financial situation threatening the livelihood of every employee. The cost of *Snow White* had vastly exceeded expectations. The studio had spent $1.48 million on the film, the equivalent of more than $25 million today, and its future depended on whether audiences would want to sit through an hour-and-a-half-long cartoon.

By December, Bianca and the entire studio staff were nervously anticipating the premiere night. The glamour of the movie's release was completely new to them — shorts never received half as much attention — and the staff fretted over how the press and public would react to the film.

On Tuesday, December 21, all their lives shifted dramatically. The animators and story artists were bunched around desks and standing in groups in hallways, excitedly discussing what might happen that evening. A few hundred of them would be attending the event, having purchased tickets early. Few of the one hundred and fifty women of the Ink and Paint department were going, despite the long hours they had labored to bring about the historic film, including creating fifteen hundred custom color shades for it. They had lovingly hand-tinted the cheeks and lips of the princess with more care than they gave to the makeup on their own faces.

But not all the women of Walt Disney Studios were excluded from the night. Besides Walt's wife, Lillian, a former Ink and Paint girl, there was her sister Hazel Sewell, now the head of the department.

Hazel had a skilled eye; she'd carefully chosen the color palette for *Snow White* and served as art director for the film. Grace was also fortunate enough to have a ticket, and her stomach fluttered in anticipation of the event.

That evening, the lucky employees arrived at the Carthay Circle Theater, a movie palace whose whitewashed walls gleamed under the arc lights brought out for special occasions. Above them was a high bell tower trimmed in blue and a neon sign that could be seen for miles. The crowd was completely overwhelming; the street swamped with thirty thousand fans. The mass of people had no hope of being able to squeeze into the fifteen-hundred-seat theater, so they formed a canyon of sorts, sitting in tiered stands along the red carpet for the mere pleasure of being part of the occasion. Advance ticket sales had outpaced any other event held at Carthay Circle, and those who couldn't get in preferred to crowd onto the streets rather than stay home.

The streets themselves were worth seeing. Walt had transformed a block of Los Angeles concrete into pure make-believe. There was a replica dwarf village nearby, its cottages complete with shuttered windows, a churning waterwheel, and flower-lined paths.

Movie stars began trickling into the theater. Marlene Dietrich and Douglas Fairbanks Jr. smiled, waved to the crowd, and posed for photographers in the bright lights. A nine-year-old Shirley Temple arrived with a dwarf character on each arm and five more behind, her height level with the costumed men as they made their way up the red carpet. A lumpy Donald Duck waved to cameras while Mickey and Minnie Mouse delighted the crowd as they hugged and kissed, their pointy noses bumping awkwardly.

The artists and writers from the studio were eagerly anticipating the film, whose every scene, made possible by one million of their own hand drawings, they knew by heart. The movie began, and following the title, a message flashed on the screen. It was a personal thank-you from their boss: "My sincere appreciation to the members of my staff whose loyalty and creative endeavor made possible this production." Below these grateful words was Walt Disney's signature. It was a compensation of sorts for the next few frames, the opening credits for the movie.

Only sixty-seven studio employees were

listed, despite the fact that hundreds had worked on the film. A lack of on-screen credit would become a painful source of discontent in the years ahead as the staff began demanding acknowledgment of their efforts. Among the many women who had worked on *Snow White,* only Hazel Sewell and Dorothy Ann Blank were named. Hazel was credited as an art director while Dorothy was the only woman from the story department acknowledged.

But resentments evaporated as the movie played, especially during the final scene, when the prince leads Snow White up a hillside, a hazy castle becoming progressively more visible through the clouds and against a pink and gold sunset. Grace glanced around the theater, eager for the crowd's reaction. Even in the gloom of the cinema, with only the projector's indirect light illuminating their faces, she could see the glistening, wet cheeks of the audience members. She had never seen, never even heard of, anyone crying over a cartoon before, but here was a whole theater of people hastily dabbing at their eyes before giving the film a standing ovation.

CHAPTER 3
WHEN YOU WISH UPON A STAR

When the studio became overwhelming for Bianca, as it had a tendency to do, her favorite place of refuge was the Los Angeles Public Library. It stuck out like a sore thumb among the department stores, hotels, and banks that lined Fifth Street in downtown Los Angeles. The urban landscape reflected the city's rapid growth over the past three decades. Thanks to the region's sunny, moderate climate, ideal for year-round shooting, moviemakers had begun flocking to Southern California in the early 1900s. At the same time, a metal forest of oil derricks started spreading across the Los Angeles Basin.

The first boom occurred in 1893 when prospectors struck oil in the area that is now home to Dodgers Stadium. By 1923, the region was producing one-quarter of the world's crude oil. The influx of new industry meant that the city was growing at a frenzied pace. Its population doubled between 1920 and 1930, rising to more than a million and making Los Angeles the fifth-largest metropolis in the United States. The swift growth was reflected in the skyline, its architecture a hastily erected mix of art deco office buildings and the low-pitched red tile roofs of Spanish colonial revival homes.

Bianca skirted the edges of multiple construction sites downtown early one morning. Around her, a mass of pedestrians was getting off the city's streetcars, a system made up of Los Angeles Railway's Yellow Cars and Pacific Electric Railway's Red Cars. It was the largest transit operation in the country, busier even than that of New York City, and choked the avenues by midmorning. Bianca was headed to the library, a rare patch of green within the growing city. A path of trimmed arborvitae and three long reflecting pools led her to the white stone steps of its grand entrance.

There was no mistaking the library for any other building in town. Its construction in 1926 marked a period of Egyptian frenzy in the United States. Just four years earlier, an excavation team had uncovered King Tut's tomb in Egypt's Valley of the Kings, on the west bank of the Nile. The discovery of the mummy of young pharaoh Tutankhamen, along with his earthly treasures, was the archaeological triumph of the twentieth century.

The Western world was soon swept up in "Tut-mania," a craze influencing art, fashion, film, jewelry, and even architecture. The Los Angeles Central Library was modeled after ancient Egyptian temples, and atop its tower rose a vibrant golden pyramid adorned with tile mosaics that could best be seen from the sky. Above the west-facing entrance, Latin words were inscribed on the stone façade: *Et quasi cursores vitai lampada tradunt,* meaning, "Like runners, they hand on the torch of life." At the pyramid's peak, covered in a shiny gold alloy, was the embodiment of these words: a hand grasping a fiery torch stretched to the heavens.

Bianca passed under these words on her way into the library, which had become in many ways her temple. It was everything the studio wasn't: quiet, respectful, and filled with women. She brushed her hand against the black marble sphinxes at the top of the staircase before heading into the stacks. Although it might seem she was merely avoiding work, she had a reason to be here. Walt had just announced that *Pinocchio,* not *Bambi,* would be their next feature film.

Although Walt had finally gotten his hands on the rights to *Bambi* a few months earlier, he had been disappointed in the animators' early sketches for it. He described the deer as "flour bags," animals without shape or dimension. Walt wanted to move away from a cartoonish look and mirror the environmentalist message of the story with a more realistic style. It was clear that the project needed more time in development.

Bianca immersed herself in the project of adapting *Pinocchio.* She sat between rows of books or sometimes found a quiet desk in the children's literature section and wrote story treatments. The studio on Hyperion Avenue boasted its own library, of course, the shelves primarily filled with the work of illustrators; many of its volumes Walt had personally selected and brought back to the United States from family holidays in Europe. Given that the team was focused on European fairy tales, perhaps it was no surprise that the artists drew inspiration from the work of Richard Doyle, Gaspard Dughet, Paul Ranson, and J. J. Grandville, among others. The staff would perch the ornately bound books precariously on corners of their old, scarred desks and emulate in their sketches the drawings they found inside. Yet among the hundreds of prized books, there were relatively few works of fiction, and so when Bianca wanted new source material for her story ideas, she was only too happy to leave the studio and head to her favorite building downtown.

Browsing through the library's novels, she had found nothing to rival the book she already had, Walt's personal copy of *Le Avventure di Pinocchio: La Storia di un Burattino,* by Carlo Collodi. First printed as a serial in an Italian newspaper and then published in its entirety in 1883, the book found immense popularity among readers in English-speaking countries as *The Adventures of Pinocchio.*

After multiple readings, Bianca knew the story — the tale of the pitiable wood-carver and his mischievous marionette — intimately. Walt had been tentatively considering it for over a year, but although he owned several English translations of the book, he turned to Bianca for a fresh take on it. He appreciated that she was the only member of the story department capable of reading it in its original Italian and then assessing its potential as a feature film. The library was a quiet place to read and work, and Bianca was soon lost in the text, her pencil flying across her notebook as she translated bits of dialogue from her native tongue.

As she delved deeper into the novel, however, she began to have reservations about its adaptability. The character of Pinocchio is, in many ways, unsympathetic. He is inherently cruel and frequently selfish, kicking the wood-carver Geppetto the very moment his creator carves his feet. In the original serialized version, Cat and Fox hang Pinocchio for his crimes and disobedience, thus ending the children's story with his vivid death: "His breath failed him and he could say no more. He shut his eyes, opened his mouth, stretched his legs, gave a long shudder, and hung stiff and insensible."

After this first serial ran, Carlo Lorenzini, who wrote under the pen name Carlo Collodi, was ready to move on from the puppet's story, but his editor Guido Biagi did not want him to. The series was immensely popular, and Biagi pleaded for its continuation. He suggested resurrecting the insolent puppet and giving him a path to redemption that would occur over twenty more installments, culminating in a fairy with turquoise hair transforming the remorseful wooden child into a real boy. Six months later, after requests from not only his editor but also readers, Lorenzini agreed to continue the serial, eventually ending his story with the line: "How glad I am that I have become a well-behaved little boy!"

Bianca loved the tale. There was something powerful and unexpected about this wooden puppet's desire for life. But although she could clearly see the possibilities, there was something missing from the plot. In those final twenty chapters, Pinocchio dreams of becoming a real boy at last, but his motivation isn't explained. As the sixteen original chapters of the story make clear, Pinocchio can do nearly everything a real boy can. He can eat, run, sing, and cause mischief like any child. In fact, Bianca realized as she made her notes for Walt, unless they animated the wood joints and strings clearly, there would be no way for an audience to distinguish Pinocchio from any other child on-screen.

So if the puppet can do all these things, Bianca wondered, *why does he want to be a boy?* They needed to give the puppet a reason to want life, a spark that would make the troublesome character sympathetic and give the story greater meaning. Bianca made a list of possibilities. It could be for love, the longing to grow up and kiss the girl of his dreams, or it could be so that he could one day become a man and not be condemned to remain a small child all the days of his existence. In her quiet sanctuary,

Bianca contemplated all the reasons one might choose to be alive.

Strange devices were taking over the film industry in the 1930s. New camera and projection motors were able to sync their shutter speeds, making possible a rear projection system that allowed inventive backgrounds to be placed behind actors. A couple could sit in a car going nowhere as the background raced behind or beside them, giving the illusion of movement. For the first time, movie studios had special effects departments that created miniature ships to fight pirate battles on the seas of a soundstage, yanked doors open with wires as if by magic, and built trick floors that made disembodied footprints appear in the snow.

Although Metro-Goldwyn-Mayer had been the last major studio to convert to sound, by the late 1930s it was leading in special effects. In 1938 Arnold Gillespie, MGM's special effects coordinator, was working on an upcoming film called *The Wizard of Oz.* He threw away the studio's lifeless rubber tornado, which looked more like a gaudy orange traffic cone than a devastating storm, and began observing the undulating wind socks that were used to determine wind speed and direction at the airport. He had never seen a tornado in his life, had never even set foot in the state of Kansas, yet he recognized something familiar in the way the sock filled with wind. It moved as if it were alive. Inspired, he took a thirty-five-foot-long muslin sock, surrounded it with fans placed at just the right angles, and proceeded to blow dust across the MGM soundstage. The tornado that he created would shock audiences when they finally saw it on-screen in 1939. Moviegoers turned to each other as they exited theaters across the country and asked in excited voices, *How did they do that?*

Walt was asking a similar question. While every live-action movie studio was clamoring for realistic special effects, he wondered how to bring realism into the world of animation. Not to be outdone by the live-action studios, he appointed an effects supervisor for *Pinocchio,* Robert Martsch. Walt's goal was to bring new techniques to the film, to create a groundswell of artistic achievement that would separate cartoon from animation and make their scenes as lifelike as a terrifying tornado fabricated from a long, dusty sock.

The zeal for visual effects was reaching into

every department of the studio. In the all-female Ink and Paint department, the women were developing "the blend." A woman in the department named Mary Louise Weiser had originated the technique using a pencil of her own invention that she nicknamed a "grease pencil." Standard pencils could only feebly scratch the glossy, nonporous surface of the cels. Weiser's pencil had a waxy exterior that the women could rub across the borders of their colors to soften their lines and create shading and depth; for example, it could tint the cheeks of a character with a diffuse, natural blush. Weiser filed a patent for the grease pencil in 1939, and eventually, its utility would reach far beyond the studio. It became an essential component of military defense and aircraft control centers in the 1950s, used to mark the locations of aircraft, weapons, and fuel on panels of glass.

In their separate workspace at the studio, the women of Ink and Paint experimented with other techniques, dabbing their cels with sponges and then rubbing the grease pencils sparingly across the surface, giving the characters' faces a youthful roundness; Pinocchio's body got a drop or two of lacquer to give it the look of real, polished pine. The women also wiped stiff, dry brushes across the cels' plastic to give texture to Figaro the cat's fur while adding vivid new colors never before seen on-screen to their palette.

While the group received little formal acknowledgment for their contributions, there was undeniable camaraderie in Ink and Paint. It was enough to make the other women of the studio occasionally wistful at their more isolated experiences, particularly Bianca, who was reminded of her own thwarted efforts in the story department.

Bianca yearned to bring emotional depth to the script for *Pinocchio* and she fretted over the puppet's character, which, despite her best efforts, remained mischievous and, she worried, unlikable. The story team seemed more concerned with creating gags for him, crafting a brash personality that echoed the original Collodi story but did not fit Bianca's vision for the film. Other characters who could balance the harsh quality of Pinocchio's nature, such as Jiminy Cricket, had not yet been substantially developed.

Other constraints weighed on Bianca. Proud of the success of her *Elmer Elephant* short, she began writing additional scripts for the character. She was encouraged by both the short's popularity and the opinion of Walt's distributor, who hinted that merchandising the elephant would likely prove profitable.

Walt, unlike the heads of other animation studios, jumped into selling character-branded merchandise early on, beginning in 1929 when a man offered him three hundred dollars to put Mickey Mouse's face on notebooks marketed to children. Walt agreed, not because he believed the venture would be particularly successful but simply because he needed the money. To his surprise, merchandising quickly turned lucrative. By the mid-1930s, the Ingersoll-Waterbury Company had sold more than two and a half million Mickey Mouse watches, and other small toys and dolls were moving quickly and bringing the studio needed income. The potential was there, yet Elmer was going nowhere.

Despite her abilities, Bianca couldn't get another script approved. She wrote one script she was particularly proud of, *Timid Elmer,* in which she enlivened the warmth of her main character with playful gags, like Elmer using his trunk to trip a monkey, that she knew would appeal to most of the members of the story department. But even this didn't work — Walt was completely uninterested. In early 1938 it seemed to

Bianca that everything she touched was fated for oblivion, discarded before she could prove its worth.

By early June, however, Walt was in agreement with Bianca on the *Pinocchio* script's troubles. He, too, saw Pinocchio as unsympathetic and viewed his stunted character development as poisoning the rest of the narrative. The gag-driven script was at its core immature and, to Walt, past all redemption. To the shock of those at the studio, Walt threw everything away. It didn't matter that the team had already worked for five months on the project, produced 2,300 feet of film, and spent thousands of dollars. They would all have to start from scratch.

The story department was in crisis. Following *Snow White,* some writers had bragged about how well they understood the complex nature of feature-length animation, but now that puffed-up confidence evaporated. Amid the general gloom and the nagging feeling that they were chasing an unattainable standard of perfection, Bianca found herself returning to notes she had made a year earlier. She was one of the few in the story department who had a smile on her face.

Walt wasn't letting the reset affect his optimism for the future of their endeavors.

Just two months after he scrapped all work on *Pinocchio,* he was ready to fund his next big venture. Money was no longer a primary source of anxiety. In the first six months after the release of *Snow White,* the studio not only paid off its debts but also grossed four million dollars. Walt, along with his brother Roy, made a ten-thousand-dollar down payment on fifty-one acres for their new dream studio in Burbank. Walt Disney Studios, which now had approximately six hundred employees on its payroll, was outgrowing its modest dwellings on Hyperion Avenue.

The current lot held two animator buildings, a soundstage, the Ink and Paint annex, and a new features building constructed just that year. Yet space was in short supply. The animators sat crammed at their desks, their elbows rubbing against one another's and occasionally causing Mickey Mouse to sprout whiskers on the top of his head, and in the story department the noise level had reached new heights. And with production ramping up on a new feature, even more workers were moving into the buildings on Hyperion Avenue.

August 1938 brought with it not just the promise of new buildings and spacious offices but a fourth woman in the story department. Her name was Sylvia Moberly-Holland, and working for Walt had been her ambition since she'd sat in a darkened theater and felt the enchantment of *Snow White* sweep over her. The film was life-altering. As soon as the lights came on, Sylvia turned to her mother and in an excited voice declared, "I've got to do that." She quickly found a job as an inker with the Ink and Paint department at Walter Lantz Productions at Universal Studios. She saw the job as a stepping-stone, a way to attain her all-consuming desire: to work for Walt Disney.

By the summer of 1938 there was a rumor circulating around Hollywood that Walt's next movie after *Pinocchio* would be a musical feature. This greatly piqued Sylvia's interest, as music had formed an essential part of her childhood, a joy she had shared with her father, a vicar in the small English village of Ampfield, where she was raised. Excited by the possibility of combining music with her art, Sylvia applied to the studios and was granted an interview with Walt himself.

This was highly unusual. Most women hired at the studio were in their early twenties, unmarried, and unattached. They were placed in a training program and only a fraction of these women would go on to join Ink and Paint. Advertisements run by the studio in the 1930s proclaimed: "Walt Disney Needs Girl Artists Now! Steady, interesting jobs for girls, 18–30 with elementary art training. No cartoon experience needed; we'll train you, pay you while you learn. Apply Disney Studios, Art Dept. Bring samples of your work." Sylvia didn't fit the criteria — she was a thirty-eight-year-old widow with two small children — but she needed this job desperately.

When she was a child, Sylvia received as a gift an early Kodak point-and-shoot box camera that she excitedly aimed at garden roses, craggy rocks, and the wild heather that grew across her native English countryside. She developed the photographs in her grade-school bathroom, much to the chagrin of her teachers, who took issue with the sinks of the girls' room being constantly filled with soaking prints.

As a teenager, Sylvia was sent to the Gloucestershire School of Domestic Science, a respectable school for young girls to learn the work of women: cooking and teaching. She lasted two years in the program before moving on to the Architectural

Association School in London, transferring from a school of all women to one that contained practically none. When she graduated, she was the first woman to join the Royal Institute of British Architects.

In the first bloom of her career, Sylvia was fortunate. One of her early projects was designing the British Pavilion at the International Exhibition of Modern Decorative and Industrial Arts held in Paris in 1925. She had her degree, meaningful work, and the love of a man named Frank Holland, a fellow student. The two married and then moved more than four thousand miles away to begin their own architecture practice in Victoria, British Columbia. Sylvia quickly made an impression in her new country, becoming the first woman accepted to the Architectural Institute of British Columbia.

In 1926, the couple welcomed a little girl, Theodora, whom they called Theo. In her home office, Sylvia leaned over her drafting table, sketching the lines of light-filled rooms while she gently rocked her infant daughter in a cradle placed at her feet. Vibrancy and joy filled their Canadian home. Frank and Sylvia were young and very much in love, and their shared passion for the elegant Arts and Crafts–style homes they designed together was eclipsed only by their excitement at their growing family.

Pregnancy and birth will often make a woman reflect on her own upbringing, and so it was for Sylvia, who, seven months pregnant with her second child, longed to see her parents in England, particularly her mother, who had never met her granddaughter. The journey was expensive, so she took one-year-old Theo with her to England, leaving Frank alone at home.

She left behind a bitterly cold December in British Columbia, with temperatures dropping to 10 degrees, far below what was typical of their normally mild winters. The streets were buried in snow, but that didn't keep Frank from Christmas shopping, his spirits high as he thought of Sylvia's imminent return. Then he fell ill. Frank lay in bed, burning up with fever. His condition quickly deteriorated as pain and pressure in his ear became excruciating. A physician's exam confirmed what was obvious to Frank: he had an ear infection. However, the doctor could offer no treatment. The bacteria spread, reaching Frank's inner ear and then infecting the mastoid process, the part of the skull behind the ear. Unlike most of the rigid bones in the human body, the mastoid process is porous, like a sponge, and filled with air cells. Bacteria can invade these spaces, leading to an infection that eventually reaches the brain. In the 1920s there was no medicine or surgery that could stop the progress of the deadly infection.

Just three months earlier, in September 1928, a Scottish bacteriologist named Alexander Fleming returned from vacation to find, in his messy London laboratory, a mold called *Penicillium notatum* growing on his petri dishes. The mold had the mysterious ability to kill several strains of bacteria responsible for human infections. Although Fleming was intrigued by the lucky accident, it would be sixteen years before researchers found a way to mass-produce the antibiotic known as penicillin. These advances came far too late to help Frank. Within weeks, the bacteria reached his brain and he died.

Sylvia returned to Canada a widow. She was twenty-eight years old and pregnant; shortly after she arrived home, she gave birth to a baby boy, whom she named Boris. In the throes of grief but with a toddler and a newborn depending on her, Sylvia tried to find a new rhythm for her life. She had always seen herself as resilient and independent, and she tapped into that inner strength as she tended to her children and planned for the future of the architecture firm that

One in a series of sketches drawn by Sylvia Holland depicting the death of a loved one and the grief of those left behind **(Courtesy Theo Halladay)**

she now ran alone. The timing, however, was not in her favor. The next year, 1929, brought a worldwide economic crash. In the midst of the Great Depression, most people were losing their houses, not building new ones. Sylvia's steady work as an architect vanished.

Years passed, but little improved for Sylvia. She received few commissions and struggled to pay the bills. In desperation, she moved to the Holland family farm outside the city, where she paid rent to her father-in-law. Then, when it seemed their situation could not get worse, Boris fell ill. The child clutched his ears and cried in pain, and when she looked into his eyes, Sylvia feared he'd suffer his father's fate. She pleaded with the doctor to do something, but the physician had nothing to offer. Ear infections were a leading cause of childhood mortality in 1930 and widely available antibiotics still more than a decade away. Yet the doctor felt deep sympathy for the panicked mother and gave her the best advice he had: "Get him to a desert climate," he told her, then added ominously, "or lose him." The next day Sylvia and her children were on a southbound train headed for the medicinal sunshine of Los Angeles.

The move meant Sylvia had to leave her architecture firm, but it also necessitated a more painful separation. In Southern California, after Boris recovered, Sylvia placed her two children in a boarding school, vowing that she would find work quickly and reunite her family. And so, with a determination that few other applicants could match, Sylvia walked into Walt's office on a clear summer day in 1938 and pulled out her sketches. Invisible to others was the nearly unbearable weight of the past few years she carried on her shoulders — the anguish of grief, the financial and emotional toll of losing her husband, the recent illness of her son, and the despair of leaving her children. Few people would still be standing after suffering the blows she had endured. It seemed that everything she held dear was riding on the success of this one meeting. Fortunately, Walt immediately perceived Sylvia's talent, and he hired her on the spot to begin work in the story department.

Although, like her female colleagues, Sylvia was paid less than her male counterparts, she still earned more than she had in her last job, where she'd gotten about twelve dollars a week. The Walt Disney Studios were known for offering higher salaries than most of their Hollywood competitors. Yet even this extra income was not enough to bring her children home. She longed for the sweetness of everyday family life, and that desire drove her to exert herself to the utmost.

Sylvia was sitting at her desk one afternoon working on story ideas when she heard Walt walking down the hallway yelling, "Anybody know how to draw a horse?" Sylvia didn't waste a moment; she jumped up and yelled, "I do!" In truth, there was nothing he could ask for that she would not immediately attempt. She walked alongside the boss, sketching quickly on a piece of

Sketch of a horse made by Sylvia on scrap paper, date unknown **(Courtesy Theo Halladay)**

paper as they made their way down the hall. In mere moments she finished the drawing and handed the horse to Walt. As a result of that one hurried sketch, Sylvia received an opportunity at the studio that no other woman had yet garnered. And it would begin at a story meeting.

Attending story meetings at the Walt Disney Studios was akin to getting one's boots stuck in soft spring mud — once you were in, it was nearly impossible to get out. Grace Huntington spent 1938 in an endless number of such meetings. They took place Monday through Saturday, often first thing in the morning, with the group poring over every detail of the script and storyboards. Grace was working on a new Mickey Mouse short and she could hardly believe the countless hours spent on what, ultimately, would be a mere eight minutes of family entertainment.

Despite a solid week of work on the Mickey short, the team of story artists had barely made a start. Until they had a finished script and storyboards approved by Walt, the animators couldn't begin their work, and the whole project hung in limbo. At nine thirty a.m. Grace and her colleagues shuffled into the room, ready to start debate over Mickey Mouse again. These walls had become as familiar to her as the seven men she shared the space with.

The group quieted down, and Peter Page, whose name was perfectly suited for his position as a writer in the department, began running through the storyboards, summarizing the action and calling out all the dialogue. His voice squeaked like Mickey Mouse's as he described how the character meets Claudius, king of the bumblebees, and is then magically shrunk to the size of a bee. The room was silent for a moment, the calm before the storm, before the other team members began to rip the story apart, attacking every facet of the plot.

Grace was quick to offer her criticism, saying, "The whole story is built on something that isn't true in the first place, because they have a king of the bees and bees are known to have a queen. Not that it makes a lot of difference, but right there it isn't true to life. The head of the hive is the queen and the males do very little except fly around and enjoy themselves." Grace looked around the room with a wry smile before continuing, "It seems to me if we had the queen of the bees it would add to the story because at the end it is the queen who is in trouble; she is captured by the wasps. If Mickey were to save the queen it seems a stronger story point. Then he can save the whole hive by beating their armies."

"There again you have a false assumption because a queen never leaves a hive," Peter responded.

Grace shook her head. "She doesn't have to leave."

They continued to argue over the short for the next few hours. Grace suggested a new approach to animating the bees in a way that would augment their story line. She tacked up her sketches of bees with light humanistic touches, their black legs dangling from their bodies. The men of the meeting widened their eyes before asking,

"No clothes?"

"No clothes" was Grace's firm reply.

Grace left the story meeting feeling they had accomplished but little. She was pleased that her work on the short, particularly sketching and writing the climactic battle scenes, would continue but unhappy about nearly everything else. Like Bianca, she was growing increasingly frustrated at how often her ideas were disregarded. Her personality was not mild — she spoke boldly at meetings, and she could be as passionate as any story man when tacking her sketches to the storyboard. Still, it seemed she had to push unusually hard for her ideas to gain traction.

The problem wasn't that Grace couldn't attract attention. A current of flirtation ran through the office, and Grace found that her male colleagues weren't interested in her story ideas, but they *were* interested in dating her. Focusing on her youth and beauty, they frequently brushed aside her writing. She complained to Bianca and then vented her feelings onto her sketch pad, repeatedly drawing an obese and overbearing Mickey Mouse. Sometimes he leered at her over her desk in her sketches, proclaiming, to the cartoon Grace's obvious horror, *I luv you!,* with menacing hands and an impish smile. Grace's desire to flee was represented in the next frame, where all that was left of her was a cloud of dust and the word *Zip!*

When she wasn't using her free time to lampoon the image of Mickey Mouse, Grace liked to sketch airplanes, which remained her passion. The shapes of her imaginary aircraft were buoyant above the clouds, and she invariably placed herself in the cockpit, a content smile on her lips, her own initials gracing the tailfin. She still dreamed of becoming a licensed pilot. On paper, at least, she was free to leave the limits of the earthly studio and take to the air.

While Bianca and Grace felt that their careers were progressing slowly, the studio as a whole continued to break new ground. In his quest to advance special effects in animation, Walt founded a new airbrush department, the aim of which was to produce realistic visual effects, particularly in the backgrounds of scenes. An airbrush uses a jet of compressed air that acts as a pump, drawing the paint from its reservoir in a cloud of tiny droplets to create a mist of color. The technique was developed in the late 1800s and first used by American

Impressionist painters, who found the gentle spray ideal for portraying the diffuse glow of natural light. Soon after that it was adopted by illustrators and muralists as well as photograph manipulators, who used the delicate application of paint to retouch or doctor images.

To lead the new department, Walt hired Barbara Wirth Baldwin. Barbara shaped the group, growing it to twenty-five men and women. There was grumbling among the male artists about having a woman as their leader. Bristling at any display of femininity, they were especially vexed when Barbara insisted that her group wear hairnets to prevent a single strand of hair or flake of dandruff from falling onto the cels. Barbara laughed off their complaints with a firmness that spoke of her innate confidence and quickly got down to the responsibilities of her job. She started by working with the massive multiplane camera housed in its own chilly studio space. Holding the nozzle of the airbrush steady, she pressed the trigger ever so gently and painted clouds directly on the glass. She was incredibly nervous while airbrushing in the studio for the first time, aware that the slightest touch of her fingers could ruin the art irrevocably.

Barbara and her team worked closely with

Grace Huntington's depiction of life as a female artist at the studio **(Courtesy Berkeley Brandt)**

the special effects animators in creating a range of visuals for *Pinocchio* that had never been attempted before and in pushing the capabilities of the multiplane camera. The airbrush allowed the film to include subtle touches, such as the haze of smoke and the luminosity of moonbeams. Barbara's team distorted the edges of goldfish Cleo's bowl with airbrushed shadows and specially fitted glasses placed on top of the camera lens. They took real twinkle lights and fastened them into a black canvas, then used the airbrush to spread gray paint over the surface so that it glowed like stardust between blazing suns. They even showed the saltwater spray of fierce ocean waves and the flickering of candlelight in the darkness, and they imbued the Blue Fairy with her heavenly glow.

The delicate artistry of their special effects contrasted with the darkness of the tale they were telling. In Collodi's original text, Pinocchio bites off a cat's paw and later kills Jiminy Cricket. Although the story department ultimately stripped away much of the horror, a dark mood clings to the film's dialogue and characters. The ominousness is reflected in its cinematography: seventy-six of the film's eighty-eight minutes are either in darkness or underwater.

The bleak concept art they were producing for *Pinocchio* reflected the fearful headlines studio employees were reading in their newspapers each morning. Bianca watched in horror in 1938 as Benito Mussolini, the dictator who ruled her native Italy, legalized a set of racial laws that stripped all Jewish Italians and other targeted minorities of their citizenship. It was clearly a grim portent.

Many employees with European ties were nervously following the news, including Sylvia, who was on the hunt for updates from England. After Prime Minister Neville Chamberlain signed the Munich Agreement in 1938, he announced that "a British Prime Minister has returned from Germany bringing peace with honour. I believe it is peace for our time. . . . Go home and get a nice quiet sleep." Instead of resting, fifteen thousand people protested in Trafalgar Square. For those who opposed Chamberlain, it was clear that instead of the peace he promised, turbulence was ahead. Perhaps it's unsurprising that, hearing of such disturbing developments, the studio artists chose to include in *Pinocchio* so many of the dark elements of Collodi's text.

Contrasted with the gloom, however, is the well-meaning sweetness of the wooden puppet. Thanks to dramatic revisions by the story department and an expanded role for

Jiminy Cricket, the film was transformed into something closer to Bianca's original concept, a tale that attempts to show what it means to be human.

The character Bianca crafted and that she advocated passionately for in story meetings was starkly different from the original wooden puppet. Her character does not arrive in the world with a malicious heart, but, like many of us hapless humans, he is frequently led into sin. He is exposed to what is arguably the worst society has to offer: thieves who take advantage of him, a man who imprisons him and threatens him with murder, even child trafficking. By making Pinocchio more like us, a flawed being trying to navigate the world as best he can, Bianca ultimately magnified Collodi's themes about the meaning of life. It doesn't matter whether one's limbs are wooden or flesh; it is not our bodies that make us human but the way we treat one another.

Bianca would receive little public acknowledgment for her contributions to the film. Neither would many others. The movie's credits, like those of *Snow White* before it, were a source of anger and resentment. Only a fraction of the artists and writers who worked on *Pinocchio* saw their names on the silver screen. Despite the stunning technological advances made by Barbara Wirth Baldwin and Mary Weiser, neither woman's name, nor that of any other female employee, was included. The absence of acknowledgment for women's efforts on the film was echoed in the paltry number of female characters, only one of whom — the Blue Fairy — spoke at all.

When Bianca arrived at work on February 7, 1940, she found the men crowded around a copy of *Hollywood Citizen News,* a local newspaper. Bianca wasn't surprised. Today marked *Pinocchio*'s release and everyone was anxious for reviews.

Bianca was settling in at her desk when one of the men called her over. "Bianca, this one's about you," he yelled. Confused, Bianca ambled over to the group and took the newspaper with no suspicion of what its pages contained.

It is no longer news when a woman takes her place in a man's workaday world. But it was news when a woman artist invaded the strictly masculine stronghold of the Walt Disney Studios. The event took place about five years ago. Until that time the only girls in the studio were the few necessary secretaries and the girls who did the inking and painting of celluloids. The girl who caused all this excitement was a young artist who, as a child, had gone to school with Walt in Chicago.

Bianca laughed at the piece, and before she gave the paper back to her colleagues, she sardonically wrote in the margin, *Who is this girl?* The reporter had found it unimportant to mention her name.

CHAPTER 4
WALTZ OF THE FLOWERS

"This is not the cartoon medium. It should not be limited to cartoons. We have worlds to conquer here. We've got an hour and forty-five minutes of picture and we're doing beautiful things with beautiful music. We're doing comic things, fantastic things, and it can't all be the same — it's an experimental thing and I'm willing to experiment on it. We've got more in this medium than making people laugh. We love to make people laugh, but I think we can do both." Walt paused as he addressed the team of writers during a 1938 story meeting. "This stuff means more, it's richer, like a painting. Excuse me if I get a little riled up on this stuff because it's a continual fight around this place to get away from slapping somebody on the fanny or having somebody swallow something."

As Sylvia listened to Walt, she found her artistic spirit reawakened. The creative pleasures of her youth that had been submerged under the weight of adult responsibility were only now beginning to bob back up to the surface. When describing his lofty ambitions for the new film, known around the studio as the "concert feature," Walt seemed to be detailing her innermost desire.

To hear Walt tell it, they weren't involved in a solely commercial endeavor designed to steal the nickels of children in exchange for a few laughs. They were being tasked with using their art to move audiences in unexpected ways. Like Sylvia, Bianca was mesmerized by Walt's words. What he was describing was the essence of why she joined the studio in the first place. Instead of writing gags, she longed to create meaningful work.

The concert feature was technically skipping ahead in line. *Bambi* would have to wait its turn yet again. The challenge of bringing an entire forest of animals to life was overwhelming the animation department and necessitating a lengthy development.

Much of Mickey Mouse's early success was due to the pioneering sound of his cartoons, so perhaps it is not surprising that Walt was intrigued by the potential of combining music with animation. A few months before *Snow White* was released, Walt had bought the rights to *The Sorcerer's Apprentice,* a popular concert piece written by Paul Dukas, a French composer, in 1897. Walt planned on using the music for Mickey Mouse's first two-reel special, a twenty-two-minute piece of animation that would feature Mickey in a wizard's hat.

With this project in the back of his mind, Walt spotted famed conductor Leopold Stokowski sitting alone at a table at Chasen's, a popular West Hollywood restaurant where Walt regularly ate, usually ordering chili. "Why don't we sit together?" Walt asked. Stokowski joined him, and Walt began describing his plans to make Mickey Mouse come alive with classical music. Stokowski was so charmed that he offered to conduct the piece for free. As they later worked out the details, the short blossomed into its own feature film, and Walt promised Stokowski that in return for the conductor's getting the Philadelphia Orchestra to work on the music immediately, Walt would put his "finest men" on the project.

They would not all be men. Early on, Walt asked Bianca to shape the film. If the studio was going to make this a feature, Stokowski would need more than a single symphony to conduct. Walt wanted someone who could listen to music with its visual possibilities in mind, and so he sent his first female story artist in pursuit of a soundtrack.

Thrilled with the prospects before her and always happy to be away from the studio, Bianca walked into a music store and asked to hear recordings of works by Bach, Beethoven, and Tchaikovsky, some of her favorite composers. The man behind the counter at first offered Bianca a meager selection, but when she explained that she worked for Walt Disney Studios, the records piled up in front of her, many more than she'd asked for.

Bianca spent the afternoon in a back room of the music store, listening. Alone in the confined space, she closed her eyes and began to contemplate how each piece could be used, the notes running wildly through her imagination. As she walked to her Oldsmobile carrying a heavy load of Victor records, she decided that the music had awoken something within her. She felt profoundly different from when she had walked in. Her exhilaration followed her back to the studio, where she listened to her music, especially Tchaikovsky, over and over again.

There was one Tchaikovsky record that

she kept coming back to. It was from the 1892 ballet *The Nutcracker.* There wasn't a recording of the work in its entirety, only *The Nutcracker Suite,* a twenty-minute-long selection from the original ballet, but Bianca found it thoroughly enchanting.

Although the whole ballet was first performed outside of Russia in 1934, it had never been produced in the United States. The delights of the ballet's score were therefore new, untasted, and Bianca relished hearing the "Dance of the Sugar Plum Fairy" and the "Waltz of the Flowers." When she tried to find the full ballet, however, she was out of luck. No vinyl recordings were commercially available. From relative obscurity, she had selected a remarkable piece of music, and she was already imagining the scenes that might form. She smiled to herself. She knew the men of the studio would not like the animation she was contemplating.

When Bianca presented the music to Walt, he was similarly struck with its magnificence. He immediately assigned Bianca to work on *The Nutcracker Suite.* With music in hand, Walt now began to look for directors. Sylvia Holland's outspokenness at story meetings and her eagerness to draw horses or whatever other animal Walt desired had made an impression on the boss. The result was that Walt decided to trust her with a role never before held by a woman at the studio. Sylvia was made story director of the "Waltz of the Flowers" sequence. As story director, she served as creative story lead, responsible for developing the characters and plotting the action. She was in charge of the storyboards and the final script. She also managed her team of story artists and worked closely with the director of the whole film. To accomplish all this, she needed an assistant, and a woman from Ink and Paint, Ethel Kulsar, was promoted to the job.

Ethel and Sylvia had much in common — they both had young children and neither had a husband. Their shared experience as strong, single mothers made them unusual not only at the studio but in society in general, where a mere 8 percent of women with children under the age of ten participated in the U.S. labor force. Finding each other was a gift. In their friendship, they each uncovered the pleasure of creating art alongside a person who truly understood what struggles life could hold.

Another woman was joining their group for *The Nutcracker Suite*. Her name was

Mary Goodrich, and, like Grace, she was an amateur aviator and a member of the Ninety-Nines, an organization for women pilots. Mary also had a love of words. In 1927, at twenty years old, Goodrich walked into the city room of the *Hartford Courant* newspaper and asked for a job as a reporter. The editor laughed at the ludicrous idea of hiring a woman but when Goodrich mentioned that she was taking flying lessons, he was struck by an idea. "If you can get the first pilot's license given to a woman in Connecticut," he told her, "I'll hire you." Mary accepted the challenge and got her license just a few months later. When she returned to the paper, the editor hired her, although he didn't intend to keep her on the payroll long. However, interest in aviation was growing, and when Goodrich suggested that she begin a daily aviation column, the editor agreed. The young reporter subsequently became the paper's first aviation editor.

While holding down her job at the newspaper, Goodrich kept pushing herself in the air. At twenty-six, she completed the first female solo flight to Cuba. Yet the accomplishment was marred by a terrifying realization: her perception of distance was faltering. One day as she came down for a landing, she misjudged the distance badly, believing that she should be hitting the runway when she was still fourteen feet off the ground. Even with corrective lenses she knew she wasn't going to pass the physical required to renew her pilot's license, and without that license, the *Courant* would not continue to pay her as its aviation editor. In one year, she lost the two occupations she held most dear: flying and writing.

She decided to make a fresh start; she moved to California, where she applied for a job at the Walt Disney Studios. The thirty-year-old was hired to work in story research in 1938. She was assigned to the concert feature, and she dived into it passionately. Writing a treatment for *The Nutcracker* sequence, she used her reportorial skills to sort through the storyboards and cut the sections that weren't working. "I sort of had to do this to get started," she wrote as a note in the beginning of her treatment. "I took the whole *Nutcracker Suite* in my hot little hand and picked out the meats one by one." Together, the group members sorted through the ballet and found a vision that matched their ambitions as female artists. They had no constraints placed on them; they were not told to mirror the story of the original ballet, and they were not required to include any specific characters. They had the whole twenty-three minutes of *The Nutcracker Suite* to do with as they wished.

In this atmosphere of friendship, Bianca found her struggles easing. Three years earlier she had proposed an animated short called *Flower Ballet.* She had sketched gleeful snapdragons and twirling thistles, but like so much of her work at the studio, the proposal had never made the leap from concept to production. Here was her chance to bring the graceful flowers to life and, even more exciting, to create new characters.

As Bianca listened to *The Nutcracker Suite,* she saw fairies dancing to the music. Under her pencil, their shining figures went flitting from flower to flower, weaving spiderwebs whose gleaming lattices, dripping with morning dew, reflected the stars in the night sky. She loved the drawings, but she knew the men of the story department would hate them; they were scared of fairies. The only exception was the Blue Fairy in *Pinocchio,* who was a fully formed woman.

Most of the studio's male artists refused to draw fairies. A few men tried, but their pixie sketches brought such a deluge of teasing and harassment that, one by one, they all gave up. Bianca rolled her eyes at their thin skins, and Sylvia was frustrated by the small-mindedness that made her colleagues abandon what she considered a bold artistic endeavor. Yet because of the men's skittishness, the fairies of the concert feature began to embody the best of the female talent at the studio.

Not all men found these sequences threatening. George Balanchine, for instance, the Russian choreographer who had just cofounded the School of American Ballet in New York City and was now living a stone's throw from Hollywood Boulevard, working with his ballet company to choreograph dance moves for film, saw Sylvia's storyboards and was delighted with them.

Balanchine had been touring the studio with Igor Stravinsky, the composer whose ballet *The Rite of Spring* was serving as the inspiration for a movement of the concert feature. The Russian composer and conductor was not impressed with how the studio had transformed his ballet into a telling of the story of evolution. The piece began in darkness, then depicted the big bang, the expansion of the universe, and the creation of Earth itself as viewed from space, a perspective that was decades away from being captured by real-life cameras. Creatures emerged from the oceans, the dinosaurs rose and fell, and ultimately humankind appeared. The human sequence would later be cut as a sop to religious creationists, most of whom would still thoroughly dislike the piece of animation that disseminated the science of evolution. Stravinsky was not fond of it either, although his dislike was founded in the artistic interpretation of his work and had no religious basis. However, he was too polite to share his real opinion with Walt. It was only later that he would call the studio's work "an unresisting imbecility."

Balanchine was having a far more pleasurable experience on the studio tour. He delighted in the fairies, who moved with the grace and fluidity of prima ballerinas in toe shoes to the "Dance of the Sugar Plum Fairy." As he gazed at Sylvia's storyboards, he recognized an untapped allure in *The Nutcracker* — its appeal to children. The images brought forth his own memories of dancing in the ballet as a youth in St. Petersburg. He saw clearly what Sylvia and the group of artists were attempting. They had taken a Russian ballet that no one in the United States had seen and fashioned it into a manifestation of beauty and glee.

This childlike wonder and inspiration stayed with Balanchine. Fifteen years later, on December 11, 1954, he would debut *The*

Nutcracker in the brand-new Lincoln Center for the Performing Arts in Manhattan. His choreography was starkly different from that of his Russian predecessors, as he made the main characters ten-year-old children instead of adults, dampening the romantic aspects of the original plot but imparting the ebullience of youth. Thanks to Balanchine's vision, *The Nutcracker* dominates American theaters every December, drawing countless children and adults into the beauty of the ballet. And yet America's cultural obsession with *The Nutcracker* would never have occurred without the women of the Walt Disney Studios.

While the tin-can quality of an old phonograph was good enough for the studio artists in Hollywood to work with, far more attention was being paid to the creation of the official music for the concert feature in Philadelphia. Walt was not content with a mere soundtrack. As he pondered a storyboard for "Flight of the Bumblebees," one of the proposed movements, he thought how wonderful it would be if the audience could feel the buzzing of the creatures around them. He imagined making the sound so realistic that men, women, and children would swat at their ears. The idea caught his fancy to such an extent that at one point, Walt considered adding smell to the mix, making the moviegoing experience so immersive that it would blur the lines between fantasy and reality.

Walt and his team of engineers called it Fantasound. Using multiple channels of optical recording — converting sound into light — on two cameras using 35 mm film, they were able to catch the signal from thirty-three microphones placed all around the orchestra, including a lonely one in the hall, listening for distant reverberations. The emphasis on recording was just half the equation, however. In order for the orchestra to be truly appreciated, Walt argued, the sound system of the theater also needed to be enhanced. The engineers determined they needed three loudspeakers behind the screen and surround-sound speakers on the walls and rear of the theater. While other films had incorporated multichannel sound, this would be the first application of true surround sound. To facilitate this, *Fantasia* would travel as a road show, with the equipment packed up in large boxes and shipped by rail to movie houses across the country. There was no denying the significant financial investment required for this new sound system, but how else could sound be made to fly across a room?

Sound engineers, musicians, and conductors experimented with the recordings, but every note relied on the story department. Each time the melody whipped around the room, it had to be tied to the action happening on-screen. Each technical advance in surround sound had to be rooted in a furthering of the story itself. The music had first inspired the story artists listening to the records at the studio. The storyboards they created then influenced the arrangement of the music chosen. After the orchestra in Philadelphia recorded the final soundtrack, each gesture in the animation was refined to ensure it matched perfectly. The art informed the technology, and the technology shaped the art, the two acting on each other in a constant, fluid exchange of innovation.

Sylvia was working closely with Bill Garity, the inventor already admired at the studio for his work developing the click track and the multiplane camera. Together they plotted each twirl of her dancing flowers. They carefully determined how the placement of the speakers in the theater would bounce each note from the viola's strings from side to side in time with a glowing trail of pixie dust on-screen, seemingly brushed over the audience's bewildered heads.

Without the benefit of pixie dust, Grace was returning home after attending her grandfather's funeral in Connecticut. Her spirits were depressed not only because of the occasion but also due to a deep-seated discontent common among twenty-five-year-olds. She felt herself growing older and yet seemed no closer to her ambition of becoming a professional pilot.

In some respects Grace was advancing. In 1939, in the midst of production on the concert feature, she managed to take vacation time in order to obtain her commercial pilot's license. Grace flew to Madison, Wisconsin, so she could take the test with an old friend who had moved there and become a civil aeronautics inspector. Even though she had to fly alone across half the country to get to him, Grace figured she would be less nervous taking the test with someone she knew.

The trip itself was arduous. This was before modern air traffic control, so Grace had to rely on radio range stations. These low-frequency transmitters emitted a broadcast of two Morse code letters, a dot-dash for A and a dash-dot for N. While these signals helped pilots understand when they were close to an airfield, they didn't give any other information, such as what direction to go. Because of this, many pilots at the time found themselves lost in the air, and Grace was no exception. At one desperate juncture she even landed at an airfield and had to ask the embarrassing question "Where am I?" Grace was surprised to find she was in Pennsylvania instead of Wisconsin. She passed the test and received her commercial license, but although she was immensely proud of the small paper certificate, she still had little hope about what opportunities it would afford her.

Even though Grace had a commercial pilot's license, no one in aviation would hire her, and no flight school would take her for additional training. When she asked Bianca for advice, exposing her fears and insecurities, the response was warm, if muddled: "It isn't so important to be doing things, dear — if only you are happy."

With her nose pressed against the chilly Plexiglas window on her Pan American return flight from Connecticut, Grace considered what made her happy. Thousands of miles below, Los Angeles looked like a fairyland, a dream of twinkling lights stretching for miles, bordered by the dark waters of the Pacific. She imagined that she was alone, flying to chase the sun, adjusting the throttle and then piercing the limits of altitude, the stars becoming clearer up ahead.

It was 1938 and not even the most powerful rockets of the age could break free of Earth's atmosphere, yet Grace believed that one day planes would not only leave Earth but propel humans into space. *How lucky to be one of those few,* she thought, then wondered how they would select pilots to operate these marvels of the future. Surely any person chosen would need experience flying as high as possible. Wouldn't it be natural to pick pilots who had already proven themselves by breaking altitude records? Up in the clouds above Los Angeles, Grace hatched a plan. *I could be that record holder,* she thought. *I could be the one headed into space.* As her plane descended to the runway, part of her imagination remained in the air.

The story department was crowded with artists sketching naked women. They worked at their desks, in the hallways, or out on the lawn, where the wind whipped the edges of their paper. Many of the characters they were developing for the concert feature were nude, from the fairies of *The Nutcracker* to the centaurs of Beethoven's Pastoral Symphony. For artists it was essential to keep in practice drawing the human form, yet in the films Hollywood produced, under the newly applied censorship laws, nudity was prohibited.

Sex and vulgarity in early 1930s films had sparked outrage. Audiences were particularly upset by the depiction of promiscuous women, such as Claudette Colbert naked in a bathtub in *Cleopatra* (1934) and a brazen Mae West in *She Done Him Wrong* (1933) slinking up to Cary Grant's character with the suggestive line "Why don't you come up sometime and see me?"

From 1929 to 1934, the pre-code era, Hollywood movies had few gatekeepers to rein in the licentiousness of their plots, and a host of strong-minded female characters showed a startling openness in their sexuality. For guidance, filmmakers could turn to a list of thirty-six Don'ts and Be Carefuls that were envisioned by a Quaker, drafted by a Jesuit priest, and ultimately compiled by former postmaster general Will Hays. The list was based in Catholic theology and aimed to restrict scenes involving nudity, illegal drugs, profanity, sex, crime, and other moral outrages, such as ridicule of the clergy. Yet the constraints were toothless; filmmakers could ignore them without penalty.

It wasn't until 1934 that political pressure brought authority to the Hays Code, also known as the Motion Picture Production Code. Finally, Hollywood had to take notice. Every feature script needed to be approved by an administrator before it was filmed. But the rules for animation were slightly blurry. No one needed to see the script prior to production, but the final film, like all others, had to be screened and approved by the trade association known as the Motion Picture Producers and Distributors of America before it could be shown in theaters.

The story department thought of these limitations not at all. Sketching the human body was as natural to the artists as twirling a pencil with their fingers. They had all studied drawing, either as part of a formal fine arts education or in the classes held at the studio, and so they were accustomed to sketching the curvature of the human form, typically with a live model in front of them.

In many ways, the story department did not consider the concert feature as being for children; at least, not exclusively. Walt had made it clear that they were creating art, the classical music acting as their muse. The animated film they produced would make the symphony beloved by anyone, regardless of musical taste or age, who was willing to listen.

Sylvia's team in the story department kept this idea in mind as they filled the screen for *The Nutcracker Suite* movement. Having no preconceived notions of the ballet to interfere with their vision, they were free to draw fairy sprites with long, slender bodies, budding breasts, narrow hips, and wings that shimmered thanks to the magic of the multiplane camera. Their sprites' dance sparks the awakening of nature and the change of the seasons. The fairies are gold, green, mauve, pink, and blue, but they wear not a stitch of clothing. Their nudity reflects their vulnerability and their pure, childlike innocence.

Nearby, however, a different portrayal of female bodies was being created. While Sylvia's predominantly female team in the story department worked on *The Nutcracker Suite,* there were six more teams developing animation for the other musical pieces. One of these was composed of the men who had spurned drawing fairies under Sylvia's direction. Instead, they drew masculine centaurs and their female counterparts, creatures they called "centaurettes." They set their story to Beethoven's Pastoral Symphony, which gave the mythical beings a grand air worthy of the glories of ancient Greece. In time to the stately composition, the half-human, half-horse creatures perform an awkward mix of comedy and flirtatious antics. The style of the character animation offers entertainment but little artistic elevation.

The centaurettes' faces are evocative of pinup girls', complete with batting eyelashes and coy smiles. From the waist up, they are nude, their movements both sensual and alluring. The pages drafted by the story department show the centaurettes preening in expectation of the men's arrival. A gathering of rosy-cheeked cupids and at least one African American centaurette, named Sunflower, wait on them to help in their preparations. Sunflower, the first African American character to appear in a Walt Disney Studios feature, stands half as tall as the rest of the herd, being half donkey instead of half horse, and her role is servile — she braids flowers into the manes of the white centaurettes and polishes their hooves. Her character was shaped in a story meeting on a late afternoon in 1938 when one writer suggested, "One girl would put nail polish — red stuff — putting it on her hoofs, you know." He mimed the action.

"That blonde is a beautiful horse. How about making the little black one fit in?" an animator asked.

"That could come during your chase — there's a little laugh there," Walt said, gesturing toward the storyboards. "Here are the girls going [through] and up comes the little black one with a watermelon — the girls are running like hell, or else the little guys have lost them, and they see their hoofs — ha-ha! They spring! And it's the little black one with a watermelon. I think they're very cute. We're not limited on our comic touches."

Sylvia focused on *The Nutcracker Suite,* where her responsibilities lay as story director, but she still tried to improve the Pastoral Symphony. Her competing sketches of the female centaurs revealed, instead of sex puppets, strong female bodies, the muscular arms of the women bent around their children; both young and old lived together, and their skin colors reflected the rainbow, but without racial bias. However, her sketches were rejected for baser representations of gender and ethnicity.

Sunflower is not a character in her own

right but rather a crude amalgam of stereotypes meant to elicit laughter. Unfortunately, her subservient depiction was not
unusual, as the animation of African American characters was almost universally demeaning and degrading in the Hollywood
of the day.

(A few years later, in 1942, Walter White,
executive secretary of the National Association for the Advancement of Colored People, would attempt to turn the tide by
negotiating with Hollywood studio executives, who, as reported in *Variety,* "promised
a more honest portrayal of the Negro
henceforth, using them not only as red-
caps, porters and in other menial roles, but
in all the parts they play in the nation's
everyday life." These pledges would never
be completely honored. Instead, it was the
rise of diverse filmmakers that ultimately
led to more accurate representations of
African Americans in film.)

The men creating the sexy centaurettes
and the servile Sunflower worked in a
vacuum of their own homogeneity. Many
would later criticize their work. Film critics
of the era described the animation of the
Pastoral Symphony as "the only unsatisfactory part of the picture"; historians have
called the centaurs "*Fantasia*'s nadir," and

numerous animators have censured the sequence.

Sunflower's presence, in particular, caused deep embarrassment in the years ahead. Walt would scrub her from the Pastoral Symphony in 1963, and studio executives pretended for decades that she'd never existed. Yet from the moment pencil sketches first formed her image, through the hours of story meetings that followed, and over the months during which she was animated, outlined, colored, and filmed, no one at the studio was strong-minded enough to put a halt to the racist depiction of Sunflower. It would be ten years before the studio hired its first African American artist.

Sunflower was drawn in an undignified manner, but she was an imaginary character; Hattie Noel, an African American stage and screen performer, suffered real humiliation. As part of the "Dance of the Hours" sequence for the concert feature, animators had the actress wear a skin-tight ballet costume, her stomach uncomfortably bulging out over a tutu. Using the woman as a model, the group of men drew hippos dancing in tutus in time to the ballet music. They snapped pictures and sketched her body and then chuckled at her "fat flesh hanging out."

One of the men callously laughing at the performer was Lee Blair, a new hire at the studio. He was as unconcerned with his position as animator as he was about the dignity of Hattie Noel. The job was merely a way to pay the bills. He was a newlywed — he had just married Mary Robinson, whom he'd met when the two were students at the Chouinard Art Institute in Los Angeles.

Mary Robinson was born in McAlester, Oklahoma, in 1911. Hers was a family of strong women. The house she grew up in belonged to Mary's grandmother and was home not only to Mary, her mother, father, and two sisters but also to Mary's two aunts. Women were the backbone of the family both physically and emotionally; they took care of the home and the children, and they brought in the income. Mary's father, by contrast, was an alcoholic who was frequently unemployed.

Even as a young child, Mary placed the highest value on artistic expression. The family moved from Oklahoma to Texas before finally settling in the tiny town of Morgan Hill, California, when Mary was twelve. When her mother told her they couldn't spend what little money they had on painting supplies, Mary shook her head, held out her hand, and said, "Dad will just drink it up anyway." In high school, Mary was class vice president and assistant editor of the school newspaper, and she graduated at the top of her class. She was the kind of person poised to leap at the throat of opportunity. In her valedictorian speech, she spoke about "self-destiny," a prescient theme, given her own complicated journey to come.

After attending San Jose State College, Mary received a full scholarship to the Chouinard Art Institute. At the end of her first year at art school, she won first prize in a nationwide contest for Cannon Mills, a textile company; it earned her a hundred dollars and the pride of seeing her design, a Trojan horse rendered in bright blues and yellows, emblazoned on towels and mats. Wherever she went, renown seemed to be waiting for her.

It wasn't just art critics who fell for her. A classmate named Lee Blair found Mary irresistible. Lee, like Mary, was a scholarship student at Chouinard, and he was just beginning to reveal exceptional talent. At the 1932 Summer Olympics, held in Los Angeles, Lee was awarded a gold medal in the drawing and watercolors category (the arts continued to be part of the Olympics until 1948).

The couple was passionate about art and their deepening relationship. "We are artists dear," Mary wrote to Lee, "and in love with art and each other. We must make these loves coincide and melt into a beautiful, happy & rich life. That is our future and is real. We'll live to be happy and paint to express our happiness." But in 1938 neither Mary nor Lee was happily pursuing the art they both loved. After graduating from art school, they made just fifteen dollars a week from selling their paintings, and they were forced to bend to commercial pressures. Fortunately they lived in Los Angeles, a city perpetually eager for artists willing to compromise their purism for money.

The newlyweds bounced from one animation studio to another. Lee was hired as an animator while Mary, in spite of her identical education and experience, was brought on as an inker. At Walt Disney Studios, Lee was assigned to work on the complex color schemes of the concert feature; Mary stayed at the Harman-Ising Studio across town, working on Porky Pig and Looney Tunes. She was promoted to art director, the position her husband had just left, and the men sang her praises and declared, "She's better than he is!"

On the weekends, Mary pushed the cartoons out of her mind and pursued her own work. She painted feverishly, her body tense as she dipped her brushes from water to paint to rag paper. One afternoon, she created dark, foreboding clouds descending on a rural landscape. Her brush captured the somber beauty of her native Oklahoma. Every artist may face struggle, but few will know suffering like an Oklahoman woman of the 1930s. As she painted, she found inspiration in the matriarchs of her family, women who labored, carrying burdens both domestic and financial, but who received little thanks or encouragement and had no chance of breaking free of their prescribed roles. Mary might have been born in Oklahoma but she didn't want to be trapped there or anywhere. It was this past that Mary was breaking free from as her brushes flew across the canvas.

Below the storm clouds, she painted a single person standing in the open doorway of a farmhouse, the form silhouetted against the incandescent light of the room inside. She called the painting *End of the Day.* The light of the painting catches the eye, but it is the portent of darkness that needs watching.

End of the Day *by Mary Blair, 1938 (Courtesy the estate of Mary Blair)*

Most story meetings for the concert feature were dynamic, even argumentative, but meetings for the "Dance of the Sugar Plum Fairy" were comparatively peaceful — at least at first. In rooms that were usually host to shouting, cartoon falsettos, and playacting, the story artists sat in silence, hands on their laps, listening intently to the music playing. A secretary sat with them, as was the custom, to record the meeting notes in speedy shorthand, but now her fingers were idle, as no transcript could record their inner responses to the Tchaikovsky score.

Although most men of the story department still rebuffed fairies, a few had finally consented to work under Sylvia's direction, and these men sat quietly, for the first time outnumbered by the women in the room. Sylvia sat back in her chair, eyes on the ceiling as the music played. Beside her, Walt was still listening to the ethereal, undulating arpeggios of the harp and the bell-like celesta, a keyboard instrument not typically heard in symphonies but used extensively in the third movement of *The Nutcracker.* They did not sketch during the meetings, nor did they present story material. All of that would come later. For now, they just listened. The score was so striking that talk became unnecessary — the music spoke for them.

These silent story meetings produced some of the most beautiful storyboards ever created at the studio. The sketches were not the work of a few hurried months but instead drew on years of ideas that had long been rejected, as Sylvia adapted Bianca's early concepts of dancing flowers and fairies. Bianca and Ethel spent hours outside on the studio lot, sketching the weeds growing through the concrete and trying to mimic on the page the way the wind blew them to and fro.

The artists aimed to saturate the on-screen world they were creating with as much natural movement as possible; they studied snowflakes swirling in the winter wind and leaves falling to the ground. Walt was so enchanted with the story Sylvia and her team had created that he insisted it deserved enhanced animation. "It's like something you see with your eyes half closed," he said during one story meeting. "You almost imagine them. The leaves begin to look like they're dancing, and the blossoms floating on the water begin to look like ballet girls in skirts." He asked the visual effects department to create a look worthy of such dreamlike imagery, acknowledging that the abstractions they were proposing would need technical prowess to translate to film.

Sylvia worked closely with the visual effects department, eager to shape *The Nutcracker Suite* into an exquisite rendering of art and nature. To this end, she brought her small group of story artists and Herman Schultheis, a member of the special effects department, to the Idyllwild Nature Center in the San Jacinto Mountains east of Los Angeles. They spent so much time at the nature center, even renting a cabin there, that they called it their "summer studio."

Spread out on a hillside, the artists observed hardy leaves quiver in the breeze, wildflowers just beginning to bud, seedpods ready to burst, and dainty mushrooms clustered together in the damp earth. While the artists stuck to their pencils, Herman Schultheis used an assortment of cameras to shoot close-ups of thistles, poppies, and pine needles.

As they watched dewdrops reflecting sunlight in the park, the members of the group considered how they could create the same effect on film. Back at the studio, the visual effects department took a hexagonal wooden stand in the shape of a spiderweb and at its center placed a pastel drawing of leaves and webs on a black background. They photographed this and then took another shot, this time with the leaves and webs constructed from minuscule metal shavings. When eight lights were placed at angles around the stand and turned on one by one, it caused the shavings to illuminate in sequence. Once the second exposure was superimposed on the first, it looked as if a fairy was lighting up one dewdrop at a time.

The challenges of effects animation were only just beginning. The animators and the women of the Ink and Paint department were struggling to draw and color the arrival of winter. In her role as director, Sylvia met with special effects, where she found a man named Leonard Pickley willing to tackle the problem. The tricky scene involved dozens of fairy ballerinas wearing shining snowflake tutus and twirling across the dark indigo of a winter night sky. The animators needed to somehow create a detailed ballerina costume that looked and moved like a real snowflake. The solution lay in an innovative stop-motion technique.

In Ink and Paint, the women traced pictures of real snowflakes. They worked from photostats, an early type of photocopy obtained from a camera connected to a microscope. The setup was placed outdoors in a snowstorm many miles from Los Angeles, where a photographer put individual flakes, one at a time, onto a glass slide, slipped it under the microscope lens, then hastily snapped a picture. The inkers marveled at the exceptional detail as they traced the outlines onto cels and then painted each stroke in luminous white. Carefully, they cut the snowflakes from the plastic. They then fastened each one onto a spool that revolved independently while sliding on an S-shaped steel track that was covered in black velvet to hide the mechanics from the camera. Frame by frame, the special effects department shot the snowflakes as they moved down the track, spinning closer and closer to the camera. The resulting images were as close to the perfection of ephemeral snow crystals as had ever been filmed outside an actual snowstorm.

The snowflakes might have been complete, but they still lacked the fairies that ushered in winter. To add these to the scene, photostats of the snowflakes were given to the animators, who drew tiny fairies at the center of each flake. They then used a wash-relief technique, in which the image was transferred to a cel photographically. An optical printer, a device that allows filmmakers to rephotograph strips of film, was then employed to merge the willowy fairies with the stop-motion snowflakes. Each cel, which accounted for a mere fraction of a second of the final film, took hours of painstakingly precise work. It was worth it. The final result transcended anything that hand-drawn animation had previously been able to accomplish and ended the "Waltz of the Flowers" with a stunning flourish.

Retta Scott left Hollywood Hills and the apartment she shared with a friend in Laurel Canyon and drove down through the San Fernando Valley, then up past dry, grassy hills and twisting oak trees. The town

146

of Thousand Oaks was tiny, a mere dot in the greater Los Angeles landscape, but it had a large draw for those in the movie industry: Goebel's Wild Animal Farm. The farm was home to a host of exotic animals, many of which were recognizable from films of the era; Leo the Lion, mascot of the Metro-Goldwyn-Mayer studio, lived there. Retta wasn't interested in the animals' cinematic potential, however. She spent hours at Goebel's with her sketch pad and pencils, drawing them as they slept, stretched, or roamed their cages. They were captive, these beasts, and yet in Retta's drawings, they were unshackled, in the open, and free to run.

At the Chouinard Art Institute, which she attended on scholarship, Retta gained a reputation for being able to depict animals with startling realism. The Los Angeles Basin was strikingly different from the foothills of the Okanogan Mountains in Washington State where Retta had been raised, in a small town called Omak. Retta grew up running around her family's fruit orchard, dodging between apple trees as she played with her five siblings while her mother, the daughter of immigrants, yelled for them in Swedish. Retta was the third of five daughters and had a baby brother seven years younger than herself whom the family all doted on.

The Great Depression stole away the Scott family farm, as Retta's father could no longer keep up with the mortgage payments. Seeking work, he moved the family to a rental home near Lake Washington in Seattle, and at first Retta worried that the city could never offer them the happiness that the open air of the country had. It was school that brought Retta joy in Seattle. Her parents, who had never attended school themselves, were astonished at her ability in her classes. She excelled in the fine arts from an early age, earning a scholarship in the fourth grade from the Seattle Music and Art Foundation to take art classes throughout her public-school education. After high school, she moved to California for college.

Retta spent her time at Chouinard unimpressed with cartoons and animation, in her opinion a coarse, childish medium that seemed to have nothing to do with her aspirations as an artist. So she was surprised when, on the verge of her graduation in 1938, Chouinard's director asked if she would consider applying to the Walt Disney Studios. He had heard that *Bambi* was being developed as a feature-length film and thought immediately of Retta and her distinct talent for drawing animals. Retta, with no affection for Mickey Mouse, warmed to the idea slowly. It wasn't the career she had initially desired, but with the Great Depression still nibbling at the country's heels, she was thankful simply to find work.

The studio turned out to be different from her expectations. Hired in the story department, she was surprised at the devotion of the artists who worked alongside her, none of whom were merely scrabbling together rough drawings as she had once supposed. Instead, they spent countless hours perfecting the aesthetics of their work. She found that many of her colleagues were Chouinard graduates like herself, all having discarded their snobbery about what constitutes art after being admitted into the warmth of Walt's inner world.

Retta, like Walt, drew people to her. Her mere presence in a room could make a person smile. With her blond curls piled high atop her head, her tiny frame, and her bubbling enthusiasm, she appeared younger than her twenty-two years, but when she spoke, those around her took notice of her assurance and intelligence. Bianca, Grace, Dorothy, Sylvia, and Ethel had primed the men of the story department, gotten them accustomed to working alongside women, and so Retta's voice, new and female though it was, was accepted.

Walt, however, was not listening. The concert feature, although it remained nameless, seemed to be consuming him. He spent little time working on anything else. By the end of 1938, he had apparently forgotten about the studio's troublesome second feature, and he stopped attending story meetings for *Bambi* altogether.

The plane shot down the runway, the propeller whining, the metal fuselage rattling. Grace pulled on the yoke and the jolting ceased as the plane rose smoothly into the gray clouds of an overcast day. She hardly looked like herself that Monday afternoon in 1939, a day she would ordinarily have been working at the studio but that she had managed to take off thanks to her hours of overtime. She wore a wool flying suit several sizes too big, fur-lined gloves, and thick socks under tough leather boots. She piloted alone, her only companions a cylinder of oxygen, a flowmeter, and a Boothby-Lovelace-Bulbulian (BLB) mask tied down firmly within reach in the space where a seat had once been. That seat, along with its cushion, the toolbox, and whatever else

Grace considered unnecessary weight, had been left behind in the hangar.

Just two days earlier, she'd received a letter from one of the physicians who had developed the BLB mask, Dr. W. Randolph Lovelace II. He originally designed the equipment to give patients anesthesia more efficiently but then adapted the mask for aviators intent on breaking altitude records. Lovelace, like so many before him, had sent Grace a rejection letter, this one telling her that the metabolism laboratory at the Mayo Clinic in Minnesota didn't need any more pilots for their high-altitude experiments. Grace had become inured to refusal at this point, but she was grateful for the advice he'd sent her about using oxygen in the air.

It was a warm day on the ground in Burbank, but the higher she climbed, the colder the air became, dropping two degrees Celsius per thousand feet of elevation. Despite the poor visibility and the chill, Grace was excited. Years of training and months of preparation had led up to this moment. With some difficulty, she'd borrowed two separate Fairchild planes from a local dealer who hoped to get some publicity from her flights. Grace then spent countless hours comparing the two planes, making careful charts evaluating their oil temperature, oil pressure, and manifold pressure. She borrowed her brother's stopwatch to record the exact amount of time it took each plane to rise a thousand feet in the air. She swapped out propellers, searching for one with less drag, and shivered in the cabin as she made her test flights. Her struggle to get to this point — the pleading for opportunity, the embarrassment at mistakes made along the way — all seemed to drop away as she got higher in the sky. She was finally doing it, going for a new altitude record for a single-engine monoplane.

Climbing above the haze over the Los Angeles Basin, or "going upstairs," as Grace called it, she reached nineteen thousand feet in fifty minutes. Even with the limited oxygen at that elevation and the risk of hypoxia, Grace was feeling fine. She had not even touched her oxygen mask. The plane, however, was not doing so well. Grace couldn't believe that today of all days, the Fairchild would act up. She tried everything she could think of but it refused to climb higher than nineteen thousand feet. She had reached the aircraft's ceiling and was now getting low on fuel. Gas weighs six pounds a gallon and Grace was carrying as little as possible despite a member of the ground crew pleading, "Grace, please take more than last trip. You came back with only about half a teacup left in the tank!" These words rang in her ears as she began her return, aware that she had not a drop to waste.

She descended as quickly as she thought safe, leaving behind the San Gabriel Mountains and flying over Pasadena on her way west toward the setting sun. When she dropped down into the clouds, visibility sharply decreased. She could see only half a mile ahead of her. She began to worry about Burbank closing their airport. If she landed under such conditions, she would be violating the Civil Aeronautics Administration regulations and potentially endangering others. She also couldn't help but remember a close call she'd had once before, flying through the valley, when she hadn't been paying enough attention and had nearly collided with a large DC-3 transport plane, avoiding disaster only by making a last-minute dive. She thought of the transport planes below her now, circling in poor weather over Burbank, and decided it wasn't worth the hazard. Although she knew she was nearly out of fuel, she decided to take the risk of flying all the way to Glendale instead.

The rubber wheels bounced down the runway as Grace scanned the airfield. She parked the plane, placed blocks in front of the wheels, and grabbed the sealed barometer, which could not leave her sight and would later be sent to Washington, DC, to officially record her altitude attempt, before rushing to a nearby phone to let her friends at Burbank Airport know what had happened to her.

Grace stood chatting with a mechanic for companionship as she waited for her friends to pick her up. Now back in the July heat on the ground, she was sweating in her flight suit. She had worn nothing underneath it and so had to stew until she could get home to change.

When the press arrived, along with her friends, there was a flurry of excitement. She posed for pictures both in the cockpit and outside the plane, a smile plastered on her face. But once she got home, feelings of inadequacy rose within her. She wished the plane had climbed higher, as it had during her test runs. She worried that all her preparation would be for naught if she hadn't attained a new altitude record. These lonely feelings stayed with her as she tossed and turned through the night.

The next day she opened the morning *Los*

Angeles Times, and there was her picture, an oxygen tube and mask hanging around her neck, alongside the headline "Woman Flyer Sets Altitude Record." Delayed feelings of happiness and accomplishment washed over her as she excitedly showed the paper to her mother. Yet her mother's gaze held not pride, but disgust. To Grace's shock, she said in a sour voice, "You're only interested in the publicity."

The locomotive was racing down the track, but no one had built a station for it to stop at. This was how the studio's development of the concert feature was advancing in the fall of 1939. Without a clear end date for the film, some artists wondered if this would be Walt's undoing, his first unfinished picture. Coincidentally, this was how Walt himself viewed it, albeit in a more favorable light. He envisioned the concert feature as a never-ending orchestral mix in which classical music could constantly be replaced and reimagined with new animation, thereby running in theaters perpetually. Yet even with this idyllic prospect before him, Walt knew the train had to stop sometime. He began having the story directors present their Leica reels, a kind of developed storyboard using filmed animated stills, in conjunction with the soundtrack.

Sylvia's nerves were on edge as she presented her second set of Leica reels to Walt. Indecision gnawed at her, not about her work on the concert feature, where she guided with a sure hand, but about whether to ask Walt for more money. She wondered if it was better to ask now or wait until she'd presented her work. Perhaps if Walt liked it, she reasoned, her raise would be higher. Sylvia, although a story director and with a family to support, made considerably less than her male counterparts. She took home thirty dollars a week. Other story directors, all men, were paid between seventy and eighty dollars a week. She had been hesitant to ask for a raise — she didn't want to appear greedy — and so she put it off again. She concentrated on her reels instead, spending long hours in the studio and then watching closely as the animation she had developed was filmed in Technicolor and then "blooped," a term for setting it to music.

Part of Sylvia's caution stemmed from the fact that a man kept taking credit for her work. One of the directors of the picture had an infuriating habit of stealing Sylvia's ideas and passing them off to Walt as his own. Sylvia could do little but watch her

One of Sylvia's colleagues admiring his newly decorated office. Halo added by Sylvia Holland.

colleague continually receive praise for work that she had performed. On February 5, she decided to take her revenge. It was the director's birthday and as a special treat, she sneaked into his office before working hours and covered the entire space with streamers of toilet paper. When he walked in that morning he was met with laughs and a sprinkle of applause. Amid the revelry, he had no choice but to smile and chuckle at the new decorations. Sylvia was laughing too, although not in the same spirit.

Urgency to finish the concert feature was

percolating throughout the studio. They had already been working on the film for three years and so the need to hurry could be felt in every department, even in promotional materials, where an artist named Gyo (pronounced "Geo") Fujikawa worked. Before she was born, her father, sure that she would be a boy, had decided to name her Gyo, after a wise and benevolent Chinese emperor. When she came into the world clearly a female, he stubbornly refused to change the name. So Gyo she became, a nisei woman from Berkeley, California, who had the easy temper and academic prowess of the emperor she was named after. When she graduated from San Pedro High School, all her friends were getting married, and for a short while it seemed she would join them; she became engaged at the age of nineteen. But ultimately she decided to break off the engagement, much to her mother's embarrassment. Her mother was so mortified that she sent her daughter to Japan for a year, hardly a punishment to Gyo, who feasted on traditional art by masters from across the centuries, including Sesshu, Utamaro, and Hiroshige, and soaked up color palettes inspired by the smoky-hued silks of kimonos.

When she came home, all thoughts of settling into a normal, domestic life had vanished, replaced by her fierce desire to become part of the art world. She received a scholarship to attend the Chouinard Art Institute and packed her bags for Los Angeles, a city that would be her home for the next decade. After graduating from the institute, she decided not to leave, joining the faculty. As a professor, Gyo helped guide countless artists, one of whom was the quiet and determined Mary Blair. It was clear to Gyo that Mary, who seemed older and wiser than her peers and had a gift for design, would find success in the art world.

After four years of teaching, Gyo realized that her own needs as an artist had outgrown her affection for the art school, and she moved on, working on murals and displays for department stores and refining her illustration style in her own pieces at home. A friend recommended her to Walt Disney Studios, where she began work in the promotions department.

Gyo's artistic style quickly drew attention. Artists, many of whom she was familiar with from her tenure at Chouinard, gathered around her desk. One of her new admirers was Art Babbitt, a top animator at the studio. Babbitt asked Gyo for a date, to which she quickly agreed. The news buzzed around the studio, and Gyo was soon the recipient of all kinds of unwanted advice and off-color warnings — for instance, that she would become pregnant before she even entered a room with Babbitt. Dating among the artists was not unusual and neither was the gossip it incited, but Gyo did not enjoy the attention. Rather than risk endless rumors, she decided to call off the date.

Gyo's career at the studio was broadening. She designed products based on the upcoming concert feature, items such as saltshakers, china sets, and glassware, and illustrated a tie-in picture book. She created a theater program for the film's premiere in select cities. The brochure was important if unusual. The concert feature would be the first American film released without credits, not even the standard "Walt Disney Presents." The lack of opening credits was meant to give the audience the sense of being at a real concert, not a movie. The film begins with the opening of a curtain, the rush of musicians taking their seats, and the sound of them tuning their instruments in preparation to play.

Opening credits for the studio's films had long been a subject of contention. Animators complained of having to fight for them, with only the most ruthless successful in getting their names onto the silver screen. The established convention at the studio was that if you produced at least one hundred feet of work, you received on-screen credit. The reality was far more complicated, particularly for those story artists whose contributions could not be measured in feet.

Sylvia was about to feel the chafe of this injustice. She was reviewing the film with Walt and a small group of directors at what Walt called a "sweatbox meeting," as employees perspired liberally while going over the raw, unedited footage, although whether the sweat arose from the small, stuffy theater or Walt's sharp criticism was never clear. Sylvia was not especially anxious at this particular meeting. She felt confident in the film they were reviewing and it quickly became clear that Walt was pleased, as he complimented her work in his usual encouraging style.

With the stressful part of the meeting over, Sylvia relaxed. The credits, though they would ultimately be printed only on a program, were thrown up on the screen for review. She glanced through the names casually, never doubting that her own would make the cut. But as the list unspooled, she was shocked to find herself omitted. Sylvia was usually calm and cool but this provocation was too much for even her easy temper. She went completely silent, stood up, and walked out of the room. "Sylvia? Sylvia!" one of the men called out after her, but she didn't turn around. It was obvious that she was livid, yet she refused to say a word to any of them. Walt, sensing trouble, followed her down the hall. "What's wrong?" he asked. The anger coursed through her and at first she was too mad to even answer. After a minute of silently boiling, however, she turned to Walt and exploded. "It's outrageous!" she exclaimed, then insisted that her work be properly credited.

Sylvia would get the satisfaction of seeing her name, though many others wouldn't. While no names would grace the screen for the concert feature, that did not mean that the struggle for credit was any less ugly or less exclusionary than on other films. For the *Nutcracker Suite* segment, for instance, credit in the program was eventually given to twenty-two artists, fewer than half of the total fifty-three men and women who'd worked on it. Sylvia made certain that not only her name but also the names of two of the women who toiled alongside her, Bianca Majolie and Ethel Kulsar, were featured prominently. Theirs were the only women's names in the entire program.

The studio still had to find a title to emblazon on the program's cover; it couldn't be known as "the concert feature" forever. The answer came from an unanticipated source, the conductor Stokowski, who would shake hands with Mickey Mouse onscreen. He suggested the name *Fantasia,* a word first tied to music in the sixteenth century and meaning a free-form composition not bound by structure. It fit their boundary-breaking film perfectly.

Oskar Fischinger showed up to the studio that Friday much as he had every day for the past nine months. He was working as an animator on *Fantasia,* but he was also an experimental filmmaker whose animation employed stunning techniques such as stop-motion, time-lapse, and intricate collages of geometric patterns. For years, his avant-garde shorts had been shown all over Europe except in his native Germany, where they were met by fierce criticism from the Nazi Party; its members called his work "degenerate." In the 1930s the Reich propaganda ministry had begun shutting down art schools, removing paintings from museums, burning books, and taking over film studios. After Fischinger defiantly criticized the Nazis in 1936, he fled his homeland and headed to America.

Tensions were increasing in Asia as well. In the summer of 1939, one hundred thousand Japanese and Soviet troops clashed on the border of Mongolia and Manchuria. As August ended, the will of the Japanese forces gave out, and after massive losses, they conceded defeat. Following this show of power, the Soviets signed a nonaggression pact with Germany on August 23, 1939. It was this alliance that spurred Hitler to storm Poland just one week later, on Friday, September 1, 1939. For many at the studio and in the city at large, it was just another weekday — but not for Fischinger. A swastika had been pinned to his office door by a few coworkers. Whether the gesture was meant as an act of aggression or a joke was unclear, but either way, the result was the same. It was the breaking point for a man who had once been questioned by the Gestapo for refusing to display that very symbol. The men who mocked Fischinger's German heritage knew little about him, as he was frequently quiet in story meetings. They would never get to learn more. Fischinger quit the studio two months later.

For those Walt Disney Studios employees who had ties to Europe and Asia, such as

Fischinger, Sylvia, Bianca, and Gyo, the news abroad had become deeply unnerving, as had the public reaction to it. Isolationists in America consisted of both progressives and conservatives, and since memories of World War I losses and the squeeze of the Great Depression were still fresh, there were few in the United States who were willing to risk the costs of entanglement.

And so, while hostilities were escalating across both the Atlantic and Pacific Oceans, the group at Walt Disney Studios continued their work and prepared for a move. Trucks were packed with furniture and boxes and festooned with signs proclaiming MICKEY MOUSE and NEW WALT DISNEY STUDIOS.

The move was two years in the making, taking Walt and his now one thousand employees from their cramped quarters on Hyperion Avenue to the new, spacious, fifty-one-acre lot in Burbank. Not everyone was sure of the studio's continued success, however. Walt's father, Elias Disney, took his son aside after a tour of the new animation building and asked, "What can it be used for?" He was worried; how would Walt sell the gigantic space if the company went bankrupt and its assets needed to be liquidated? "Well, this would make a perfect hospital," Walt replied. The building would henceforth be known as "the Hospital."

Elias Disney's concerns for his son's business seemed less silly after the studio's move was completed in early 1940. The company, try as it might, could no longer ignore the effect war was having on its business. Even in the midst of terror, those Europeans who were still at liberty to do so were continuing to go to their neighborhood movie houses, happy to escape reality and sink into a theater seat that could drop them into a world of illusion. Micky Maus in Nazi Germany, Mickey la Souris in France, and Topolino in Italy received equally warm receptions, though in each case, the escapades of the character were bookended by very different newsreels and propaganda films.

Despite Mickey's continued popularity, the money from ticket sales was not being sent back to California. War had cut off payments from the studio's distributors. And so Walt announced that they would have to slash one million dollars in expenses and fire three to four hundred employees. The cuts ate at Sylvia's peace of mind. Walt had just given her a raise of twenty-five dollars a week, and her assistant, Ethel, had received a raise of ten dollars a week. The money she had fretted over requesting for months was now in her hand but her future in animation was more uncertain than ever.

With violence escalating overseas, Walt decided that the world premiere of *Fantasia* would be a fund-raiser, with "music you can see and pictures you can hear," held at New York City's Broadway Theater. The event took place on November 13, 1940; tickets sold for ten dollars each — an astronomical price for a movie ticket at the time — and 100 percent of the profits raised went to the British War Relief Society.

Fantasia was the second film the studio released in 1940, the first being *Pinocchio* in February. The reviews for *Pinocchio* were glowing; the *New York Times* declared, "*Pinocchio . . .* is every bit as fine as we had prayed it would be — if not finer." But the box office did not agree. The film had cost twice as much to make as *Snow White,* more than two million dollars, but the returns were far smaller, only about one million by year's end. It was a staggering deficit that made Walt pin his hopes on *Fantasia*'s release.

At the Los Angeles premiere, held two months later at the Carthay Circle Theater, Sylvia walked down the red carpet with her daughter, Theo, now thirteen years old. The years of struggle and pain were finally giv-

167

ing way to deserved pride and celebration. She smiled as she watched Deems Taylor, the composer who acts as an emcee in the film, introduce the music for her work. "It's a series of dances taken out of a full-length ballet called *The Nutcracker,*" Taylor explained. "It wasn't much of a success and nobody performs it nowadays."

Sylvia's only regret was that her family in England would not get to see her work — there were no plans for *Fantasia* to be distributed overseas. Even with this disappointment and the impending cuts, Sylvia felt her career was advancing. She had exciting new projects in the works, and Walt had just promised her a promotion and another raise, one that would finally give her the financial security she longed for.

Bianca did not attend the premiere, and she would never see the completed film. Even as some of her best and most inspired artwork was finally reaching the silver screen, she was falling into a depression. She began to isolate herself even more profoundly from her coworkers, many of whom, particularly the men, were envious of her portfolio. In the quiet solitude of her new office, she got into the habit of drinking port wine by the bottle, the telltale smell of the sweet alcohol filling the small room.

The alcohol stole away not only her pain but also her consciousness, leaving her in a hazy gloom. And in the distance, the darkness that was spreading in 1940 was coming for all of them.

CHAPTER 5
LITTLE APRIL SHOWER

The artists working on *Bambi* gathered around a pile of sketches. No one knew where the drawings had come from, but all agreed that they were terrifying. The hunting dogs seemed to leap off the page with thick, muscular bodies and arresting eyes. In the sketches, the snarling beasts corner the doe Faline. Bambi then charges in, using his antlers to fend off the vicious animals in scenes that burst with action; the dogs' backs arch in pain and Bambi's antlers are framed perfectly in each shot to highlight their strength. The artists looked at one another and asked, "Who did this? Whose drawings are these?" The animators all assumed that the mystery artist was a man. But no one took credit. It seemed as though the sketches had fallen from the sky. Then Retta Scott walked in. Here was their culprit — not a man at all but a young woman with blond curls piled on top of her head and a host of ideas on how to make the attacking animals even more frightening.

Walt Disney Studios had just moved into its new home in Burbank, and for Retta, the move had come not a moment too soon. The story group working on *Bambi* back on Hyperion Avenue had been relegated to a small outbuilding on Seward Street that they called, not affectionately, "Termite Terrace," as its walls had started curving inward; the place was literally crumbling. The Burbank studio, in contrast, with its three-story streamline moderne design, was like a palace. Walt had personally worked on the architectural plans, helping to create the massive eight-wing building that was formed from two side-by-side H-shaped structures with plenty of windows so that natural light flowed into the offices. The animators and concept artists were on the ground floor; directors, background, and layout artists were on the second; and the story department and Walt's office were on the third.

If you took a private elevator up to the roof, you entered an entirely different world. Getting off the lift, one was confronted by a mural of fourteen nude women surrounding a single man. Known as the Penthouse Club, the space offered a bar and restaurant, a barbershop, a massage table, a gym, steam baths, beds, and billiard and card tables, as well as a large uncovered area popular for nude sunbathing. The exclusively male club required substantial dues, and there was a strict selection process to join. An employee had to make more than two hundred dollars a week, an amount attained by only a small number of animators. It was a new era of elitism at the studio, one that rankled many of the artists, who had previously viewed their group, crammed together in ramshackle buildings on Hyperion Avenue, as a family.

Retta worked on the third floor in the story department, creating her sketches for *Bambi.* Walt was finally turning his attention back to the forest feature; he'd confessed, "I haven't felt that *Bambi* was one of our productions." Four years earlier, when Bianca had first started writing story treatments for the film based on the novel, she had noted the book's message of peace and the beauty inherent in its descriptions of the natural world. But it also had a political message that was even more necessary now that war was escalating in Europe and Asia.

Devastation was spreading across the globe in 1940, but the United States was shutting its eyes. Felix Salten, the author of *Bambi,* had always been conscious of surrounding danger. Born in 1869, Salten was the grandson of an Orthodox rabbi. When he was only a month old, his family, seeking tolerance of their Jewish faith, moved from what is today Budapest, Hungary, to Vienna, Austria. Following the Enlightenment that had pervaded eighteenth-century Europe, in 1867 the city had begun granting citizenship to its Jewish residents, something many European cities refused to do. This sparked a mass migration of Jews to Vienna in search of social and economic opportunities.

As a young artist, Salten was a passionate Zionist, writing articles and giving speeches advocating a homeland for Jews in Palestine. When the Nazis banned *Bambi* in 1936, they declared the work "a political allegory on the treatment of Jews in Germany." They were only partially correct; the meaning of Salten's work goes far deeper.

In *Bambi: A Life in the Woods,* Salten illustrates the dangers of cultural assimilation. Several animals in the book advocate saving themselves from humans by bending to their will and joining forces with them. For the animals who submit to the cruel hunters, however, things do not work out well. Gobo, a sickly young buck, tells Bambi,

"I don't need to be afraid of them anymore. I'm good friends with them now." Gobo believes that the halter he wears will keep him safe, but when he naively approaches a hunter in a meadow, the man shoots him dead. Even the vicious dogs that Retta sketched with such skill play complex roles in Salten's book, as animal collaborators with the very hunters they despise. Bambi's father describes their beliefs this way: "They pass their lives in fear, they hate [Man] and themselves and yet they'd die for His sake." It was no coincidence that *Bambi* was finally coming together at the studio in 1940. The story was a response to the rise of fascism, a tale that those employees who closely followed events abroad felt fervent about telling.

When Walt saw Retta's sketches for *Bambi,* made as part of her work developing the script, he was so overwhelmed by her talent that he decided to do something unprecedented: he made Retta an animator. She was the first woman to join that elite group. If the story department was "the heart of the organization," as Walt said, then the animators were the lifeblood coursing through it, each artist handpicked by Walt. Being promoted to animator was no minor accomplishment. Many men and some women worked as "inbetweeners," cleaning up the animators' drawings and making the repetitive sketches that linked together their work and gave the characters movement. It was a job that someone might occupy for years before becoming an assistant animator and, eventually, a character animator. Even those who made it to the top had to consistently perform in order to maintain their position. Retta knew that her prowess in the story department had steered her into a spot only a select few occupied.

An in-house write-up of Retta's promotion read jokingly, "The Animators had always hoped that their pleasurable existence wouldn't be marred by the entrance of a mere girl into their working lives." Retta reported to her new department to find that her male colleagues had mockingly decorated the space for her, hanging ruffled, feminine curtains and placing a lace doily on her chair.

Retta was not working solely on *Bambi;* she was pitching in wherever help was needed. She began animating the centaurettes for *Fantasia,* her precise hands drawing the lines already dictated by her male colleagues. The Pastoral Symphony sequence was past the point of redemption, and all Retta could do was bring her own skill to the flawed scenes before her.

In 1940, opportunities were expanding for women at the Walt Disney Studios. Retta was the beacon, lighting the path to the animation floor that other women hoped to follow. There were only five other women working as inbetweeners and assistant animators at the time; one of them was artist Mildred Fulvia di Rossi, "Millie" to her friends.

Millie had created terrifying sketches of Chernabog, a monster in the *Night on Bald Mountain* sequence in *Fantasia.* In drawing the winged creature in hues of cobalt, with white glowing eyes and long claws, she found an affection for the beast. Millie and Retta, the women of the animation department, were creating the studio's most terrifying monsters. And more were coming.

With women carving a permanent place for themselves in animation, a memo was circulated in the department asking men to watch their language and stating that "it has always been Walt's hope that the studio could be a place where girls can be employed without fear of embarrassment or humiliation." An influx of women was similarly arriving in the effects and story departments. Of the 1,023 total employees

176

working for the studio, 308 of them were women. Most of them were still confined to Ink and Paint, but more than a hundred were spread out over other departments. In the proportion of women employed, Walt Disney Studios outperformed any other major Hollywood studio and even most American workplaces of the time, where, on average, a quarter of the workforce was female. Walt was determined to grow these numbers further and started to take steps to do so. The other men at the studio, however, observed Walt's new hiring practices with trepidation.

One of the women hired in 1940 was Mary Blair. After three and a half years, she was fleeing the Harman-Ising Studio, where she felt that one of her coworkers, Joe Barbera (later a founder of Hanna-Barbera Productions), wouldn't leave her alone. He allegedly made passes at her and often wrapped his arms around her waist and refused to let go, even in the middle of the office. Mary hated the daily harassment and begged her husband, Lee, to find her a job at Walt Disney Studios, where he had been working for the past two years.

Lee got her a job in the character-model department, where artists made three-dimensional figurines of characters to aid the story artists and animators. It was an odd fit for the painter who preferred to work in watercolor. When Mary's talents were finally recognized, she was sent over to the story department. They were working on a new project tentatively titled *Lady,* and Mary started sketches of a puppy with floppy brown ears for the canine coming-of-age story.

When Mary entered her new workspace, her mouth fell open. There were women everywhere. It couldn't be more different from Harman-Ising. Even her boss, Sylvia Holland, was a woman. While Bianca found Sylvia to be somewhat overwhelming and called her a "mother hen," Mary saw in Sylvia the soul of a sympathetic artist. Under Sylvia's direction, Mary began working on "Baby Ballet," part of a proposed *Fantasia* sequel. The men considered drawing babies as unmanly as animating fairies, and they refused to work on it. The women were unafraid and so designed the sequence together. Mary and Sylvia created a multicultural group of infants who emerged from a large shared bed to dance playfully together. There was pleasure in the work, but not nearly enough freedom. While her husband enjoyed artistic liberty at the studio, Mary felt stifled in her more modest role.

Working alongside Mary, a male artist named Tyrus Wong shared her feelings of being underestimated. Tyrus had been born Wong Gen Yeo in a small fishing village in China. In 1919, at age nine, Wong left China with his father and set out for San Francisco, which promised more stability and economic opportunity. Wong said good-bye to his mother and sister tenderly. He would never see either of them again.

When immigrants arrived in San Francisco, they were separated by nationality. Wong watched wide-eyed as Europeans and those traveling first class were allowed immediate entry into the city. He and his father, as well as other Asians, some Russians, and those arriving from Central and South America, were shipped over to the Angel Island immigration center, between Alcatraz and the Golden Gate Bridge.

In 1922, the commissioner-general of the U.S. Bureau of Immigration declared Angel Island to be filthy and unfit for human habitation, describing "the conglomeration of ramshackle buildings which are nothing but firetraps." He wrote, "The sanitary arrangements are awful. If a private individual had such an establishment he would be arrested by the local health authorities." Angel Island was originally envisioned as "the Ellis Island of the West," but at Ellis Island, only 2 percent of those seeking refuge were barred from entering, and most were admitted to the United States within a few hours of landing, whereas at Angel Island, roughly 30 percent of immigrants were turned away, often after they'd spent months as detainees.

This first experience of American racial prejudice for Wong and his father was the result of the Chinese Exclusion Act of 1882. The country's first significant law restricting immigration, it put a moratorium on all Chinese laborer immigration and marked the first time an ethnic group was targeted by the U.S. government.

After two weeks, Wong's father was admitted to the United States, but he had to leave his son behind at Angel Island. Finally, after a month of detention, the boy was permitted to gather up his belongings and board the ferry. He was finally free, but life was not necessarily easier. Wong and his father lived in the Sacramento Chinese Community Center, and Wong attended the local elementary school. Finding his personal name, Gen Yeo, difficult to pronounce, one of his teachers changed it to Tyrus. He struggled at school, especially as he had to learn English along with his other subjects.

After two years, his father moved to Los Angeles in pursuit of work, leaving Tyrus behind at the community center. The eleven-year-old found work in a grocery store, where he bought the ingredients to make his own dinner after his shift. At age fourteen he joined his father in Los Angeles, happy to no longer be alone and finding a tenuous balance between school and work. At night, after dinner, his father would train him in Chinese calligraphy. With no money for ink or paper, they would dip their brushes in water and paint on old newspaper. For a few moments the beautiful words were visible, but then they would evaporate, vanishing into the air.

A career in the arts seemed as elusive as those disappearing words until one summer, while still in junior high school, Tyrus learned he had received a partial scholarship to the Otis Art Institute in Los Angeles. Despite the significant financial strain it would entail, he was determined to attend. He found comfort in unexpected places at Otis, not only in his classes on life drawing, painting, and illustration but in the cafeteria where he worked as a busboy and where an elderly waitress insisted on feeding him

181

leftovers. The school gave Tyrus paints and canvases and also helped him find work designing signs for local businesses. His father, looking at one design for which Tyrus had earned twenty-five dollars, told his son how proud he was of him. It would be the last words of artistic admiration Tyrus heard from his father, who would die shortly afterward, before Tyrus finished school.

After graduation, like many other artists in the 1930s, Tyrus worked as a painter for the Works Progress Administration. At a restaurant where he waited tables, he met a young woman named Ruth Kim, and they were soon married. Now a husband and soon to become a father, Tyrus had to find a better-paying job and someplace to live. He looked for weeks for an apartment, but no landlord would rent to the young Chinese couple.

A steady job was just as difficult to obtain. Applying to the Walt Disney Studios, Tyrus cited his education and exhibitions at the Los Angeles County Museum and the New York World's Fair. Even with these impressive credentials, he was hired as only an in-betweener, not an animator. His first day on the job, he was referred to by a racial slur, and the work was tedious. But then he learned of the new picture the studio was making: *Bambi.*

Tyrus read Salten's book and was inspired by the writing. At night he began sketching, drawing in pastels the natural beauty of the forest, a lone deer the only animal visible. He brought the sketches to the art director on the film, who showed them to Walt. The reaction was immediately positive: "It looks like we put you in the wrong department," the director said. Tyrus would soon be sitting in on story meetings, creating concept art that set the film's style, making storyboards, and designing backgrounds. His art instilled *Bambi* with mysterious splendor — the light-dappled leaves in the forest, early-morning mists, shadowy thickets — and captured the poetry of Salten's work.

Tyrus was not the only Asian American working at the studio. Cy Young, born and raised in Hawaii, the child of Chinese immigrants, had joined the studio early on and by the early 1940s held an influential position as a special effects animator. There were also Bob Kuwahara, a story artist; Chris Ishii, an assistant animator; and James Tanaka, an animator, among others. Yet Tyrus was often mistaken for a busboy in the cafeteria, and at story meetings he was frequently quiet, preferring his work to speak for him. His studio file gave his height, weight, and marital status along with one short sentence summing up his strengths: "Good on inspirational sketches, but of an oriental variety with that type of treatment."

While Tyrus was slowly breaking free of the studio's biases and low expectations, Mary found her own ambitions still stymied. The projects she was working on were interesting, particularly a feature about a little girl named Penelope, a time traveler who explores the world. But unlike Tyrus, Mary had no creative control over her projects or the gratification of seeing her work on-screen. Her confidence was faltering, but she found Tyrus's impressive work soothing. The hundreds of paintings he had produced as concept art for *Bambi* were in a completely different style from her own, yet she loved the soft brushstrokes of his backgrounds and the delicate forms of his deer. The two worked near each other on the third floor, and when they heard someone yell, "Man is in the forest," a line from *Bambi,* they knew Walt was coming out of his office and heading their way. They hurriedly put their best sketches on top of the piles on their desks, eager to impress.

Grace, like Mary, felt that her real purpose

was elsewhere. In 1940 she was looking for a way to escape the studio and enter the world of aviation. She wrote to as many people as she could, searching for work. The rejection letters that flowed in were too numerous to count. Fortunately, her many hours in story meetings had taught her how to handle rejection. And so she simply kept her head down and kept sending inquiries. She joined the American Rocket Society and asked questions about jet propulsion and rocket ships. She wrote to famed engineer and physicist Dr. Robert Goddard, who told her about a group of students at the California Institute of Technology interested in rocketry, so Grace wrote to them as well. The students, known as the Suicide Squad, would become the forefathers of modern rocketry and space exploration, but these young men didn't know what to make of a bold female pilot.

She dreamed of seeing the curve of the Earth from above, writing of her hopes in her journal:

I have realized that interplanetary travel will never be realized in my lifetime . . . So far, only twelve miles above the earth have actually been explored. We can guess what is higher, we can surmise by scientific conjecture, but until someone has been higher, all the supposed knowledge is only a guess. This exploration would not be useful just for the future of interplanetary travel. It would add to man's knowledge . . . I can learn to handle a plane at high altitudes and in this way be of help to scientists and engineers who need some pilot to bring down actual data to them. In the future perhaps it will be a rocket ship or balloon that will bring down this important data, but the pilot of the contrivance, whatever it may be, is most apt to be chosen from the ranks of pilots who have had experience in the stratosphere. If I can build my experience and name, I might, slim as the chance is, be chosen.

These dreams seeped into Grace's work at the studio, where she was developing dialogue for *Bambi.* The story department grappled with how to convey the philosophical meaning of the book. Unlike *Snow White* and *Pinocchio,* there was no dramatic arc to guide the film. Instead, the narrative rose and fell like the life cycle of the forest itself. The department wanted to evoke emotion and mix in traces of humor but without the cheap gags the Mickey Mouse shorts relied upon.

186

At story meetings Walt enumerated the many ideas their early research had dug up. From Bianca's early notes, made after watching the birth of a fawn, he proposed animating the first shaky steps of a newborn. Some of his other ideas were not as charming. In a critical scene on the storyboard, Bambi's father takes his son to see the dead bodies of human beings in order to show him that man did not have unlimited power over nature. Walt suggested showing the charred bodies of the hunters after they'd lost control of the fire they started in the forest. The story department dismissed the idea, feeling that the imagery would be too intense for many adults, much less children. Ultimately, humans would never be shown at all, not even their shadows.

Striking a balance between staying true to the novel and adapting it for young audiences was proving increasingly difficult. The story department was particularly concerned over the death of Bambi's mother, a scene that stirred deep emotion for all who had read it in the novel. They discussed showing Bambi's mother dead in the snow but decided it would be too much. Even without that image, the scene still worried Walt; he asked the team, "Do you think it's too sad, too gripping?" They painstakingly went over each line spoken between Bambi and his father, everyone contributing ideas on how to shape the moment without over-sentimentalizing it. They didn't take it lightly — this would be the first death depicted in a Disney film. They finally decided Bambi's father would say a single line: "Your mother can't be with you any-more."

"And as the stag goes off," said Walt, standing in front of the storyboard, "why, this little guy is going along there, trying to be brave and going on off into this blizzard, followed by the big stag . . . and pretty soon, they have disappeared and there is nothing but this snow falling."

It was Tyrus's art that showed the story department how to trim their script. Ulti-mately the movie would have a mere one thousand words of dialogue, less than a fifth of *Pinocchio*'s script. Tyrus's paintings, not words, conveyed the emotional resonance of the story. For some, the scenes in the final film would prove overwhelmingly emotional. When Walt's nine-year-old daughter, Diane, saw the completed feature, she cried and asked her dad, "Why did you have to kill Bambi's mother?"

The long-pushed-aside feature was finally

getting the attention it deserved. At the studio, the sweet smell of hay filled an entire soundstage, where two young orphaned fawns, shipped by train all the way from Maine to Hollywood, nestled on the ground. The deer, named Bambi and Faline, slept while more than a dozen artists sat around on folding chairs and benches, sketching them. An instructor in animal anatomy, Rico Lebrun, was on hand to assist the group. Their goal was to create a lifelike image of the deer, starkly different from the cartoon animals drawn for *Snow White*. Retta was frequently the only woman sketching with the men. They all took turns feeding the orphaned deer, giving them baby bottles filled with cow's milk.

Even those who weren't nursing fawns had baby animals taking over their sketch pads. Sylvia was designing a sequence set to a song called "Little April Shower." She drew not only the deer but also rabbits, quail, squirrels, skunks, and birds, all scurrying through the woods. The piece had been written by Frank Churchill, already well regarded at the studio for his ability to write music based on a simple story idea. His original score for *Snow White* — which included "Whistle While You Work," "Heigh-Ho," and "Someday My Prince Will Come"

— had been nominated for an Academy Award. Sylvia was immediately drawn to the rhythm of "Little April Shower," which evoked the feeling of being caught in a storm. The staccato sound of the wind instruments was reminiscent of the beating of raindrops. Between the orchestral sounds, the song was punctuated by real thunderclaps. To create the howl of the wind, Churchill composed a section inspired by Gregorian chants; it had no discernible words, merely the rise and fall of the choir's voices.

Sylvia strove to give the sequence a genuine look, showing how a rainstorm moves through the forest. She and her team aspired to a spiritual interpretation of nature that captured the very essence of Salten's writing but without using any words. For this to work, she needed a lot of action occurring in a small amount of time. She used quick edits to move from one animal to another: the quail rushing through the brush, the squirrels and mice hurrying to their homes, and Bambi and his mother nestled together in the thicket. Sylvia kept the tempo of the action consistent with the music, choosing camera angles to highlight both the beauty of the forest and the drama of the storm. Working on *Fantasia* had taught her the power music could have in telling a story.

Accuracy in representing the physical world was key to communicating its splendor. Sylvia, together with the special effects department, made sure each raindrop adhered to physical laws. They fell as elongated spheres and splashed into the water, making ripples. To achieve this effect, the group photographed water falling in the dark with a spotlight trained on the cascade. They enlarged the images so that each splash was frozen in time and then traced over the photograph, rendering the drops in all their intricacy. The ripples created by the falling water were made, not with ink, but with lacquer layered in rings directly on the cels. These were subtle details that Sylvia didn't expect the audience to fully see and appreciate, but combined, they lent realism.

There were moments of excitement too. With each lightning strike, the team used an X-ray effect, making the forest momentarily glow and highlighting the veins of the leaves on the trees. The final result was striking. Story direction, story research, script writing, art direction, and scene timing — it seemed there was nothing Sylvia couldn't do.

Retta, however, was still learning. While most animators had inbetweeners to perform the menial task of creating the transitional sketches that form the action of each character, Retta had only herself to rely on. She had been assigned no assistants. She didn't even have a proper desk of her own yet and was working in one of the secretary rooms.

Like any new animator, she leaned on the seasoned artists around her, and they helped her refine her skills. She put in long hours creating hundreds of sketches of her evil dogs. The creatures seem to pile up on one another as they move ferociously up the slippery cliff where Faline stands frightened. They attack with the flow of an ocean wave over the rocks and then engulf Bambi, biting his neck and legs. The only woman in the animators' room had created the fiercest creatures in the forest.

Retta drew her sketches with paper and pencil before she traced them in india ink. Once finished, she gave them to the Ink and Paint department, where the women traced her work with quill pens that were incredibly sensitive. When walking down the corridor outside their rooms, the Ink and Paint artists shuffled their feet rather than lifting them and putting them down so that nary a vibration would cause the pens to quiver. The cels they were tracing the sketches onto had traditionally been made of cellulose nitrate. The long chains of sugar molecules that make up the compound cellulose form all plant-cell walls, everything from the trunks of trees to the fluffy buds that bloom across cotton fields. When cellulose nitrate is mixed with camphor, it results in a clear, flexible plastic, ideal for the animator's pen. Unfortunately, it is also highly flammable; it has even been known to spontaneously combust. Walt was always eager to adopt new technology, and the Disney studio was one of the first to switch to a new and more stable plastic: cellulose acetate.

Performing both the animator and inbetweener work was exhausting but also superlative training for Retta. With her eagerness to learn and her guileless personality, she was quick to make friends among the animators. On weekends she often went out to sketch with Marc Davis and Mel Shaw, two other young animators.

She was making friends elsewhere in the studio too. Retta and Mary Blair quickly went from being casual acquaintances to best friends. They had much in common; both young women were art-school graduates who'd felt apprehensive about using their considerable talents to draw cartoons.

Retta had made peace with this decision and had found satisfaction in her work, but Mary was still unsure. She sometimes felt she didn't belong there. Mary frequently invited Retta over to her house, where they talked about their motivations and desires. Nestled in the Hollywood hills, the one-bedroom home Mary shared with Lee was snug and peaceful. It was only five rooms, but it had glass walls that opened up to a forest, making it feel much bigger. A small, detached studio was the perfect place to paint, a haven for Mary.

Mary and Lee's house might have been small, but that didn't stop them from entertaining. Their parties were legendary, packed with friends from the studio and the art world standing around the oversize fireplace or out on the terrace, the lights of Tinseltown twinkling below them. Lee made pitchers of martinis as he complained about the cloying cuteness of *Bambi,* then passed around cocktails with stacked olives. Mary and Retta formed a close bond on these nights, drinking, laughing, and smoking cigarettes in the cool evening air. Retta was outgoing and fun-loving, telling stories and teasing her coworkers. Mary was quieter, more serious. She remained aloof from the crowd, modesty shrouding her feelings and ambitions. Their differences drew them together.

The artists working on *Bambi* were more relaxed than usual. In story meetings, Walt made clear that they were in no rush. He encouraged all the artists to focus on the refinement of what they were creating, saying, "The main thing is the slower pace. Move it with a sure, steady pace rather than hurrying it so we get into messes and [compromise] on quality." The film had already been in production so long that more time seemed inconsequential. Particularly when Walt had just decided on another feature — and this one would have the muscle of an elephant.

CHAPTER 6
BABY MINE

A twisting gray trunk reaches out from between the bars of the cage to rock a lonesome elephant baby. The eyes and ears of the mother are obscured but everything you need to know about her emotional state is conveyed in the way she holds her little one, in the twitch of her muscles, and the distraught bend of her trunk. Mary Blair watched Walt looking at her sketches with a flutter of anxiety. He didn't have to say a word. If Walt merely raised an eyebrow, she knew she was in trouble. But instead, a smile formed on his lips.

The pace of *Bambi*'s production had been glacial, but the feature *Dumbo* was moving swiftly and surely. The writers and artists were working with a slim volume, *Dumbo the Flying Elephant,* by Helen Aberson and Harold Pearl. The children's book was a mere thirty-six pages and printed as a roll-a-book, an uncommon format in which the words and illustrations were printed on a scroll of paper in a box. The scroll was then unrolled by the reader using a small wheel. There was scant material to work with, but the story department managed to turn the minimal lines of text into a treatment of over a hundred pages. None of it would have been possible without Bianca.

The feature they were writing leaned heavily on Bianca's *Elmer Elephant.* She had written numerous scripts for the character, but the little elephant with a big heart who didn't fit in had made it into only one short despite his popularity and the merchandise bearing his image. Among the other animal children, Elmer is an outsider, taunted for his trunk. When flames in her tree house surround Tillie the Tiger, it's Elmer who comes to the rescue, using his trunk as a fire hose to save her. The elephant who overcomes ridicule, who uses his awkward physical features to help others, had always been the basis for a powerful narrative, but it had taken this long for Walt to recognize it.

Story artist Mary Goodrich worked on the script, keeping Bianca's themes in mind. Goodrich had just written a treatment for the Hans Christian Andersen fairy tale "The Snow Queen." The title character initially

197

appears in the fairy tale in the form of a snowflake; it grows in size "until at last it turned into a woman, who was dressed in the finest white gauze, which looked as if it had been made from millions of star-shaped flakes. She was beautiful and she was graceful, but she was ice-shining, glittering ice." Alas, the project was stuck in development, so Goodrich turned to *Dumbo,* glad to work on a story that was moving to production so rapidly.

Much of *Dumbo*'s appeal at the studio lay in this speed. Thanks to Bianca's previous work, the script was temptingly simple. "Dumbo is an obvious straight cartoon," Walt said. It could be made much as the *Elmer Elephant* short had been, without the complexity of their recent features. Unlike *Bambi,* there was no extensive animal anatomy to study, as the animals would be drawn as caricatures. The backgrounds would not have Tyrus Wong's impressionistic quality — they would be simple watercolors. There would be none of *Pinocchio*'s involved special effects, which had taken years to develop, nor would the feature require the artistry and interplay with music that *Fantasia* had. It would be cheap and quick to make.

Cost was paramount in Walt's mind because the studio was drowning in debt. The phenomenal success of *Snow White* had proved difficult to replicate, and while the company was proud of its beautiful new space, it lacked the resources to pay for it. It wasn't for lack of trying. The studio's efforts on *Pinocchio* had been extreme; story, animation, and special effects had all combined to produce a truly memorable film. Unfortunately, it wasn't making much money. *Snow White* had earned millions, but *Pinocchio* was still in the hole.

Mistakes had been made with *Pinocchio* right from the start. Walt and his brother Roy had spent an enormous sum to make *Pinocchio,* $2.6 million, whereas *Snow White* had cost only $1.5 million, so they decided to raise ticket prices. They charged $1.10 a head, more than twice the price of a typical theater ticket. Adults and families wavering about what movie to see would simply pick the cheaper option. Walt lowered prices in response to the lackluster ticket sales, but the damage had already been done.

This snafu, however, was nothing compared to what was happening overseas. The grip of World War II was tightening across Europe, and American cinema was just one of its victims. While *Snow White* had been dubbed in twelve languages, *Pinocchio* was

199

dubbed in only two. The critics had praised it highly, the *New York Daily News* calling it "the most enchanting film ever brought to the screen," but it quickly became clear that the movie was a financial flop.

With *Bambi* still in production and *Fantasia* slowly tiptoeing to release, Walt needed cash fast, and it seemed that *Dumbo,* with only a smattering of effort, could be the answer. Four years after writing the story treatment for *Bambi,* Bianca watched the feature get bumped yet again, this time to make way for an awkward elephant based on her own design.

The film had no special effects or attempts at sophisticated artistry, so capturing the emotional impact of the story was critical. The team had little time for character development — the movie was their shortest yet, just sixty-four minutes, far less than the hour and a half of *Snow White* and *Pinocchio.* To build a world in one hour and make the film more than an extended Silly Symphony cartoon, they had to portray the characters in an endearing fashion and give the simple script poignancy.

One of Mary Blair's greatest strengths as an artist was the emotion she was able to render in a single scene. Her watercolor paintings conveyed distinct stories with strong, lifelike characters, their feelings evident on their faces. In her sketches for *Dumbo,* she harnessed this talent, framing shots in such a way that the bond between mother and child emerged clearly.

Hunched over her desk now with paper and pencil, Mary worked on the "Baby Mine" scene. In it, Dumbo is visiting his mother in solitary confinement at night. Since she is locked in her cage, the baby elephant can't see her face, so he slips his small trunk questioningly through the bars. His mother tries to reach him, but the chains fastened around her feet hold her in place. She can only stretch her trunk back through the bars in response, the movement filled with deep longing, until she finally touches his face. Their trunks twist together and tears seep from Dumbo's eyes as the lullaby "Baby Mine" plays. Mary worked closely with Frank Churchill, the in-house composer of the stirring melody. The scene itself is only a few minutes long, and yet, thanks to Mary's concept art, it perfectly communicates the enduring bond between mother and child. When Dumbo's mother cradles her son's small body with her trunk and rocks him in time to the music, the love and despair felt by the pair are captured more completely than any dialogue could describe.

Mary knew about longing. As she created the scene, she was experiencing her own heartbreak. She was able to conceive, but she had had several early miscarriages, and the doctors could not explain why, leaving Mary feeling helpless and full of yearning. At the time, it wasn't the kind of thing women talked about, even to each other, despite the high prevalence of first-trimester miscarriages. She could not grieve openly for the loss of her babies, so Mary channeled her sorrow into her sketch pad and brushes. She painted the scene between mother and child in a dark, moody palette, the images destined to become iconic. Yet at the edges of her paper, the watercolors pooled like tears running from her eyes, betraying her own sorrow.

The emotional scenes of the film were coming together well, the whole staff working speedily, but Retta soon noticed that the colors were off. In the studio, the cels on which the animators' drawings had been traced and colored by the Ink and Paint department looked vibrant. On film, however, the images seemed dull; the elephants became a washed-out gray, barely distinguishable from the muddy backgrounds.

The excitement of the circus in all its color and action had faded into a boring homogeneity.

A decade earlier, in 1930, few working in the film industry could have predicted the enormous impact color cinematography would have on entertainment. Actors complained that color washed away the mysterious dance of shadow and light that black-and-white features had; projectionists criticized color's technical difficulties, and executives noted that the technology had no bearing on ticket sales. Among the few early believers in the power of color were Walt Disney and his group of artists.

In 1932 Walt secured an exclusive contract for a new three-strip color process. Making a color picture required a camera with a double-prism beam splitter right behind the lens. A portion of the light that came through the lens was reflected by a gold-flecked mirror and sent through a magenta filter, which removed the green light and transmitted the red and blue light onto two 35 mm strips of film, one sensitive to red light and one to blue. The rest of the light passed straight through a filter that transmitted green light only onto a third strip of film. The three strips made for a bulky camera that weighed between four hundred and five hundred pounds, and the process yielded three sets of exposed film. While each one looked like regular black-and-white film, the gray tones differed depending on the color filter; blue elements appeared white on the blue-filter film; red elements appeared white on the red-filter film; and green elements appeared white on the green-filter film. Each strip of film was then dyed with its complementary color — the blue was dyed with yellow, the green with magenta, and the red with cyan. The whitest portions of the film would absorb the least amount of dye, so that meant that, for instance, the red elements would absorb very little of the cyan dye. The three strips would then be layered one on top of the other to form a color palette that was vivid and not at all true to life. The movie was now "in glorious Technicolor," as the advertisements proclaimed.

Walt's early negotiations had been with Herbert Kalmus, who, along with two other men, formed the Technicolor Motion Picture Corporation in a railroad-car laboratory in Boston and named the technology partly after Kalmus's alma mater, the Massachusetts Institute of Technology. Walt's exclusive license to use Technicolor for animation had run out but his close relationship with the company continued. When Walt complained to Kalmus that they were having difficulty with washed-out color, an unusual problem to have with the normally intense, saturated hues of Technicolor, the company sent Natalie Kalmus to help.

Natalie was no longer married to Herbert at the time. The two secretly divorced in 1921 but continued to live together and develop the Technicolor technology. When a studio used Technicolor, it did not simply buy the cameras; the technology came with a team of more than a dozen technicians who ran the cameras and processed the film. The service also included a color director, who would read the script, make a chart of colors for the film, and discuss with the production crew — particularly the costume and art departments — which colors would go best together.

Technicolor was tricky to work with. It required extensive set lighting and an intimate knowledge of the technical capabilities of the process. Technicolor often dictated the look of a film. For *The Wizard of Oz,* for example, Dorothy's classic slippers, whose heels she must click together three times, were originally supposed to be silver. Some historians have noted that in L. Frank Baum's original book, *The Wonder-*

ful Wizard of Oz, the silver slippers and the gold tone of the Yellow Brick Road can be read as representing the contentiousness between the gold and silver standards that dominated the banking world of 1896. But the political interpretations of the novel would be lost to the wonders of color film, as silver in Technicolor would look like nothing at all. With Natalie Kalmus consulting on the movie, the shoes were changed to ruby red, which would contrast nicely with the Yellow Brick Road.

Natalie Kalmus called herself the "ringmaster to the rainbow" and as such played a critical role in many films of the era. She made decisions about makeup, pushing for more natural skin tones so that cheeks, eyes, and lips wouldn't look oversaturated. She changed lighting and sets and replaced costumes, such as those in *Gone with the Wind,* for which she insisted on more muted tones to balance the vivid Technicolor process. She occasionally went behind the camera and played the role of cinematographer, taking particular interest in how color influenced emotion and elevated tension in a scene.

But the self-assured, capable Kalmus was not always welcome on film sets. She clashed with makeup artists and set designers, who, from their stage experience, were accustomed to making far bolder color choices. Producers and directors also resented working with such a powerful, opinionated woman. On the set of *Gone with the Wind,* director David O. Selznick complained, "We should have learned by now to take with a pound of salt much of what is said to us by the Technicolor experts. I cannot conceive how we could have been talked into throwing away opportunities for magnificent color values . . . We might just as well have made the picture in black and white." In the 1940s, most filmmakers did choose black-and-white. Only 12 percent of Hollywood films were made in color.

But at the Walt Disney Studios, Natalie Kalmus was appreciated. The shade constraints Technicolor imposed on live action largely evaporated in the medium of cartoons. Here, the potential of color was wide open. With no inherent pigment to get in the way and no annoying need to adhere to reality, animation was Technicolor's best friend. Except for *Dumbo.*

Like Retta, those who worked with color at the studio, especially in the Ink and Paint department, were worried about how lackluster the elephants looked. They talked over the problem of paint colors at teatime, which the all-female department was treated to twice daily — a uniformed maid served them from a china pot, and occasionally a platter of Lorna Doone shortbread cookies was provided. The department's isolation was magnified in the new Burbank studio; it was housed in a building on the other side of the lot from Walt and the animation and story departments. The separateness of the building, complete with its own lunchroom and outdoor patio, soon led to its nickname: the Nunnery.

The women of Ink and Paint wore silky smocks and thin white cotton gloves so that no bit of lint or fingerprint would mar the smooth surface of the plastic they worked with, although they each wore one glove with the ends of the thumb, pointer, and middle fingers cut off so that the fabric wouldn't interfere with the grip on a paint-brush or quill. The inkers were nicknamed "the Queens" due to their ability to trace the animators' sketches while not making a scratch on the easily marked surface of the cel plastic.

Every detail of how paint was applied had been addressed. The colors themselves were manufactured in-house, and the artists made sure not to add too much water to their paint pots before applying the paint with fine sable-hair brushes. They used the most vivid colors first, pulling the paint close to the edge of the ink lines and then dabbing with a rag to blot the excess liquid. The paint appeared custardy in texture before the planes of glass hovering below the multiplane camera pressed down on the cel, releasing a hidden vault of moisture that gave a smooth, opaque finish to the art.

Producing its own paint not only saved the studio money but also ensured stringent quality control. The pigments' chemical composition, surface tension, reaction to humidity and temperature, and suitability for use on cellulose were all carefully optimized. Given this and their own diligence, the women of Ink and Paint knew that their colors were not to blame for *Dumbo*'s dull palette. Nor did the difficulty seem to be with the cameras. The problem must lie with the cels themselves.

The studio's recent switch to cellulose acetate had been heralded as a significant advance in safety. But the reduced fire hazard came with an unexpected cost: colors weren't popping the way they used to. The studio turned to Natalie Kalmus and her ingenious color wheel. To simplify their experiments, the Ink and Paint department chose just one hundred and fifty colors, a fraction of the thousands used previously, but the limited palette dovetailed with the minimalism of *Dumbo*'s story and animation style. With Technicolor in mind, Ink and Paint played with shades of gray, finally selecting the perfect hues so that Dumbo and his friend Timothy Mouse could stand out on-screen.

Financial woes at the studio deepened. Given how his feature films tended to drag in development, Walt needed cash to keep his doors open, so in 1940 he decided to make a move he had long avoided: taking his company public. The decision would allow Walt to raise money by offering shares of the studio, bringing in banks and investors willing to take a chance on an enterprise that had been incorporated only two years earlier. But with this move came a new transparency. The way the company spent money, particularly on salaries, was now open for all to see. Employees of the Walt Disney Studios found a surprise lurking in the numbers. In 1940 Walt took home two thousand dollars a week, and that did not include his stock options. It was an enormous sum, even by Hollywood standards.

The introduction of Wall Street changed

the atmosphere at the studio. The illusion that they were a family of artists all sharing equally in lean times, working toward a common ambition and against the establishment, was shattered. In the lavish new offices, resentment stirred. Walt might be bringing home a comfortable salary, but many on the staff were not.

As part of the New Deal, President Roosevelt had been pushing to protect labor in the United States. During FDR's reelection campaign in 1936, a young woman in Bedford, Massachusetts, had pushed toward the president with an envelope in her hand. A police officer held her back but Roosevelt told one of his aides to get the envelope from her. It contained this note:

> I wish you could do something to help us girls . . . We have been working in a sewing factory . . . and up to a few months ago we were getting our minimum pay of $11 a week . . . Today the 200 of us girls have been cut down to $4 and $5 and $6 a week.

It was a poignant impetus for the president to institute protections for workers, including women and children, who had previously been largely ignored. As part of the

Fair Labor Standards Act of 1938, Roosevelt outlawed oppressive child labor and instituted the country's first minimum wage, twenty-five cents an hour. Roosevelt also defined what a fair workweek should look like. He first considered a thirty-five-hour week reasonable but ultimately compromised on five eight-hour days, a forty-hour workweek. American workers were getting needed protections and higher salaries to boot. Employers, however, found much to criticize in these new rules.

Employees at Walt Disney Studios, especially those in the story and animation departments, worked far more than eight hours a day and certainly were not confined to five days a week. Saturday meetings were as common as the Snow White special, a popular chicken-salad sandwich available at the cafeteria. Salaries varied widely; a small number of top animators brought home two to three hundred dollars a week, while a woman in Ink and Paint earned a meager twelve dollars. The average artist at the studio made eighteen dollars a week, slightly higher than the median male income of the era.

The animators at the Walt Disney Studios were not the only ones dissatisfied with their lot. In 1938, the Screen Cartoonists' Guild was formed in Los Angeles, led by Bill Littlejohn, an animator working on the new Tom and Jerry shorts for Metro-Goldwyn-Mayer. As the guild's ranks grew, so did its reach, and Walt, employer of more animators than any other studio in town, was in its sights.

The tidal wave of turmoil about to wash over the studio started slowly. Demands began to increase, and although Walt made promises and even cut his own salary, he gave his staff no extra money. The public offering had not gone well. Stocks initially valued at $25 a share quickly plummeted to $3.25 a share.

At the same time, *Fantasia,* the studio's artistic darling, was proving a disaster. Finally released on November 13, 1940, it was introduced as a road show, moving among only thirteen theaters. This was due to the expense of the surround sound, or Fantasound, that the movie required. Fantasound necessitated eleven amplifier racks, dozens of loudspeakers, four hundred vacuum tubes, and a team of specially trained technicians to maintain and operate the equipment. The system weighed fifteen thousand pounds and took more than a week to install. At a cost of eighty-five thousand dollars per theater, it was an investment that few movie-house owners were willing to make.

Not only hampered by limited screenings, *Fantasia* was also eviscerated by critics, with *Newsweek* stating, "Where Disney misses is in the creation of the smirking centaurs, the 'art calendar' cupids, the coy and flapperish centaurettes, and the comic-strip Bacchus, who all desecrate the Olympian background chosen for Beethoven's Pastoral Symphony." In the *New York Herald-Tribune,* columnist Dorothy Thompson wrote, "The illustrations of the Beethoven 'Pastoral' are sufficient to raise an army, if there is enough blood left in culture to defend itself. . . . The clean, pure sounds — the unbearably clean, pure sounds — fall about us while we gaze on the raspberry and marshmallow Olympus, and the pure, strong music seems to be dropping cold and frustrated tears." Then as now, the weakness of *Fantasia* lay in the misguided, and later considered sexist and racist, Pastoral Symphony scene.

The film had cost $2.3 million to make, a million more than *Snow White,* and it seemed the studio would never recoup the loss. It was now imperative to hurry *Dumbo* and even the idealistic aspirations of *Bambi* along. Under such pressure, Walt had little incentive, and even less capital, to respond to the needs of his staff. The studio was $4.5 million in debt to Bank of America, and the freedom to raise salaries Walt had enjoyed just the year before was now gone. The stockholders had effectively seized control of his company, and unless something dramatically shifted, they would be the ones to have final say on all future feature projects. Walt's studio was no longer truly his.

The focus on money jarred some artists, many of whom could make more as clerks at retail stores than they made working at the studio. Mary Blair was as discontented as most of the employees around her, but for different reasons. She wanted only a decent salary and cared nothing for seeing her name on-screen. But she still felt removed from the studio, as if she didn't belong. It was only when she sat next to Retta, the two of them sketching a live elephant named Mabel brought in to aid the artists, that she found happiness in her job.

Unlike Mary and Retta, Bianca felt life at the studio was nearly torture. Story meetings, always a wearying exercise in personal criticism, had become even more intense. Instead of smoothing her path, Bianca's success in *Fantasia* and her inspiration for *Dumbo* had hardened the men to her, and they took every chance to heap on more disparagement. She knew her ideas had potential, and yet she couldn't advocate effectively for their production.

Bianca was working on two projects, both based on stories she loved: *Cinderella* and *Peter Pan.* It seemed to her that *Cinderella* had the same dramatic potential as *Snow White* had had — a princess in distress, with the promise of evocative imagery. They could use animals in the story, and there were scenes she was sure would create dramatic tension. On her sketch pad she drew Cinderella running down a dark flight of steps in a voluminous blue dress, a glittering slipper lying behind her.

She was also working on a character from *Peter Pan* that was of particular interest to her. Bianca had always been drawn to fairies, and here in the book was a mischievous one named Tinker Bell. She drew the tiny fairy again and again, giving her an impish expression and surrounding her with flying children and golden fairy dust.

Bianca had been developing the projects for years at the studio without gaining traction. Her newest story treatments didn't draw Walt's notice. She wondered if the only way to get him interested in her ideas was to have them presented by someone else.

Feeling frazzled and unappreciated, she decided to take a vacation and refresh her artistic sensibility. When she'd first moved to Los Angeles, she felt the city was "young, beautiful, and full of angels," but now she was desperate to leave town, if only temporarily.

But when she returned to the office after her vacation, she was confused. Her office was not as she had left it. Her pencils, sketchbooks, and story notes were all gone. Sitting at her desk was a man she had never met. In astonishment, she backed out of the room, believing that she must have made a mistake; perhaps she had entered the wrong office. But no, this was her room. In the hall one of the men saw her stunned expression and told her, "You know you're fired." But Bianca hadn't known. No one had bothered to tell her. And her high-school friend Walt did not take the trouble to say goodbye.

CHAPTER 7
AQUARELA DO BRASIL

Grace was usually gentle as she pulled back the throttle during takeoff, but today she threw caution aside, opened up the mechanism, and let the plane climb as fast as she dared. She passed the Burbank tower at one thousand feet and kept pressing. She was leaving disappointment and pain back on the ground behind her. It was 1940 and she had left the studio abruptly after she was offered a job that felt like a dream dropped from the sky. Yet only weeks later, after she'd quit her job at the studio, her prospects were crushed by the rising threat of war. Archibald M. Brown of Fairchild Aircraft rescinded his recent offer of employment, explaining in a letter that it was due to "circumstances beyond everyone's control with the possible exception of Adolf Hitler."

Grace was devastated, but in her grief, she became more determined. She decided to go for another altitude record. A twenty-year-old with the patriotic name Betsy Ross had recently tried to set a new record for light planes but came up short, reaching eighteen thousand feet in the sky above Pennsylvania. Grace knew that she could beat not only Ross's attempt but also her own previous record set in 1939. If she did, then perhaps someone would finally hire her. From a dealership interested in publicity, she was able to borrow a plane, a Taylorcraft two-seat painted a sleek black with red trim. Grace nicknamed it "Black Beauty."

Forty-five minutes before takeoff, Grace began stretching her muscles and breathing pure oxygen out of a mask. It was a new technique for removing nitrogen from the blood and avoiding the effects of rapid changes in atmospheric pressure. Grace cleared her mind as she walked to the plane, her brother Charles beside her, carrying her oxygen tank.

After takeoff, she climbed quickly through the air above Burbank until it seemed she was barely moving at all, her altimeter oddly stuck at 21,000 feet. When she looked at the more sensitive altimeter she had brought on board, however, she noted that it read 22,750. She was startled. She hadn't expected to reach any higher than 20,000 feet.

She knew now that she was going to make a record, and she wanted to keep going, keep pushing higher, and really see what she was capable of. At the high elevation she was feeling no dreaded light-headedness or nausea, only a growing sensation of boredom, when she suddenly heard *boom*.

There was no worse noise a pilot could hear. She ran her eyes over the plane and equipment. She knew it could have been the motor backfiring or perhaps a broken cable, and so, while trying to stay calm, she searched for the cause of the frighteningly loud sound. The answer was staring right at her. The windshield was cracked. She saw the break splitting the glass from top to bottom. If the windshield caved in now, Grace might completely lose control of the plane. She examined the glass carefully from her seat and thought it looked fairly intact. She decided to take her chances and press on.

It was then that Grace noticed just how cold she was. Her more sensitive altimeter had stopped registering the changing altitude, but it was obvious from the temperature that she was continuing to climb. It was twelve degrees below zero, and Grace's hand shook as she gripped her pencil and, from habit, tried to note the false unchanging altitude in her notebook. Even with her windshield cracked and her body shivering, Grace kept going up; she started descending only when her fuel gauge told her she had just enough in the tank to get home.

After she landed, the first question the press asked was "How high did you go?" With a smile on her face, Grace responded, "The altimeter registered 22,750 feet." She wouldn't know that she had reached 24,311 feet, breaking the previous record by more than 4,000 feet, until the official barometer was sent to Washington and analyzed. She had come back down to Earth with no job, no security concerning her future in aviation, and no exact answer to what altitude she had attained, but she felt just fine.

Everything was not fine at the studio. Grace's departure left a hole in the story department. Her colleagues, particularly the women she worked with, felt the loss keenly, even though it was not a surprise. For years, Grace had talked of finding her fortune in aviation, despite her talent for writing scripts and putting together storyboards. But Grace's work had made an impression on her employer; it was clear that the ambivalence about hiring women Walt had expressed when he first brought Grace in four years earlier had dissipated.

The strides being made by women at the studio were not confined to the story department. In the early 1940s Walt instituted a new training program to bring women from Ink and Paint into animation. If you were a woman working for Walt Disney Studios, you suddenly had unprecedented opportunities in the animation industry, opportunities that existed at no other studio in town.

The only other animation studio of the era with similar openings for women was Japan Animated Films, later renamed Toei Doga, based in Tokyo. Like the studio in Burbank, the company was unusual in that it hired women directly into the animation department. It was their female employees, such as Kazuko Nakamura and Reiko Okuyama, who would later become the mothers of anime and give life to a genre elegant in its blend of emotion and art.

The rise of women in the workplace, no matter what side of the world it occurred on, was frightening to some men, and they approached the perceived threat much as toddlers would a monster under the bed — by crying about it. Just as, over the centuries, some Americans have blamed immigrants for siphoning jobs away from them, a subset of male employees blamed women for stealing work they felt was right-fully theirs, and some of the men at the Disney studio accused Walt of hiring women only as a way to save money, as they could be paid so much less. In this environment of fear and unhappiness, Walt gathered all his employees at the Burbank studio on February 10, 1941, to address these complaints directly.

Another ugly rumor is that we are trying to develop girls for animation to replace higher-priced men. This is the silliest thing I have ever heard of. We are not interested in low-priced help. We are interested in efficient help. The girls are being trained for inbetweens for very good reasons. The first is to make them more versatile, [so] that the peak loads of inbetweening and inking can be handled. Believe me when I say that the more versatile our organization is, the more beneficial it is to the employees, for it assures steady employment for the employee, as well as steady production turnover for the studio.

The second reason is that the possibility of a war, let alone the peacetime conscription, may take many of our young men now employed, and especially many of the young applicants. I believe that if there is to be a business for these young men to come back to after the war, it must be maintained during the war. The girls can help here.

Third, the girl artists have the right to expect the same chances for advancement as men, and I honestly believe that they may eventually contribute something to this business that men never would or could. In the present group that are training for inbetweens there are definite prospects; and a good example is to mention the work of Ethel Kulsar and Sylvia Holland on *The Nutcracker Suite,* and little Retta Scott, of whom you will hear more when you see *Bambi.*

It was a strong defense of the value of women independent of wartime or economic pressure, and Walt's words buoyed the confidence of Sylvia, Ethel, and Retta in particular. For many of the men, however, there was little Walt could say to quell their fears. They were simply not ready for such radical change.

Whether or not they were ready, upheaval was coming for all of them. In early 1941, although the United States was still ostensibly uninvolved in the violence and destruction occurring in Europe and Asia, it was clear to most Americans that the fragile stability of peace could not last and that they had best prepare for war.

Life at the shiny new studio in Burbank was also poised for turmoil. All spring Walt had been meeting with leaders of the Screen Cartoonists' Guild and members of his staff who were demanding a more equitable approach to salary and screen credits. Like many studio heads, Walt resented having to speak with Herb Sorrell, who was a powerful union organizer and leader and particularly skilled at negotiation. In public, Walt blamed Communist forces for the unrest, but in private he took personal offense at the position of some of his favorite animators.

Chief among these was Art Babbitt, the animator who'd drawn the wicked queen in *Snow White* and created the character of Goofy. Babbitt couldn't claim that he was unappreciated. He was one of the highest-paid animators at the studio and saw his name frequently in the credits. He lived a lavish lifestyle complete with a large home, servants, and three cars. It seemed preposterous to Walt that the studio that had given him so much should be the target of his antipathy.

Babbitt, for his part, viewed his position

of power in the studio as giving him a responsibility to aid the less privileged artists around him. He didn't confine himself to the men but spoke to as many studio employees as he could, frequently visiting the Ink and Paint department. In fact, Babbitt claimed that concern over the health of one inker, who had passed out at her desk because she was unable to afford lunch, had prompted his involvement in the union.

On May 28, 1941, the meeting became ugly. Sorrell yelled at Walt, "I can make a dust bowl of your studio!" The shouts and threats yielded neither side what it sought. As the angry meeting broke up, Walt turned vindictive. He immediately fired Art Babbitt and sixteen other pro-union artists. It was the ammunition the union needed to strike.

On the morning of May 29, everything changed. Hundreds of employees stood blocking the studio entrance on Buena Vista Street with signs that read THERE ARE NO STRINGS ON ME, ARE WE MICE OR MEN?, and IT'S UP TO WALT TO CALL A HALT.

Suddenly, the employees were divided by their loyalties, and some friendships were destroyed over union sympathies. Walt's niece Marjorie Sewell was working at the studio as a painter and rooming with one of her coworkers, an inker, and as they fell on

226

opposite sides of the strike, the tension at their home was high. Sewell would drive her roommate to the studio in the morning, drop her off outside to protest, then drive through the gates to work.

Many single women at the studio did not have the financial means to join the strike no matter what their personal feelings about supporting the union were. Retta drove across the picket line with her heart heavy. She knew that some of the anger she witnessed was reserved for her. The men were irate that she had dared to take a job that they felt belonged to them. She had not been an animator long and was fearful of losing her prized position, and she couldn't afford to go on strike even if she wanted to. As she drove through the throng of hundreds, men began to pound on her car, yelling, "What are you doing here? You should be home having babies!"

Sylvia was also nervous about her job prospects in light of the strike. She could not jeopardize her employment — everyone in her family was counting on her income. One close friend at the studio, however, felt differently. Ethel Kulsar, also with two young children to support, decided to join the picket line. For two women who had so much in common and had worked together so closely, the separation was deeply felt. Their relationship was just one of many fractured in the strike.

Sylvia, unlike Ethel, had no outside family to aid her, and she knew that without her income, she could lose her children. She would rather accept meager wages and endure long hours than risk that. She was already making about sixty dollars less a month than she had been promised in her last promotion and it seemed likely that the cuts would continue. She didn't blame Walt for the tumultuous conditions. Instead, she blamed the company's lawyers for not finding a way to compromise with the strikers, and she did her best to keep working.

There was much to do. Before striking, Ethel Kulsar had written a story treatment for "The Little Mermaid," by Hans Christian Andersen, and Sylvia now spent long hours storyboarding the film and taking the helm during story meetings with Walt. She was outspoken in her vision, frequently dominating the meetings, and Walt was as impressed with her confidence as he was gratified by her loyalty.

Neither Sylvia nor Mary Blair nor Retta would join the strikers, but for Mary in particular, the ensuing chaos distracted her from her work as an artist. She didn't want to be drawn into long discussions about money and screen credit; she would rather be at home painting. Abruptly, she resigned, feeling she was making the best move artistically for her career.

With multiple vulnerabilities confronting the Walt Disney Studios — financial strain, employee unrest, and a world war on the horizon — Walt thought it seemed like a good time to leave town. An opportunity had presented itself from an unlikely source: the State Department. The U.S. government wanted to send Walt and a few select studio employees on a goodwill tour to South America, hoping to impede the political inroads that Nazi Germany was making throughout the continent.

In 1940 Nelson Rockefeller wrote a memorandum to President Roosevelt expressing fear that the United States would lose its dominance politically and economically in the hemisphere because not enough was being done to secure interests in Latin America. Trade between Axis powers and Latin America was considerable, with platinum, copper, and cotton all being sent to Europe. There was also concern about securing the Panama Canal and its strategic link between the Atlantic and Pacific Oceans. In response, FDR formed the Office of the Coordinator of Inter-American Affairs (OCIAA), with Rockefeller at its helm, overseeing a new era of cooperation, propaganda, and securing key trade interests. The office's work was not solely for wartime but was meant to extend far into the future.

One of the OCIAA's earliest endeavors was to flood Latin American countries with U.S. culture, disseminating movies, magazines, and advertising, and even sending celebrities below the equator. It then tightened its grip on news sources. Newsprint was in short supply during the war, and the United States as well as countries in Latin America relied almost exclusively on imports from Canada. With most newspapers reduced in size due to rationing, the OCIAA was able to suppress unfavorable printed sentiment about the United States by supplying paper rag only to those sources friendly to its interests. Intelligence gathering also intensified, as the need for keeping abreast of political and economic changes was paramount.

Sending Walt Disney and his crew of merry artists on a tour of South America was just one facet of a many-layered plan to snatch control of the continent out of the hands of Nazi Germany. The Roosevelt administration imagined that the trip would yield new feature films celebrating Latin America, leading to closer diplomatic ties, and therefore offered not only to pay travel expenses but also to underwrite the films that resulted and even give Walt a guarantee on them: if the studio didn't recoup its expenses after they were released, the federal government would pay for them. This was all Walt needed to hear. An escape hatch for his financial problems had magically appeared at just the right time.

Almost immediately after she resigned, Mary regretted her decision. Lee, along with a small group of artists, had been chosen to accompany Walt on his tour of South America. Mary was consumed with jealousy. *If only I hadn't quit,* she thought, *I could have been going on this adventure.* Lee shook his head, but Mary's father had an idea. "Well, Mary," he said, "why don't you get yourself fixed up and go over to the studio and make an appointment with Mr. Disney and tell him that you want to go too?" Mary liked the advice, and she walked into Walt's office and, with genuine humility, asked if she could accompany her husband. Walt said yes, and he also put her back on the payroll; Mary left the office in raptures. She was an employee again and about to embark on her first overseas journey.

As the buses lined up for Walt and his select group of artists to leave, some loyal employees gathered outside to wave goodbye wistfully to the group. Sylvia was there, sitting on the steps as Walt came out of the building. He stopped in front of her. "Aren't you going?" he asked.

"No, I wasn't invited" was Sylvia's meek reply.

"You're not going?" Walt said, genuinely surprised. There had evidently been some mix-up, although Sylvia would never get an explanation. She watched them go, wishing she were part of their group and jealous of the travel and experiences that awaited them.

International travel was not common for Americans in the early 1940s, and so the novelty of the trip tickled their curiosity. The team consisted of eighteen people, including Walt and his wife, Lillian, and was dominated by members of the story department, among them Lee and Mary Blair. There was only one animator, Frank Thomas, and one musician, Chuck Wolcott. They were all young; even Walt was a fresh-faced thirty-nine-year-old with only a few wrinkles, perhaps from recent stress, on his smooth forehead.

In 1941, few aircraft could make an extended cross-country flight. Because of this, Walt and his artists hopped from city to city, going through Fort Worth, Nashville, and Jacksonville before landing in Miami. They left Miami in a Pan American seaplane and flew to San Juan, Puerto Rico. From there, they flew to the small town of Belém, Brazil, then on to Rio de Janeiro.

Globalization had not yet shrunk the world and so everything they encountered was new to them. They had never tasted the sweet tartness of the guava fruit or the rich heartiness of feijoada, a black bean stew. They had never seen fashion like that worn in Brazil, with its bright colors and beaded jewelry. Yet of all these experiences, it was the music that mesmerized them the most. In Rio, the artists heard a live samba for the first time. Its pulse-like rhythm, with origins in Angola and the West African slave trade, was part of the Brazilian cultural identity. Mary Blair wore an orchid behind her ear as she moved to the claves and drums pounding out the rhythm, her exhilaration building as she twirled around the floor. The samba held so much energy that the group stayed up all night dancing, heading back to their hotel only as the stars faded into the brightening sky.

Walt stayed at the opulent Copacabana Palace, its pearly stone façade mere steps from its namesake white-sand beach, while the rest of the artists stayed at the Hotel Gloria, located in a middle-class neighborhood of the city. The place suited them well, for while Walt visited with President Getúlio Vargas and assorted foreign dignitaries, his days packed with parties and dinners, the artists were free to explore. They spent their time strolling the streets of curved mosaic tile, sitting at outdoor cafés, and sketching the sharp profile of Sugarloaf Mountain against Guanabara Bay. The country was energetic and vibrant, and their sketches were inspired by the heartbeat-like tempo of the samba, colors exploding across their landscapes. Mary felt unprecedented freedom in her sketching, painting a macaw parrot in contrasting vertical stripes of bright pink and yellow, a bow tie around its neck.

One night the group sat around the lobby in their formal dinner attire, and a steward called out, "El Grupo . . . El Grupo Disney." They all laughed at the moniker that described them so well and insisted on using the name for the rest of their trip. That evening they were ushered to the Cassino da Urca, a luxurious casino where Carmen Miranda had performed before she left for fame on Broadway and in Hollywood. Tonight the ballroom was decorated with items from *Fantasia,* and the stage glittered as musicians and dancers gave the audience a taste of Carnaval, the largest pre-Lent celebration in the world.

Contrasting with the cultural delights and raw beauty of Brazil was the news coming from home. Without access to newspapers in English, the group had become somewhat insulated — a welcome respite. Still, letters and telegrams told them that the studio had been completely shut down due to the strike. As of this moment, the members of El Grupo were Walt's only working artists, and they were far from home. Back in Burbank, the beautiful new offices, filled with hundreds of desks, stood empty and silent.

Walt and El Grupo closed their eyes to the studio's miseries as they flew to their next stop, Buenos Aires, Argentina, where they would spend a month of their three-month trip. This time they stayed together at the Alvear Palace Hotel and converted a large penthouse space there into a miniature studio filled with storyboards, a Moviola, and easels with sketchbooks. On an adjoining open terrace, they hosted folk dancing and folk music, with Walt delighting in the malambo, a rhythmic step dance originated by gauchos, South American cowboys.

With the studio closed in Burbank, some of the travelers felt that, artistically, nothing was waiting for them back home. They dreaded returning to their workplace and its troubles. A dawning realization that their futures might very well lie in the success of their current endeavor spurred them to embrace the culture surrounding them. They explored the city and countryside, making new friends and creating art.

One morning they drove two hours to a ranch in the small town of El Carmen, Argentina, where long tables were set up in the center of a blossoming peach orchard in preparation for an *asado,* or outdoor barbecue. Mary drank cocktails in the early afternoon with the rest of El Grupo as they waited for Walt to emerge in traditional gaucho clothing, complete from *esporas,* spurs, on his boots to a bright red *lenço,* a scarf, tied around his neck. The afternoon was relaxed as they listened to live music and later watched Walt riding a horse in front of a spirited crowd of Argentine artists. There was a dreamy, unreal quality to the afternoon that seeped into the sketches

Mary later drew of gauchos and horses, the colors of her paintings often at odds with reality.

As happens to many travelers, Mary discovered her own sense of self in South America. The trip completely altered the course of her artistic life. She found her palette while traveling, creating shades and contrasting colors that would forever become part of her identity and her art. Before Mary left on the goodwill tour, her watercolors had occasionally been confused with those of her husband, Lee. After she returned, her work was never again mistaken for another artist's.

Mary perceived her role at the studio differently as well. She was no longer an outsider, allowed through the studio doors only because of her husband. The trip had made her one of Walt's inner circle and given her a higher appreciation for the artistry that drove their animation. As the studio's value was rising in her opinion, Walt was gaining new appreciation for Mary. The colors and sketches she developed on the trip were like nothing he had seen before. She would brazenly place reds and pinks next to one another, then throw in eccentric patterns that few other artists would dare combine. Her portraits were moving, especially those that captured the sweet innocence of children. Walt was transfixed. He had a new favorite artist.

Lee watched Walt's increasing partiality to his wife with a wary eye. This, after all, was supposed to be his trip; Mary had had to plead to come along. Jealousy welled within him. It was uncommon for a wife's talent to be prized over her husband's, and the experience made Lee feel slighted, even though he continued to adore Mary.

From Argentina, the group split up — some people took a plane across the Andes to La Paz, Bolivia, others traveled to northern Argentina, and those individuals who feared altitude sickness headed west to Santiago, Chile. The plane that flew to La Paz, passing over the snow-covered mountains at eighteen thousand feet, was not pressurized, so the artists were surprised to learn that not only could they not smoke, but they had to be prepared to use the red tubes positioned in front of their seats for oxygen intake if they became woozy.

After the plane landed in La Paz, Mary suffered from altitude sickness, but she didn't want to waste time resting. Instead, she explored her surroundings armed with pencils and a sketchbook before embarking on a bumpy llama ride. Next they were off

238

on a boat trip across the wide blue waters of Lake Titicaca. The adventures were exhausting, but Mary had no intention of slowing down.

Walt and his wife took the SS *Santa Clara* back to New York, but Mary, Lee, and several of the other artists kept going. They toured small towns in Peru and then made their way to the capital city of Lima. After that, they flew to Mexico City, where they attended a bullfight, and then finally hopped planes back to California. The world they were returning home to, however, would feel as foreign as the countries they had just traveled through.

CHAPTER 8
YOU'RE IN THE ARMY NOW

The strike lasted all summer. Sylvia, who was not part of the group that went to South America during the shutdown, bore the scars of the experience. In July, she learned that the arbitrators negotiating with studio executives would increase pay only for those employees striking; those remaining loyal to the company would receive no salary increase. It was difficult to even talk about the situation with her colleagues. A memo sent by Roy Disney on July 24, 1941, stated, "Any discussions of union activities or infractions of established company rules on company property during working hours will be considered cause for immediate dismissal." Sylvia doodled unhappily on the back of the pink memo, feeling wary and tense about her future.

Tumult continued both inside and outside the studio walls in late July as the remaining employees hatched a plan to stage their own walkout. Soon, however, negotiations fell apart once again. Sylvia kept working, and despite the tension, she found moments of creative freedom. Her former director on *Fantasia* had long been a thorn in her side, taking credit for her work, trying to keep her away from Walt, and editing her sketches with a heavy hand. Now, the strike had carried him away, and Sylvia felt relief at his absence.

Before Walt left for his South American tour, he had called Sylvia into his office and charged her with writing her own script. It was a sign that she was advancing rapidly and might soon be given even more responsibility. While she might have preferred the excitement of the goodwill tour, her adaptation of *The Little Mermaid* was providing plenty of interesting challenges. Like much of the studio's original source material, the tale was dark. In it, the youngest daughter of the widowed sea king falls in love with a prince. Longing to be human, she makes a deal with an evil sea witch, trading her voice and tongue for a pair of legs. In the original story, the legs she receives are incredibly painful. Each step she takes with them is as excruciating as stepping on the blade of a knife and has a similar effect, as her magical appendages bleed. The ending is not a happy one. The prince marries a neighboring princess, and the little mermaid must choose between slitting his throat or evaporating into the oblivion of sea foam. Ultimately she spares the prince's life and dies. However, instead of becoming sea foam, she ends up in purgatory, which she can escape if she performs good deeds for three hundred years. Only then can she earn a spot in the kingdom of heaven among the humans.

Peeling away the ominous elements of the story, Sylvia recognized its raw potential. She had begun the adaptation while Walt was still in town, but in his absence she delved further into the mix of tragedy and romance. Her storyboard and script focused on the plight of the little mermaid, who is nameless in the original story and who Sylvia believed deserved a happier ending. Right from the beginning she felt strongly that music would be essential to the film. She proposed that the opening scenes be choreographed to a symphony that would lead the camera deeper and deeper into the sea, past fish and sea creatures, straight to the sea king's majestic palace.

The thrill that these moments of inspiration gave Sylvia were not to last. On August 15, 1941, without being given any notice or pay, Sylvia learned that the studio was shut down. She drove to the studio anyway and stood openmouthed as she looked at the empty parking lot where a thousand cars had once lined up in neat rows. She was filled with despair. Her children depended on her and she felt as though her life was a constant struggle to give them the stability they needed. But no matter how hard she worked and despite the progress she had seemed to be making, everything kept falling apart. She had finally had the freedom to write a script, had shaken off an annoying director, and even received a raise. Now it was all gone.

Perhaps most frustrating to her was the studio's inability to explain to its employees what was happening. She was released from employment in the shutdown, but she had no idea what that would mean and whether she'd be able to return to work. She knew only that no paycheck was coming her way.

On September 12, 1941, although Walt was still in South America, a settlement was finally reached. A full-time employee would receive a doubled salary, and the studio would take a more equitable approach to screen credits. These benefits, however, came at a cost. As part of the agreement with union leaders, the majority of studio employees would be laid off; half of the laid-off employees would be strikers and half non-strikers. Sylvia felt the injustice keenly. She waited, hoping she would be one of the lucky ones brought back inside the studio walls.

Walt was no longer truly in charge. Because the studio was so deeply in debt to Bank of America, the bankers were pulling the strings. *Dumbo* was completed and *Bambi* nearly there. The non-striking studio employees had been working long hours in Walt's absence to finish the films. Walt could not afford to start production on another feature — apart from the South American projects, which were subsidized by the government — particularly in the midst of war. Yet he might have kept some staff on to work on future projects, anticipating the need for scripts and storyboards in the years ahead. Instead, in the changed atmosphere, the studio chose to keep only a skeleton crew of 288 artists to work on the South American features and shorts. The other 1,200 artists were told they were temporarily laid off, but they were given no guarantees of future employment.

The beautiful Burbank studio was altered as well. Half the animation building was closed, its spacious interior unnecessary for the small number of artists remaining. The rest of the studio was handed over to the Lockheed Corporation, an American aircraft manufacturer preparing for the country's seemingly inevitable involvement in the global conflict. The paths, trees, and lawns, once a lush landscape in which employees could stop and rest, were now blocked off by barbed wire and security guards.

Sylvia had not been one of the small crew of artists kept on at the studio. As the weeks turned into months, she gave up hope of ever returning to the work she loved. She needed money and could no longer wait for a job that might be permanently gone. Even with her experience and skill, however, Sylvia couldn't find a job at another studio. There were more than a thousand animation employees freshly on the market, all of them looking for work. And most studios in town were uninterested in hiring women for story and animation departments, no matter the women's qualifications. For Sylvia, the well of opportunity had run dry.

She found a job at the Desert Sun School in Idyllwild, California, an elite preparatory school for grades one through nine. Offering a resort-like campus and a wealth of activities, the school attracted the children of celebrities; over the years, Frank Sinatra,

Peter Sellers, Fred Astaire, and the Lockheed family all sent their children to the educational institution. Sylvia's employment there had an added benefit: her children could attend at a reduced rate.

But despite the job's advantages, life did not get easier for Sylvia. The school was understaffed and so she worked fourteen-hour days. She woke at five thirty a.m., the air still cold, and lit fireplaces throughout the building to get the classrooms heated and ready. She taught classes in the morning, and in the afternoon she saddled horses and instructed children in riding, ferrying the kids from the school to a ranch near the Salton Sea. In the evenings she watched the kids in study hall. It was lovely to have more time with her children, but the exhaustion was overpowering. She yearned for her old life at the studio and the artistic freedom it had once afforded her.

With similar reasoning as Sylvia, Tyrus Wong also chose not to join the strike. His allegiance was not to Walt, whom he had never met, but to the studio itself, which had given him unprecedented independence on *Bambi.* Like Sylvia, he had a young family to support, a wife and a three-year-old daughter, and knew from experience that jobs in animation could be difficult to obtain.

The studio shutdown was a dramatic turn of events, but Tyrus assumed that his influence and long hours on *Bambi,* as well as his loyalty to the studio, would result in his getting his job back. Behind the scenes, however, a group of strikers jealous of his talent and unreasonably angry that he had taken the company side were plotting against him. Although Tyrus's expressive visual style was essential to *Bambi,* the film was nearly complete. Despite his artistry, Tyrus was fired. The experience was shattering, but Tyrus quickly pushed away his resentments and began looking for work. The search would not take long. With his *Bambi* sketches and two original storyboards in hand, he walked over to Warner Brothers and was promptly hired.

Retta Scott, too, was among the non-striking artists at the studio. She felt great affection for Walt, whom she viewed as a second father. Her own father was more than a thousand miles away in Seattle, and with her limited resources, Retta rarely got to visit him. With her family so far away, she delighted in her relationships at the studio, especially with Walt, who called her

"Little Retta" and sometimes stopped his car and offered to give her a ride if he saw her walking to work in the morning. He praised her work in story meetings and chided her only when he saw her feeding the stray cats at the studio. The animals had made the move to Burbank along with the artists and seemed to be a permanent part of the studio's landscape. Walt did not mind their presence, but he preferred them to eat rodents rather than food given to them by his employees.

Like Tyrus, Retta worked long hours on *Bambi* during the summer of 1941. The animators' room was nearly empty, and only three artists remained — herself, Eric Larson, and Art Elliott. She drew over fifty-six thousand dogs for *Bambi,* then, because they were so short-staffed, did the cleanup work single-handedly, taking her rough sketches and transforming the lines into clean, crisp drawings that were ready for the Ink and Paint department.

That summer Retta was not just behind the scenes but on-screen as well, appearing in a promotional film called *The Reluctant Dragon,* released on June 20, 1941. More an advertisement for the studio than a feature in its own right, it consisted of a live-action tour of the Walt Disney Studios, with a visitor roaming the grounds, going into the camera room, stopping by the story and animation departments, and even saying hello to the women of Ink and Paint. It also included four animated shorts dropped in at intervals. Filmed prior to the strike, the movie presented a studio starkly different from the current reality. Yet seeing Retta smiling on-screen from the studio's life-drawing class, one of a group of animators sketching an elephant, girls in theaters across the country were inspired. Retta's presence shattered preconceived notions and, for the young women watching, offered proof that their gender need not be a hindrance to a creative career.

The next project was *Dumbo,* and Retta worked furiously, animating the film in record time considering the minimal crew. Every day was drudgery; long hours, with little relief from friends and coworkers, and anger and resentment specifically directed at her as she entered and exited the studio each day. She did not even have the comfort of her best friend, as Mary Blair was a world away. Despite the atmosphere of misery, Retta was not easily beaten down. She laughed in the face of her misfortunes and tried to make the best of her difficulties.

Not all the news was bad. Thanks to Retta

and the hardworking remaining staff, the studio was able to finish *Dumbo* on time, although just barely. The film was completed just two and a half weeks before its New York City premiere, October 23, 1941. The critical reviews were positive, and the *New York Times* declared the film "a fanciful delight." From their experience with *Pinocchio* and *Fantasia,* the staff knew that praise from critics did not necessarily mean ticket sales, but Walt, newly returned from South America, was hopeful this film would help pay down debts and give the studio enough financial stability to bring staff back.

Like Sylvia and Tyrus, Retta was shocked at the shutdown. Unlike them, however, she was one of the few artists immediately rehired, as her work was absolutely necessary for the feature films they were completing. Alas, Retta's good fortune was not to last. The studio had gotten everything it needed from the young animator, and with the company's future still uncertain, executives had little reason to keep her on. On November 24, the artist whom Walt had warmly praised only four months previously, the first credited female animator of the studio, was fired.

In the fall of 1941, unlike most of her colleagues, Mary Blair returned to the studio she had once hastily quit confident of her employment, as were all the other members of El Grupo. The studio was a sad, empty place, to be sure, but there was much to rejoice in. She was coming home full of inspiration, her sketchbook replete with images, her mind bursting with ideas.

As planned, the artists who had gone to South America began turning their months of travel into films celebrating the diverse cultures of the continent. Unfortunately, as no new features were in the works, the story department had been stripped down and there were few people left who could put together a nuanced storyboard. The animators, though talented, were more adept at gag humor, using the slapstick movements of their characters to evoke laughter without the need for words.

The studio was further handicapped by the fact that most of the artists working on the picture, which would be known as *Saludos Amigos,* hadn't been to South America and so were re-creating scenes they hadn't witnessed firsthand. Without artists to provide the finesse the studio had once been capable of, the South American culture was lost in translation.

251

■ ■ ■ ■

Early one Sunday morning in December 1941, a surprise attack on Pearl Harbor in Hawaii took twenty-four hundred lives and changed the fate of the nation. Most Americans stayed near their radios with no thought of carrying on normal life. But that morning, while many Californians worried that they were next in line to be attacked, Walt, who hadn't yet heard the news, was working. He had a story meeting scheduled.

That fateful December day, Walt was discussing a feature he had been hoping to make for years based on the 1865 novel *Alice's Adventures in Wonderland* by Charles Lutwidge Dodgson and published under the pseudonym Lewis Carroll. He had no money to develop a new feature and yet he was optimistic that they would somehow find a way. Oblivious to the impending chaos of their world, Walt and a group of story men discussed the plot. At one point, Walt said, "Oftentimes the best sense is nonsense. I'd like to finish the whole thing by coming out with some bit of nonsense that makes very good sense — the implication would be 'There. That's what we've been trying to tell you.' "

The riddles of Lewis Carroll could not distract Walt from reality for long. The next day, the U.S. Congress officially declared war on Japan, and days later, Germany and Italy declared war on the United States. The delightful absurdities of *Alice in Wonderland* had to be set aside. The South American feature now took on new importance. It was more than a film; it was a hand reaching across continents to potentially warm the hearts and gain the political sympathies of the United States' neighbors.

Mary's sketches for *Saludos Amigos* captured the vibrancy she had experienced in Brazil, but her work was only one part of the larger project. The movie would be a package film — a collection of related shorts — each of its four sequences endeavoring to illustrate the spirit of one of the countries El Grupo had visited. Between the segments, real footage of the trip was incorporated, and Mary Blair, smiling on an airplane, stood out from the male artists on the trip. With a cartoon plane moving across a map of the continent, the film took the reverse course of their route, going from Lake Titicaca to Chile to Argentina and ending in Brazil.

Alô Amigos, the Portuguese title of the film, premiered in Rio de Janeiro on August

24, 1942. It would be six months before an English-language version of the studio's shortest picture, at forty-two minutes, would be shown in North America. The delay was deliberate, the exclusivity meant to underline the fact that the film was primarily intended to entertain South American audiences and hopefully strengthen ties between the Americas. The film yielded mixed reactions, bringing in a modest profit for the studio along with praise and criticism from both sides of the equator.

The Chilean segment failed to capture the rich culture El Grupo had encountered during their time in the country. The short's hero is a young mail plane named Pedro on his first trip across the Andes. The plane struggles with the weather and altitude before heroically delivering the mail from the high plains of Mendoza, Argentina, down to Santiago, on Chile's coast.

Many Chileans found the puerile plane a disappointing character. One of those Chileans was René Ríos Boettiger, a former medical student who in the 1930s had traded in his stethoscope for pencils. In 1941 he met Walt in Santiago, where Boettiger was working as a cartoonist under the pseudonym Pepo. The meeting was cordial, but Boettiger's amicable feelings vanished after he saw *Saludos Amigos* in 1942. In response, he decided to create his own character, one that would properly represent the country he loved. Boettiger selected the condor from the Chilean coat of arms, and in 1949, the comic *Condorito* was born, the protagonist an endearing rascal who frequently falls to the floor with a *plop!* His popularity would far outstrip that of *Saludos Amigos,* reaching readers across the world as an influential ambassador for the land of the Andes.

It wasn't solely the Chilean segment of *Saludos Amigos* that was lacking. The representation of Argentina was similarly dissatisfying to many. It depicted the character Goofy learning the ways of the gaucho, the national symbol of Argentina. While the beginning of the short depicts the elements of traditional gaucho clothing, the rest of it is composed of typical gag material as Goofy struggles with his lasso and saddle.

Only in its last segment did the film approach its aspirations. In time to the beautiful song "Aquarela do Brasil," written by Ary Barroso in 1939, the short unfolds from the perspective of a paintbrush, seemingly held by the audience, capturing in watercolors the luscious beauty of Rio de Janeiro. The animation is free and artistic, with

255

greater ambition than its predecessors. Unsurprisingly, it is also the only short in which Mary Blair's influence and style are displayed.

It was Mary's brush that made bananas turn into yellow-billed toucans, flowers burst into color against a pitch-black sky, and twinkling lights shine along the shore of the city. Even the Urca casino where Walt and El Grupo spent a glamorous evening made an appearance. The sequence celebrates the wild beauty and urban sophistication of Rio de Janeiro that the artists adored. It also introduces José Carioca, a Brazilian parrot who becomes fast friends with Donald Duck and who would return for the studio's next Latin American film, *The Three Caballeros*. Thanks to Mary's concept art, the piece was extraordinarily beautiful, a visual love song to the country that had transformed her as an individual and as an artist.

"It isn't exactly like anything the Disney boys have ever done," wrote Bosley Crowther in his 1943 review of the film in the *New York Times*. In his praise of the Brazil sequence, where he complimented the "exquisite sequence of animated watercolorings," Crowther managed to completely overlook Mary Blair, even though her face and name were right there on the screen.

Hours after the bombing of Pearl Harbor, the Federal Bureau of Investigation in Los Angeles was sent into action, rounding up individuals and freezing the assets of over a thousand Japanese community and religious leaders. For those of Japanese descent living in the United States, regardless of citizenship, persecution was imminent.

Two months later, on February 19, 1942, President Roosevelt signed Executive Order 9066, which stated, "War requires every possible protection against espionage and against sabotage." He instituted military zones that would be used as internment camps for all persons living on the West Coast who were one-sixteenth Japanese or more. The United States was not alone. Similar violations of civil rights were being committed in Canada, Mexico, Peru, Brazil, Chile, and Argentina.

Fear reverberated around the studio as some employees became apprehensive over the uncertain fate of their colleagues. Walt was particularly concerned for artist Gyo Fujikawa, who had been born in California but whose parents were from Japan. In anticipation of the danger that could befall her, Gyo decided to transfer from the studio in Burbank to the company's offices in New York City, where she could continue her work as an illustrator. Prejudice existed on the East Coast too, but at least there was no danger of internment. Gyo left, grateful for Walt's consideration, but she was soon consumed with guilt when she learned that her parents had been sent to the Rohwer Relocation Center, an internment camp in Arkansas.

Although New York City had become her sanctuary, Gyo often had to travel outside its borders. She returned to the studio in Burbank at regular intervals and even bravely went to Arkansas to visit her family. Her fellow travelers questioned her heritage on these trips, suspicious that she might be a Japanese spy. Gyo would laugh and say she was Anna May Wong, a Chinese American fashion icon and Hollywood movie star.

Walt dropped into Gyo's New York office one day and asked, "How are you doing? I've been worried about you."

"I'm doing okay," Gyo replied. Gaily making light of her situation, she said, "If people ask me what nationality I am I tell them the truth or give them big lies, like I'm half Chinese or half Japanese, or part Korean, part Chinese, and part Japanese."

"Why do you have to do that?" Walt said, enraged. "For Christ's sakes, you're an American citizen!" Gyo understood his point perfectly. His words captured her own ambivalence about hiding her identity. Walt's outburst strengthened her self-confidence, and from that day on, when someone asked where she was from, she said simply, "I'm an American."

While Gyo was falling in love with the bustle of New York City, Sylvia had at last received the call to return to the studio. With modest profits coming from its most recent features, the studio was slowly rebuilding, and Walt needed a story department if it was to have a future. Sylvia was buoyant at seeing that her friend Ethel was back too. Now that the strike was over, the divisions that had separated them seemed less important. Yet she had little hope for resurrecting their script for *The Little Mermaid.* There was no way the studio was ready to invest in an expensive new feature. Unfortunately, in comparison to the projects they had worked on previously, the jobs currently on the table were far from inspiring.

Sylvia's skills were being distinctly under-utilized; she was plotting advertisements for Coca-Cola that included playful gnomes that stole away bottles of the soft drink. The partnership between the two companies began when Walt advertised *Saludos Amigos* on a radio show sponsored by Coca-Cola in 1942. The association was fortunate for Walt, who badly needed money. Advertising did not ignite the passion of his artists, but for the moment it was helping to keep the doors open and the lights on.

As Sylvia had feared, there were no new animated feature films being developed. The once-bustling story department, whose job had been to develop a fat portfolio of new ideas, scripts, and storyboards, was eerily quiet. Other than the government-backed South American features, the studio was working on nothing but its animated shorts, some commercial projects such as the Coca-Cola campaign, and propaganda films commissioned by branches of the military and the U.S. government.

With so few resources, Walt had let go of the features, the films that had defined the studio since the release of *Snow White* five years earlier. Their artistry and storytelling were simply too expensive. Walt began assessing the potential of live-action films, a more economical alternative to animated features. Overwhelmed by personal and professional struggles, he nevertheless knew that he had to find a fresh approach to the timeworn medium of actors in front of a camera. Fortunately, one of his oldest colleagues had returned to help him do just that.

A technology called the optical printer had been in development since the turn of the twentieth century. Early on, it was used primarily to duplicate film. The original film was placed in a projector with a movie camera mechanically linked to it. Using a lens, the film was projected directly onto new, unexposed film, creating a copy. The technique was like taking a picture of a picture — imperfect in terms of quality, but it got the job done. However, the potential for effects inherent in the setup was apparent from the beginning. Filmmakers immediately began zooming in on different areas of the film they were interested in or cutting out those they wanted to get rid of.

The idea of altering the film being produced was as old as the movies themselves. As early as 1898, the filmmaker Georges Méliès used mattes, pieces of glass painted black, to keep certain parts of the film unexposed. He would then rewind the film, remove the original matte, cover everything else to protect the original shots from being double-exposed, then project new images onto the clean film. With this careful process, he created footage that seemed to alter reality; for example, in one scene, he appeared to pop his head off his body, set it on a table, and then continue talking.

Movies that relied on the wizardry of mattes and optical printers, such as the original *King Kong* in 1933 and *Citizen Kane* in 1941, were increasing in popularity. Yet as exciting as the technology was, the devices were not yet available commercially. Movie studios that wanted to take advantage of the magic of optical printers had to build them in-house.

At the Walt Disney Studios, Ub Iwerks was the man in charge of visual effects. One of the first animators to draw Mickey Mouse was back after his own animation studio had closed its doors a few years previously. Iwerks was building an optical printer that had the potential to combine animation and live action. The new technology would come in handy for the second film developed from the Latin American goodwill trip, *The Three Caballeros.*

Walt's directors had originally filmed a scene in the movie using a rear projection screen with animation running behind Aurora Miranda, a Brazilian singer and actress and younger sister of the legendary Carmen Miranda, and a few dancers. Donald Duck was projected onto the screen so that it looked like he was at her side, and the unlikely pair danced to a samba. But the scene lacked realism, and the artists were unhappy with it. Only by using the optical printer could they truly combine Miranda's moves with that of her cartoon costars, Donald and the parrot José Carioca. Thanks to the technology Iwerks had engineered, the animated characters broke free of the background and looked like they were moving in front of and between the dancers.

Mary Blair played a key role in designing numerous scenes in both of the Latin American movies. Her drawings of children, a whimsical train, and unusual plants and flowers, along with her bold color choices, provided some of the films' most striking features. Mary's talents were highly praised, and she was no longer in direct competition with her husband at the studio. Lee had been drafted into the army and sent to Camp Livingston in northern Louisiana. Lee wrote to Mary telling her of his escapades, life in the military, and his new friends and professing his love for her. Yet he rarely asked about her work and life, and as is often the case, the distance between them exposed the faults in their relationship.

The person closest to Mary during the war years was not Lee, but Retta. With her husband gone, Mary found the house lonely, so she invited her friend to move in with her. The two were now both living and working together, as Retta had been rehired at the studio in the summer of 1942. She was happy to be back, for in her months away she had struggled to find creative endeavors. Along with animator Wolfgang Reitherman, known as Woolie to his friends, she had painted large canvases of military aircraft for local officer clubs and had put together a picture book about a bomber plane titled *B-1st,* although they couldn't find a publisher. Woolie had a reputation at the studio for dating female colleagues, including both Grace and Retta. Retta and Woolie dated during the layoffs but when Woolie was rehired at the studio, they parted ways. Retta found work illustrating an airplane-parts catalog until she finally got her job back too.

Retta returned to the studio on August 12, 1942, one day before her work reappeared in American movie houses. On August 9, the long-awaited *Bambi* premiered in London, as a show of support for the city in the midst of World War II, and it was released in New York a few days later, on August 13. Among the fifteen animators credited, Retta was the only woman. It was the first time a female animator had ever been credited in Hollywood feature animation.

The critical reception to *Bambi* was mixed. *Variety* proclaimed, "*Bambi* is gem-like in its reflection of the color and movement of sylvan plant and animal life." *Variety* also admired Sylvia's thunderstorm for its "glow and texture." Retta was proud of the abundance of praise for her work; *Time* had called her dogs "the most terrifying curs since Cerberus."

Yet many hunters came out against the movie, and an article in *Outdoor Life* called it "the worst insult ever offered in any form to American sportsmen." In a different vein, a review in the *New York Times* complained that the animation was too realistic, saying of Walt's latest production, "His painted forest is hardly to be distinguished from the real forest shown by the Technicolor camera in *The Jungle Book* [the 1942 live-action film]," and asking, "Why have cartoons at all?" *Bambi,* like *Pinocchio* and *Fantasia,* would be an unequivocal failure at the box office, losing approximately one hundred thousand dollars in its first theatrical run.

Retta was thinking not of studio profits but of her own paycheck when she returned to work. She found an environment very different from the one she remembered — everything was smaller. Not only the staff and the grounds, but also the projects; they were far more limited in scope. No longer were the group members indulging in lengthy storyboard meetings in which they debated topics like the moral lessons central to a particular character. Their focus was on educational shorts, commercial projects, military propaganda films, and a small number of features, although these seemed unlikely to ever leave the studio walls. More upsetting still was her humbler position in the studio hierarchy. Before Retta was laid off, she had been a top animator, but when she was hired back, she was told that she could return three salary grades lower as an assistant animator or move over to the story department. Both options were demotions, so she reluctantly chose the story department, where she felt she'd have a greater chance of creative freedom.

But Retta would soon learn that artistic expression was not to be found in the projects currently under development.

When she returned to the studio, a nonfiction book called *Victory Through Air Power,* by Alexander P. de Seversky, was number one on the *New York Times* bestseller list. Released mere months after Pearl Harbor, the book was causing a sensation. The author had served in the Imperial Russian navy and in 1918 had been sent as an envoy to the United States. The timing was providential — it allowed de Seversky to escape the chaos of the Russian Revolution and the rise of the Soviet Union. With no wish to return to his home country, de Seversky offered his services to the War Department and was soon assistant to General William "Billy" Mitchell. The two men had much in common, as they both passionately believed that the future of combat depended on military aviation and that no other force, neither battleships nor troops, was nearly as critical. Mitchell felt so strongly about the dominance of air strategy and the need for a separate U.S. Air Force (which was not formed until 1946) that he was openly insubordinate, accusing the Navy and War Departments of "incompetency, criminal negligence, and almost treasonable administration of the national defense" in a 1925 press conference. After being court-martialed for his outspokenness, Mitchell ultimately resigned his commission and left the military.

De Seversky invented and patented many aeronautical instruments (including a gyroscopically stabilized bombsight and a device that allowed for air-to-air refueling) and started an airplane company that manufactured a fleet of nimble military aircraft. In 1939, however, its board of directors, frustrated at the business's lack of profit despite multiple military contracts, forced de Seversky out.

Although he'd been removed from his own aircraft company, de Seversky remained a passionate proponent of aerial warfare. He wrote articles and gave lectures on the subject, and in 1942, his book *Victory Through Air Power* was published. The book, advocating for a separate air force and an aviation-centered strategy, drew both fierce criticism and warm praise, igniting a public debate about how war should be waged. Walt, like many, found de Seversky's arguments persuasive. In fact, he was so convinced that he felt compelled to bring its contents "far beyond the limited audience of the book-reading public."

With the war ongoing, speed was the chief consideration at the studio when adapting the book. The film needed no finesse from the optical printer; it included scenes of de Seversky and General Mitchell speaking directly to the camera, and basic animation carried the rest of the action, each thesis of the book illustrated with maps, planes, and submarines. Retta spent long hours animating arrows indicating battleships, airplanes, and supplies moving from the Americas and throughout Europe and Japan. She joked that the film necessitated so many of her arrows that it should be called *Victory Through Arrow Power.*

While she missed the artistic wonderland of the studio during the early production on *Bambi,* Retta knew that her workplace was reflective of a changing world. Everyone's life was altered, and the dreams she had cherished after graduating from Chouinard had to make way for new realities. At night Retta was happy to have Mary's company, and the two of them drank cocktails on the large porch that had once hosted wild parties.

While Retta's recent experience illustrating airplanes proved useful for the film, many in the studio regretted that Grace had left. Her expertise in aircraft would have been a rich source of knowledge for the film. Grace had hoped that leaving the studio would finally bring her the career in aviation she longed for. Yet World War II, rather than opening doors in the field for her, was shutting her out. First, her job at Fairchild Aviation was withdrawn. Next, her many inquiries for jobs as part of the war effort were rebuffed. Grace thought she might find work ferrying planes from the United States to Great Britain, as she knew women in England were performing similar work, and yet no one would hire her. With frustration she watched as men with less flying experience than herself were hired as copilots while her applications were continually passed over.

In the midst of this disappointment, Grace met Berkeley Brandt Jr., a pilot with a commercial license like herself. He flew for United Airlines and had an employment history and opportunities that Grace could only dream of. The two fell in love, and in late 1941, Grace was married in a white lace dress with a long train. Marriage did not dim her hopeful prospects for the future, but the continued prejudice she encountered against female pilots did.

"It is a total war," Grace wrote in her diary. "It seems as though it should be the right time for every able-bodied person, man or woman, to help. Now more than ever even though I am married I feel that I can and should be of service, but still there are no opportunities."

The film version of *Victory Through Air Power,* released in July 1943, was advertised with the tagline EVERY VITAL QUESTION YOU'VE ASKED SINCE PEARL HARBOR . . . ANSWERED AT LAST ON THE SCREEN! The film showed the horror of the Pearl Harbor bombing in animated Technicolor, and for the audience, the images of destruction, occurring so recently on American soil, were distressing. Yet Walt chose to keep violence in the picture. This was not timeless entertainment for all ages; this was a propaganda film.

The message of the film divided its audience. Many were persuaded by the animated scenes of airplanes dropping bombs across Europe and Asia that an air force was needed, and others were angered by the film's shallow depiction of the significance of the navy and army. One of those who found its message ill-considered was President Roosevelt's chief of staff, Admiral William Leahy. Attempts to have the film screened at the White House, one of Walt's chief ambitions, were blocked.

He had better luck across the Atlantic,

271

where Winston Churchill not only viewed the feature but appeared to find its message persuasive. When Churchill met with Roosevelt in August 1943 to plan the D-Day invasion of France, he asked the American president if he'd seen it. When Roosevelt replied that he hadn't, Churchill insisted that a fighter plane rush a print of the film to them, and they watched it twice in two days. Walt had accomplished his ultimate goal of sending its message to those in power.

What role the movie played in shaping future tactics is unknown, although it seems likely that it only reinforced the already growing reliance on aviation among military planners. A year after the film's release, June 6, 1944, D-Day marked the largest aerial operation in history, with transports, bombers, reconnaissance planes, fighter planes, and troop-carrier planes all playing critical roles in the storming of the beaches at Normandy.

Although many women worked on *Victory Through Air Power,* including Retta and Sylvia, the only one to receive screen credit was Natalie Kalmus, the ever-present color director, brought in for Technicolor consultation. Although the strike had sought to democratize how artists were credited, the results were as subjective as they'd ever been. Retta was not credited for her work on *Fantasia, Dumbo,* or *Victory Through Air Power.* Other artists were similarly denied on-screen acknowledgment. Tyrus Wong, whose color palette and visual style defined *Bambi,* was listed as merely a "background artist." The artists who benefited from the hierarchy of on-screen credit were those who were favorites of Walt's, such as Mary Blair.

In red pastels, Retta drew an impish creature donning a flight helmet and goggles. Its mischievous grin made Mary laugh when she saw it, but the author who had described the troublemaking character would not find Retta's sketches quite so amusing. The creatures were called gremlins, and Royal Air Force pilots in England had dreamed them up during World War II to use as all-purpose scapegoats for the many mechanical failures of modern aircraft.

Roald Dahl, a flight lieutenant in the RAF during World War II, wrote a story about the creatures, "Gremlin Lore." As a boy, Dahl had enjoyed writing stories, but his instructors did not believe the young man possessed any extraordinary talent. One of his English teachers wrote in a report, "I have never met anybody who so persistently writes words meaning the exact opposite of what is intended."

Dahl had been a combat pilot, but after suffering numerous injuries, he was sent to Washington, DC, as a military attaché. At his desk job, he wrote adventure tales of his experiences, including "Gremlin Lore," which told of a band of endearing trouble-makers. As an officer in the RAF, he could not have his stories published without the approval of the head of the British Informa-tion Services in the United States, Sidney L. Bernstein. But Bernstein wasn't merely a government liaison; he was also a well-known English movie producer with con-nections to Walt Disney. Believing that the story Dahl had written had the potential for adaptation, he sent a copy to Walt on July 1, 1942.

Nearly everything Walt and the studio were working on was related to World War II, and although wary about the fleeting nature of war entertainment, Walt tele-grammed less than two weeks later that he wanted to secure the rights to the material. Dahl was an unpublished writer and so had few demands, his only stipulation being that he should have the "opportunity to pass upon the general characterization and technical details," a seemingly inconsequential line that would later prove challenging to Retta and the studio.

Dahl's story was sold to *Cosmopolitan* magazine that September, and Walt Disney Studios was slated to create illustrations for the piece. In many ways, the published story was a test run; the hope was that its popularity would pave the way for a feature film. The fervor for gremlins, however, grew far more quickly than the studio expected. The legend had made its way to American airmen stationed in Great Britain, and by late 1942, articles about the devious creatures were being published in dozens of magazines.

Retta drew her gremlins as both rascally and adorable, small in stature with barely visible blue-tinged wings, too-large boots, and green horns on their heads. Her drawings portray creatures that resemble naughty children playing in dress-up clothes. Dahl was not amused, writing, "If only I had been able to come down and talk with you about them, I know I could have, at any rate, given you an accurate description of what they looked like." The twenty-six-year-old writer was insistent that the creatures should wear green bowler hats instead of flight helmets and goggles, citing his personal observations on the airfield.

Dahl traveled to Burbank and spoke with the studio artists, describing with minute exactness how gremlins should look and act. He wasn't the only pilot to visit — Walt put out a call asking available RAF airmen to come to California, and dozens of pilots arrived to offer tales of the gremlins and eyewitness accounts of their appearance and behavior. The depiction of the creatures became so complex that in the story department, the staff made a chart to organize the vast array of guidelines governing gremlin behavior. The artists listened to the men sympathetically, hiding their surprise that these military professionals, all of whom appeared sane, talked with certainty about seeing creatures scampering around their planes. Retta and Mary worked together from the detailed interviews and research, Retta sketching while Mary developed the color palette.

Even as the story treatment and artwork were taking shape, the physical appearance of the gremlins was still hotly debated. Not only did Dahl continue to have strong notions about what his characters should look like, what clothing they should wear, and how they should behave, but a clause in the signed contract required both his approval and that of Britain's air ministry.

Between the studio's difficulties with revisions for the film and Dahl's displeasure at their design, the project ultimately became more trouble than it was worth. The storyboards were scrapped, and production for it shut down. Dahl's story, however, would still be published in *Cosmopolitan,* under the pseudonym Pegasus, and would later be published as a book, the proceeds of which were donated to the RAF Benevolent Fund.

Many within the studio's walls were beginning to feel as though everything they produced was destined for failure. *Pinocchio, Fantasia,* and *Bambi* had lost millions at the box office. *Dumbo,* even with its reduced production costs, barely broke even. *Saludos Amigos* and *The Three Caballeros* (released in 1944) had earned a small profit, but *Victory Through Air Power* had lost half a million dollars. Training shorts commissioned by the U.S. government were helping to keep the studio afloat, but the threat of bankruptcy lingered. With their meager staff and suppressed creativity, the artists at Walt Disney Studios were starting to think that animation, an enterprise that relied on hand drawings and the artistic spark, was antiquated and couldn't possibly turn a profit.

■ ■ ■ ■

In a small apartment in Queens, New York, Chester Carlson was also beginning to give up hope. Carlson had graduated with a degree in physics from the California Institute of Technology in 1930, but in the wake of the Great Depression he was unable to find work in his field. After applying to eighty-two different companies, he finally took a job at the Bell Telephone Laboratories in New York City. The low-paying job soon grew dull, so he transferred to the company's patent office, where, even if he couldn't create inventions, he could at least protect them. He found working with the attorneys in the office more tiresome than he anticipated, however, primarily because of the paperwork involved. Drawings of each invention had to be copied by hand several times in order to correctly file the patent. With his poor eyesight and rheumatoid arthritis, Carlson spent much of his time there in misery. He began to dream of a machine that would be able to copy a document with the push of a button.

The fantasy was not his alone. A Hungarian physicist named Pál Selényi was publishing papers on the nature of light and performing experiments to electrostatically attract ink to an insulated surface. Inspired by Selényi's published studies, Carlson began playing with the techniques in his kitchen, occasionally starting fires in the Astoria, Queens, apartment he shared with his wife and mother-in-law.

On October 22, 1938, Carlson had his first success. Along with another physicist, the Austrian refugee Otto Kornei, he wrote in ink the date and his location on a glass microscope slide: *10.-22.-38 Astoria.* He rubbed a handkerchief on a sulfur-coated zinc plate in order to build up an electrostatic charge, just as a child might rub a balloon on her head to build up static electricity. He quickly laid the glass slide atop the zinc plate and shone a bright light on it for five seconds, then removed the slide and sprinkled, as if it were fairy dust, lycopodium powder on the plate. When he blew off the loose powder, what he had written remained clearly visible: *10.-22.-38 Astoria.*

Carlson and Kornei improved their technique, and Carlson used his expertise in the area to quickly file a patent on the process. He assumed that the next step, finding a business partner with money to invest, would be simple. This was not the case. By

1942, he had been rejected by dozens of companies, including IBM, GE, and RCA. Carlson began to question whether electro-photography would ever be valued by the business world. He couldn't know it at the time, but the invention he lamented ever finding a home for would eventually trigger a revolution at the Walt Disney Studios.

CHAPTER 9
ZIP-A-DEE-DOO-DAH

In the cool night air of Mexico City on December 9, 1942, Mary watched children gather in front of the Basilica of Our Lady of Guadalupe. They formed a procession, some of them carrying pictures of Joseph, Mary, and the angel Gabriel, others holding candles, their small hands cupped around the naked flames to protect them from the wind. They walked through the streets slowly, their voices echoing off the buildings as they sang "Canto Para Pedir Posada," the sweet melody that marks the Mexican Christmas tradition of Las Posadas. The song is a conversation between Joseph and the innkeepers of Bethlehem in which he pleads for lodging for himself and the pregnant Mary, about to give birth. During Las Posadas, the children go from house to house asking for shelter. Voices inside sing in response, at first saying there is no room. Finally, at a designated house, the door is opened to welcome them and the final verse is sung by everyone together. Inside the house, a party is held, the children letting out happy shouts as they swing at a piñata.

Mary was not religious but she felt incredibly moved by the beauty of the tradition. As she sketched the scene, she experienced a breakthrough moment in her artistic development. She had drawn a few young people during her travels in South America, sketching faces that conveyed sweetness and innocence. The many children she drew in Mexico were similar in their stylized nature but with rounder cheeks and more expressive faces. Mary brought a level of empathy to the pieces that underscored her connection to the scene, the bright colors reflecting the participants' joy as they walked through the streets. Mary's depiction of children in her artwork would never be the same.

Walt was struck by her work. "You know about colors I have never heard of," he told her. While Mary was thrilled at the praise, she could feel the jealousy of her male coworkers, who bristled at the attention Walt gave her. In their displeasure, they called her "Marijuana Blair," a nickname that mocked her eccentric color choices.

But Walt's admiration was lasting and

sincere. Very few pieces of artwork by studio employees were displayed at his home, but Walt loved Mary's watercolors so much that two of her paintings of Peruvian children, both concept drawings for *Saludos Amigos,* hung in the Disney house in Los Angeles. It wasn't solely her art that made an impression. Diane and Sharon, Walt's daughters, regarded Mary herself with awe and admiration.

Mary left her twenties the way a snake sheds its skin — with a shiny new sense of self. She was thirty-two in 1943 and had attained confidence and focus, and not only artistically. A natural sophistication emerged in the way she looked, acted, and dressed. She designed and sewed her own clothing, creating a unique style. Her bold wardrobe included capes, scarves, neckties, and unusual hats. She played with tailoring, often using the lines found in men's clothing and wearing jackets and pants. With her high cheekbones, short bangs, French perfume, and quiet, worldly demeanor, she made an impression not only on Walt's young daughters but on almost everyone else who met her.

By 1943 Mary's life had become a blur of airfields, suitcases, and the melodic tones of the Spanish language. After traveling to

South America in 1941 to prepare for *Saludos Amigos* and then to Mexico with Walt and a few other artists in 1942 for material for *The Three Caballeros,* she was sent to Cuba to do some work for a third planned feature, tentatively called *Cuban Carnival.* Cuban diplomats, citing the vast numbers of American tourists to their shores in the 1940s, were disappointed to have been left out of *Saludos Amigos* and had requested an animated celebration of their culture.

Mary got off the plane in Havana and, accustomed as she was to the dry climate of Southern California, was immediately struck by the humidity. She was traveling with a small cadre of artists and without Walt, so unlike the expedition to South America, where Walt's presence lent a formal air to events and appearances, she now had the freedom to sketch and write, meticulously documenting the culture she was immersing herself in.

Relishing the independence, she let her own inclinations and instincts guide her. She sketched furiously over the course of five weeks as she traveled the country, visiting cigar factories, strolling through fields of sugarcane, and twirling in her heels in dance halls.

Walt had given her the freedom to work

Mary Blair (center) making new friends in Cuba in 1943 **(Courtesy the estate of Mary Blair)**

as a concept artist, creating the look and feel of the films she designed. Her travels were an essential part of this process, inspiring her first rough outlines for upcoming features. A story artist was responsible for creating storyboards and writing scripts, but her work was often more like a cinematographer's — she captured specific scenes and chose a color palette that communicated the emotion the scene should have. The roles she played were frequently diverse; in addition to concept art, she created background art for some films, and for others she served as an art director, which she described as "an idea-creating position," adding "you either have it or you don't."

Mary and the story department staff worked closely together to come up with ideas for a new film. As Mary was performing her magic on the concept art, the story department would build a storyboard and then begin working on the script. Mary's art acted as a foundation, creating a look for the film, the set, and the characters that the animators could build from. However, the ideas coming from the story department were a mere trickle compared to the mighty river that had once flowed from the group. When Mary was home from her travels, she and Retta would discuss their frustrations at the limited prospects before them, martinis in their hands.

In 1943, with *Victory Through Air Power* nearly complete and training videos for the military in constant production, there was little to inspire Retta, Sylvia, and the group of artists who remained in the studio. Retta was working on the shorts *Tuberculosis, Cleanliness Brings Health, Infant Care and Feeding,* and *Hookworm,* while Sylvia was shaping *The Story of Menstruation.* Yet even with their meager budgets and limited subject matter, both women managed to bring exceptional artistry to their work.

Sylvia was zealous about describing to young women the scientific nature of hormones and their impact on the growing female body, information accompanied by anatomically accurate animation. In many ways the piece was radical. Talk of menstruation in the 1940s was taboo, and frank discussions of female human biology were rare. Misconceptions surrounding menstruation lingered from past generations; many women referred to their periods as "the curse" and believed themselves to be unclean and unable to participate in normal activity during it.

Sylvia's piece was being produced at a time of innovation in feminine-hygiene products. After World War I, nurses realized that the cellulose bandages they had used on soldiers were more absorbent than cotton and began making menstruation pads from the material. By the 1940s the pads were widely available and sold, along with sanitary belts to hold the material in place, by companies like Kotex and Modess.

Although tampons in one form or another had existed for centuries, with the earliest use documented among Egyptian women, the product wasn't commercially available in the United States until 1933. A doctor named Earle Haas applied for a patent on November 19, 1931, for his "catamenial device," a piece of compressed cotton that could be inserted into the vagina using two pieces of telescoping cardboard. After failing to get manufacturers interested in the product, he sold the patent to a woman named Gertrude Tendrich, who formed the Tampax Sales Corporation. She was its first president and began to sell the product in retail stores as an "invisible sanitary napkin." As the United States entered World War II, the popularity of tampons grew, since they were marketed to those with "active" jobs in the war effort.

In the short film, Sylvia didn't shy away from frankly discussing female anatomy, preferring candor to conventional modesty. The short would be shown in high schools throughout the 1940s and 1950s, and for many young women, it was their introduction to reproductive biology.

Although these projects offered a sense of purpose, Sylvia was happy to leave them behind when Walt told her the next feature she would be working on would be musical in nature. Her face lit up with delight at the prospect of allowing music to once again influence her work. She was working with fellow writer José Rodriguez on a new package film called *The History of Music.* The two had previously collaborated on *Victory Through Air Power. The History of Music* could not have been more different. Sylvia drew a wise owl to explain the evolution of musical instruments and the technical aspects of their design that created a "toot, whistle, plunk, and boom." While she happily filled her studio space once again with symphonies, another new feature film was finally emerging from old storyboards.

Story development at Walt Disney Studios was a competitive sport. Writing was just the beginning of the process. For the story to thrive and enter production, the writer needed to be a strong advocate for his or her work, someone who could be thoroughly persuasive during story meetings. That description did not often apply to Bianca, so her projects made it to the screen only after torturous effort. Bianca's story treatment for *Cinderella,* written in 1940 and accompanied by her drawings, at first seemed to be just another failed proposal. Yet with the dearth of new ideas being generated by the diminished department, Bianca's take on the classic tale gleamed like a glass slipper left on a dark staircase. Walt brushed the dust off the file and began rereading her work.

Bianca's adaptation captured the essence of the age-old fairy tale, which crosses cultures and traditions. Variations on the story have been found in the literature of ancient Greece, Tang-dynasty China, and seventeenth-century Italy, and there are more than five hundred European versions. "Cendrillon," published in French writer Charles Perrault's *Tales of Mother Goose* in 1697, would grow in popularity thanks to his additions of a fairy godmother, a pumpkin that turns into a carriage, and a glass slipper. Some later adaptations would intensify the cruelty in the plot. The Brothers Grimm version, called "Aschenputtel," published in 1812, had the stepsisters cut off parts of their own feet in order to fit into the lost slipper, filling the shoe with blood. Even at the happy ending, when Cinderella is marrying her prince, birds swoop down to peck out the eyes of the cruel stepsisters, leaving them forever blinded.

It is unsurprising that Bianca preferred to adapt the less disturbing French version when writing her script. While the simple story required little finesse, there were still changes Bianca felt would improve the film.

Given the studio's adeptness at animating animals, Bianca decided to create a large supporting cast of helpful creatures. Both the animals and their relationships with the central character offered a fresh take on the tale. Mice in the original stories were merely pests caught in traps, but in Bianca's script, the mice are Cinderella's friends and a key plot device.

At the end of Perrault's story, after the stepsisters fail to fit their feet into the glass slipper, Cinderella shows up and says simply, "Let me see if it will not fit me." Feeling the need to bring tension to the scene, Bianca had the wicked stepmother lock Cinderella in a cellar from which she cannot escape; her pet mouse Dusty must take the glass slipper in his paws and lead the king's men to the dark prison. Bianca's script ends not with a wedding but with the image of Dusty now living in a gem-encrusted mouse hole.

Bianca brought other animal characters to the script as well, including a pet turtle named Clarissa and a cruel cat named Bon Bob that belonged to the stepsisters. With its cast of animal characters, Bianca's screen adaptation of *Cinderella* was an ideal fit for the studio. The timing, however, was not perfect. It was 1943, and few people were interested in lighthearted princess stories. Money was still tight, as Walt and Roy were able to meet their current expenses but had been unable to pay down their debt. Nonetheless, Walt threw caution to the wind, anticipating better days ahead, and convinced the bankers to give the project a budget of one million dollars. He then assigned two of his best story artists, Joe Grant and Dick Huemer, to supervise work on the feature. The men were not excited about their assignment. They did not share Walt's love of fairy tales and preferred working on an original story of their own. "I never liked pictures where you knew how it was going to end," Grant complained of the project. Reluctantly, they resurrected the words and drawings from Bianca's last days in the story department.

Progress on *Cinderella* was soon interrupted by another feature. In early 1944, Walt decided that *Song of the South* would be the studio's next big project. The film was based on Joel Chandler Harris's *Uncle Remus: His Songs and His Sayings,* published in 1880.

The book is a collection of African American oral folklore supposedly told to Harris. In 1862 he began working outside the small town of Eatonton, Georgia, as a typesetter's apprentice for a local newspaper. Describing himself as "forlorn and friendless," the fourteen-year-old Harris started spending his free time among the slaves working on the nearby Turnwold plantation, particularly enjoying the compelling stories told by a man named Owen Terrell.

The Civil War ended in 1865, but no one would have known it from observing the cotton fields surrounding the Turnwold plantation. In 1865, President Andrew Johnson reverted property to its prewar owners and granted governmental freedom to southern states. Although four million slaves were now free under the Thirteenth Amendment of the Constitution, state governments in the South enacted "black codes" that restricted the movement of African Americans and ensured their exploitation as a labor force. At the plantation, Harris saw little change. African Americans performed the same work, lived in the same cabins, and told many of the same stories they had under slavery.

Harris began writing down the tales of Brer Rabbit, a hero who frequently outthought his foes Brer Fox and Brer Bear. The stories can be traced back to the Akan folk traditions of West Africa, whose enslaved people carried the tales throughout the Americas to symbolize how a small creature, by virtue of his intelligence, can triumph over stronger, larger animals. In Harris's collection, Uncle Remus, a former slave, tells the stories nightly to a young white boy visiting his grandmother's plantation. Harris portrays Uncle Remus as having "nothing but pleasant memories of the discipline of slavery." For years after, children and adults alike would assume Joel Chandler Harris was a black man, someone like Uncle Remus, when in reality he was more akin to the white boy in the book. By publishing these stories, Harris not only usurped the culture of African oral folklore but also whitewashed the history of slavery in the United States.

In spite of these offenses, the book was incredibly popular at the turn of the twentieth century, quickly making its way into children's libraries across the country, including Walt Disney's. With fond childhood memories of the stories, he purchased the rights to the book in 1939 and assigned a few members of his story department to work on the adaptation. With so much to distract the studio at the time, little attention was paid to the book, and it wasn't until five years later that Walt's interest in the project was rekindled. Part of its attraction was that the film could now benefit from the optical printer. With hand-drawn animation still unbearably expensive, combining it with live action and thus saving money while also furthering a new technology was appealing. But unlike in 1939, there was no longer a large staff of writers to let loose on it, so Walt hired Dalton Reymond, a writer and professor at Louisiana State University in Baton Rouge, to begin the adaptation.

Reymond wrote a sixty-page treatment that mirrored the book's narrative. It was allegedly full of racial bias and stereotypes, including the dialects associated with slavery in the South. It was obvious to Walt that this would not do, so he decided to bring in another writer to help balance the final screenplay. But instead of hiring an African American, as might be expected, he hired Maurice Rapf, a Jewish man and avowed Communist living in New York City.

Rapf was hired primarily because of his disgust for the project. He thought making the film was a mistake and that it would inevitably embrace overt racism. "That's why I want someone like you to work on it," Walt said to him. "You're against the black stereotypes. Most of us, even if we have no racial bias, commit booboos that offend people all the time. Because you are sensitive to the problem, maybe you can avoid it." The argument convinced Rapf, so he and Reymond spent the summer of 1944 bickering as they tried to write a screenplay.

The world was slowly shifting and the stereotypical characters the studio had relied on in the past, such as Sunflower in *Fantasia* and Jim Crow and his gang in *Dumbo,* were no longer acceptable. In the fall of 1944, after the studio announced *Song of the South* as its next project, multiple leaders of the African American community as well as Joseph Breen, an official film censor, warned the studio's executives that any adaptation of Uncle Remus would be met with protest given the book's racist tone. In-house publicist Vern Caldwell alerted the film's producer to this, writing, "The negro situation is a dangerous one. Between the negro haters and the negro lovers there are many chances to run afoul of situations that could run the gamut all the way from the nasty to the controversial." Yet even with these substantial warnings, Walt pressed on, seemingly oblivious to what lay ahead.

Before the screenplay was written, Mary was sent to Georgia for ten days to create concept art for the film. Her paintings illustrate the red-dirt roads and pink magnolia trees of the South. Yet amid the beauty in her work, there is darkness. In some aspects it is reminiscent of the suffering she captured in her watercolors of the dust-bowl era. Instead of the pure, sanitized happiness described in the Uncle Remus stories, tragedy tinges the lives of African Americans in Mary's scenes. Beside a green field of blooming flowers, an African American woman and her child walk a red-dirt path to their home. In the background, dead trees are silhouetted against a yellow sky. In a cotton field, the fluffy white blossoms look as light and inviting as cotton candy, but they are juxtaposed against a dark thorny background, communicating a sense of inescapable sorrow as former slaves begin to harvest the crop.

Even her paintings of Uncle Remus express unmistakable sadness. In one, he walks hunched over a cane, shadows lengthening around him over a flowery landscape. Behind him, separated from the bright splendor of summer, are the crops of the plantation laid out in rows as dark as death itself.

But despite the profound contrasts Mary depicted, the animators on the film used

only the cheerful imagery from her paintings — trees full of pink, shimmering blossoms; red-dirt roads; green, rolling hills —
leaving behind all trace of tragedy. The
choice to exclude all indications of injustice
and hardship was evident throughout the
film, in both its appearance and content.

As Mary traveled through the South, the
screenwriters were sinking deeper into
disagreement. Rapf made changes both
large and small, editing out pejorative terms
and altering the characters and setting so it
was clear that the story took place after the
Civil War. He even inserted a date, 1870, to
clarify that the African Americans in the
film were not slaves. He attempted to
indicate in the script that Brer Rabbit was
an African American character, as defined
in the oral tradition, and the opponents he
was outsmarting were white. Unfortunately,
most of these changes would be discarded.
By the end of the summer, the two writers
were at each other's throats and Reymond
insisted his cowriter be taken off the project.

Walt put another progressive writer on
Song of the South and assigned Rapf to
work on *Cinderella*. Rapf was not sorry to
leave the abysmal project behind, especially
after he read through Bianca's treatment of
Cinderella. From her initial script and draw-

ings, he began to create a character very different from the studio's previous princess, Snow White. Perhaps it was his Communist beliefs that inspired him to model her as a worker. He wanted Cinderella to earn her rewards, to go out and get her prince instead of just passively waiting for him. He particularly liked Bianca's touch of having the girl locked in a cellar by her stepmother, which meant Cinderella had to fight to overcome her oppressors. Rapf changed the setting, having her trapped in an attic after a violent rebellion against her stepfamily. The story department felt that was going too far and ultimately removed the violence, and yet the scene crystallized a key part of the main character's motivation and cemented Bianca's vision for the finale.

Nonetheless, work on *Cinderella* was crawling in 1944. The war was still going on and the studio was now teetering on the brink of economic ruin. It was unclear whether the banks that held the studio's debt would even allow the film to be made. Yet most of those in the story and animation departments longed for a return to feature-length animation. Even though so many of their previous efforts — *Pinocchio, Fantasia,* and *Bambi* — had been commercial flops, the creative freedom they had enjoyed while working on them could not be matched by either the package films or the new live-action hybrids.

The fight against fascism abroad cast a harsh light on the deep inequities in the United States. It was impossible to ignore the hypocrisy of a country fighting for freedom and equal rights overseas while it treated its own citizens shamefully. With this in mind, during World War II, the NAACP called for an end to discrimination in the armed forces. Walter White, executive secretary of the organization, made several trips to Europe in order to boost the troops' morale. When back on American soil, he advocated for institutional changes, met with President Truman, and drafted Executive Order 9981, which desegregated the armed forces and abolished discrimination on the basis of race — although it wasn't signed by the president until 1948.

The NAACP and many other black organizations' leaders were calling for change in civilian workplaces as well. The representation of African Americans in film was among the many areas targeted for radical upheaval. The NAACP had long opposed racial stereotyping in film and had staged massive protests when *The Birth of a Nation,* a blatantly racist movie that glorified the Ku Klux Klan, premiered in 1915. In 1937, White had written personally to David O. Selznick, offering to send the producer research papers that refuted the version of the Reconstruction South described by author Margaret Mitchell in *Gone with the Wind.* He suggested that Selznick hire "a person, preferably a Negro, who is qualified to check on possible errors of fact or interpretation."

In 1942, White and influential politician Wendell Willkie had met with studio heads at Twentieth Century Fox to insist on an end to the typecast subservient roles played by black actors, and for years, there had been concerted efforts to fight racism. Nonetheless, roles for African Americans had not significantly expanded since the minstrel shows that dominated American entertainment in the late nineteenth and early twentieth centuries. Cinema had been segregated, both in studios and on-screen, since its inception, with only a few filmmakers, such as Oscar Micheaux, depicting the complexity of life in the African American community. With Uncle Remus in the spotlight, it was clear that the time for action was now.

■ ■ ■ ■

In 1945 the studio turned its attention from Uncle Remus to focus on world events. On May 8, 1945, the front page of the *Los Angeles Times* declared, "Full Victory in Europe." After the news broke, celebrations erupted in the streets. The city even launched a 445-foot "victory ship" from the harbor of the Port of Los Angeles.

Inside the studio, the mood was euphoric. There was much to celebrate. For many employees, their first thoughts were of their loved ones in the military and the hope that they'd be coming home soon. Still, for many on the West Coast, the events of the Pacific theater were equally as urgent as those of Europe, if not more so. It wasn't until August 14, after nuclear bombs were dropped on the Japanese cities of Hiroshima and Nagasaki, that Japan surrendered and World War II effectively came to an end. It was the first and only use of nuclear weapons in armed conflict, and it killed hundreds of thousands of people, most of them civilians. The aftermath of this decision would have far-reaching consequences for decades to come. But with the devastating war finally at an end, many around the globe were able to start rebuilding.

In Burbank, prospects seemed to brighten. The artists were excited about the potential for new projects in their future. For the past four years, 90 percent of their work had been government- and military-related. They were all ready to move on. But other worries were now emerging — for instance, female employees were concerned about their jobs. The number of women working in the animation department had shot up even before the war began, but women knew that the men coming home from war would expect their jobs back. From comments made by supervisors, they believed it was likely that the end of the war would also mean the end of their employment at the studio.

Most service members returning home were hoping to find some normalcy in the day-to-day life they remembered from before the fighting began. Yet for African American servicemen and -women, the world they were returning to was a little too familiar. Attitudes on race had not changed in the United States, and in the South, even those African Americans in military uniforms were denied entry to restaurants that German prisoners of war would have been welcome to eat in. Other injustices persisted;

African American veterans received unequal access to the benefits of the 1944 GI Bill of Rights, particularly the ability to obtain low-interest home loans.

In his 1943 poem "Beaumont to Detroit," Langston Hughes passionately expresses this inequity and the experience of fighting a war on two fronts: against Hitler and against Jim Crow. In 1946, Nazi Germany had been defeated, and the fight against racial segregation was finally gaining momentum.

On November 12, 1946, James Baskett, the first African American to star in a Walt Disney production, appeared on-screen singing "Zip-a-Dee-Doo-Dah." The song was inspired by the slavery-era folk song "Zip Coon" and in 1947 won an Academy Award for best original song. Baskett, who also voiced Brer Rabbit for the film, later received an honorary Oscar for his role as Uncle Remus, the first African American male actor to win an Academy Award.

For the *Song of the South* premiere, however, Baskett was deliberately excluded, as was one of his costars, Academy Award winner Hattie McDaniel. Because the premiere was held at the Atlanta Fox Theatre in the segregated South, neither actor could attend. On the marquee that night, the words

WORLD PREMIERE WALT DISNEY'S "SONG OF THE SOUTH" IN COLOR glowed, and below that were the names of the film's stars — except for its African American actors. Under this banner of racism, an all-white audience streamed through the theater's front doors.

In Eatonton, Georgia, coincidentally where the author of *Uncle Remus* hailed from, a young Alice Walker went to see the movie based on childhood stories passed down through generations. Sitting in the colored section, along with seemingly her whole town, she found no enjoyment, only grief. In a 1981 talk to the Atlanta Historical Society, later published in a book of essays, she described the effect of Walt's movie: "In creating Uncle Remus, he placed an effective barrier between me and the stories that meant so much to me, the stories that could have meant so much to all our children, the stories that they would have heard from their own people and not Walt Disney."

Black leaders organized protests of the film, surrounding theaters in California and New York and carrying signs that read WE WANT FILMS ON DEMOCRACY, NOT SLAVERY; DON'T PREJUDICE CHILDREN'S MINDS WITH FILMS LIKE THIS; and WE FOUGHT

FOR UNCLE SAM NOT UNCLE TOM. The *California Eagle,* an African American newspaper, played a key role in organizing protests in Los Angeles. The paper was owned and operated by Charlotta Bass, a woman committed to using her power in publishing to promote civil rights activism. When describing the reasons for the planned protest, the newspaper reported, "The dialect for Uncle Remus could not even be read by the actors who saw the script."

Ebony ran a photo editorial calling the film "lily-white propaganda" that "disrupted peaceful race relations." Other critics of the era agreed, and a review titled "Spanking Disney" in the *New York Times* addressed Walt directly: "For no matter how much one argues that it's all childish fiction, anyhow, the master-and-slave relation is so lovingly regarded in your yarn, with the Negroes bowing and scraping and singing spirituals in the night, that one might almost imagine that you figure Abe Lincoln made a mistake. Put down that mint julep, Mr. Disney! It doesn't become your youthful face."

Walt Disney Studios couldn't say it hadn't been warned. Walt had known for years that the film's release would provoke an immediate and powerful response. Even Maurice

Rapf, credited as a writer on the film, joined in the criticism, perhaps hoping to distance himself from the project he had once attempted to improve. The film would earn money but not enough to significantly ease the studio's financial distress. As a result of the loud protests surrounding it, *Song of the South* would die a quiet death, never to be released in any video format in the United States.

At a shareholder meeting in 2010, Bob Iger, CEO of the Walt Disney Company, called the film "antiquated" and "fairly offensive" and dismissed the possibility of a DVD release in the near future. Yet others view the film in a different light. During her 2017 induction as a Disney Legend — an honor recognizing individuals who have made extraordinary contributions to the Walt Disney Company — actress Whoopi Goldberg urged the studio to rerelease *Song of the South.* "I'm trying to find a way to get people to start having conversations about bringing *Song of the South* back," Goldberg said in an interview, "so we can talk about what it was and where it came from and why it came out."

Mary Blair's sensitivity toward race in the segregated South shines through in her concept art for the film, although her nuanced depictions were not ultimately used by the animators. And yet, Mary could have tried to do more. At story meetings when racist depictions were discussed, she sat completely silent. During a discussion of the tar-baby sequence, a part of the film that relied on racist stereotypes and later raised justifiable indignation in theaters, Walt asked, "Could it be a thing where he says 'Get the fire going good . . . get the tar good and hot,' etc., singing about what they're doing? The bear could interrupt for some of the dialogue, but he's singing about what he's doing. That's a typical negro thing." Mary did not comment. At the next meeting, Walt asked the room, "You feel the tar-baby thing works all right?" and she again said nothing.

Early in her career, Mary had created a piece titled *Sick Call.* In the drawing, an African American man lies on a cot unconscious while an elderly white doctor leans over him. A second African American stands behind the doctor, terror contorting his face. The work is poignant, the two black characters drawn with a tender sympathy that makes the viewer wonder what events preceded the melancholy scene. If Mary had brought this sense of humanity to the story meetings in addition to her *Song of the*

Sick Call *by Mary Blair, circa 1930s* *(Courtesy the estate of Mary Blair)*

South concept art, might she have swayed Walt? We'll never know.

Even though there was a gradually shifting perspective on the use of stereotypes in film, the lack of diversity in both the story and animation departments was hindering not only *Song of the South* but also the future of animation at the studio. There was no relief in sight. In 1948, two years after *Song of the South* was released, Walt Disney Studios hired its first African American animator, a man named Frank Braxton. He was brought in as an inbetweener, a job with an exceedingly high turnover rate. Like many of his cohorts, Braxton decided not to stay in the position, leaving for unknown reasons after only two months to look for work in animation elsewhere.

Soon afterward, Braxton befriended Benny Washam, a Bugs Bunny animator who worked at Warner Brothers Cartoons. Washam decided to advocate for his friend; he walked into the office of Johnny Burton, the production manager, and said, "I hear Warner Brothers has a racist policy and refuses to hire blacks." Burton spun around and yelled, "Whoever said that is a liar! It's not true." "Well, then," Washam replied, "there's a young black animator outside who's looking for a job. Guess he's come to the right place." Braxton quickly became a valued animator in director Chuck Jones's group, and in 1960, he was elected president of the Los Angeles chapter of the Screen Cartoonists' Guild.

CHAPTER 10
SO THIS IS LOVE

"The Greek word Muses means the Mindful Ones," Sylvia wrote in her notebook. She filled pages documenting her research on the nine muses and their domains: Calliope, the muse of epic poetry; Clio, history; Euterpe, lyric poetry and music; Erato, love poetry; Polyhymnia, sacred song; Melpomene, tragedy; Thalia, comedy; Terpsichore, dance; and Urania, astronomy. By 1946 she had written numerous treatments and scripts for a feature about the Greek muses and was determined to find a home for it at the studio. The nine muses consumed her days and nights as she played with how to use them most effectively as narrators in the short films the studio was working on.

As a rule, Sylvia hated the shorts, and for the most part, she had little respect for the writers and animators who created them. She called their brand of comedy "sadistic,"

311

as it relied on violence and hateful stereotypes to elicit laughter. It simply wasn't her style, nor was it the type of comedy the studio wanted in its feature films. Sylvia threw herself into her current project, coloring her muses in bold shades of black and red and adding intricate architectural details in the backgrounds that no other artist at the studio would have conceived of.

Her work often followed her home. Her daughter, Theo, now a teenager, was working full-time as a painter at the studio. She would come home with her mother in the evening, ready to relax after a long workday, but she could tell from a twinkle in Sylvia's eye that she wasn't ready to leave her work behind. One night, Theo saw her mother set up her opaque watercolors and brush the paint onto a sheet of black construction paper. Sylvia was visited by a muse that night, one that guided her hand, making brushstrokes in a style that was not at all her own. She filled page after page, creating more than a dozen paintings of a couple dancing, a Parisian cityscape behind them. The experience would leave a lasting impression on her, and in a page of her notebook she scrawled, "We are Muses," apparently writing to no one but herself.

The sequence Sylvia painted that night

would become the "Two Silhouettes" segment in the package feature *Make Mine Music,* released in 1946. It seemed that her future was secure; her salary had been raised to ninety-five dollars a week, and the freelance work she had been doing for *Walt Disney's Comics* magazine had doubled. After years of struggle she was finally able to live comfortably with her children. Yet this façade of stability was about to crash down around her.

On August 1, 1946, the studio laid off four hundred and fifty employees, 40 percent of their total staff. "The union trouble we were dreading has hit us with a bang," Sylvia wrote in a letter, adding, "I am now laid off." The Screen Cartoonists' Guild had demanded a 25 percent raise for all employees and threatened a strike if the studio did not comply. The studio responded that the funds were not available, a plausible defense considering the meager profits made by Walt's last few films, the massive debt still controlled by Bank of America, and the fact that a few months later, Walt would request an emergency million-dollar loan from RKO Radio Pictures, the studio's longtime theatrical distributor. Unyielding negotiators and hot tempers brought the situation to a head in late July. On Monday,

July 29, everyone received a raise, including Sylvia; her pay was bumped up to a hundred and twenty dollars a week. The good fortune was temporary. A few days later, nearly half the studio staff was laid off. This time, Sylvia wouldn't come back.

In the home they had shared for the past few years, Mary and Retta drank until they could no longer stand. The room seemed to spin as the women consumed martinis and talked late into the night. The two friends would soon no longer be roommates in the house where they had plotted and debated untold animation scenes. In the ashes of the gutted story department of 1946, nearly every individual who had brought creative force to the features of the past decade had been fired. Retta, once the darling of the animation department and then an employee of the story department, was now gone.

Many employees, including Sylvia, were hoping they'd be rehired, but Retta was giving up all expectations. She had met someone — Benjamin Worcester, a naval submarine commander. The two were getting married, and now Retta and Mary toasted their friendship and Retta's nuptials. Retta soon left California for Key West, Florida.

Although Retta felt that a chapter was closing in her life, her work for Walt was not yet over.

Unlike Retta, Mary didn't know where she was going to end up. She had been traveling frequently on assignments for the studio and visiting Lee often at his base in Virginia. She felt like a vagabond without a true home.

Lee was discharged from the U.S. Navy in 1946, and while Walt was eliminating staff with all the discrimination of a farmer using a dull machete, he was also courting Lee. Walt wrote to him, asking him to come back to his work at the studio. Perhaps Lee didn't wish to return to the place where his wife was so highly valued, or possibly he doubted the long-term stability of Walt's company, or maybe he was just ready to strike out on a new path. In any case, Lee decided to stay on the East Coast, where he and two partners formed Film Graphics, a company that produced television commercials, a relatively new field.

In the 1940s, television was cinema's annoying little brother, always trying to horn in on American visual entertainment but doing nothing more than pulling on the pigtails of his big sister. The television set had been introduced to the United States at the 1939 World's Fair in New York. The machines were expensive, costing around six hundred dollars each, about the price of a new car, and there existed only a single broadcast station, based in New York City.

During World War II, television-set production was banned, as the cathode-ray tubes necessary for their manufacture were needed for U.S. military technology and radar development. A poll in 1945 found that the majority of Americans had no idea what a television was. For Lee to take a chance on the rising popularity of the medium in 1946 was a tremendous risk. Mary wasn't worried; she loved Lee and would follow him down any path, no matter how uncertain.

Walking down Fifth Avenue to her new Manhattan apartment, Mary let the crowds of rushing people move around her. Even in the middle of a packed city sidewalk she felt like the only woman in the world. She had just received the news she had despaired of ever hearing: her baby had a heartbeat. In the 1940s, before pregnancy tests were common and obstetrical ultrasounds developed, prenatal care was limited to the latter months of pregnancy. Mary had never made it that far before, her miscarriages occurring, as most do, in the first trimester. The repeated heartbreak of loss had robbed her of hope, so this time, when Mary suspected she was pregnant, she tried to push the thought from her mind. But now here she was, five months along and, after seeing the doctor press his stethoscope to her belly, full of anticipation. Mary was thirty-five, a decade older than the average first-time mother in the United States, but the added struggle to conceive a child only made the moment that much sweeter. The baby growing within her was the fulfillment of her deepest wishes.

For many women in 1946, motherhood was a thief, stealing away the careers they had begun during the years of war. More women were having babies following World War II than previously, and fewer were working outside the home. This was not by choice — 94 percent of women of color and 75 percent of Caucasian women had planned to keep working following 1945. Employers, however, were averse to letting women continue to work, particularly those married with young children. Four and a half million women lost their jobs after the war.

Mary was not one of those millions. Even though she now lived three thousand miles from the studio in Burbank, Walt was not willing to give up his favorite artist. He allowed her a freedom that few other artists ever received — he permitted her to work remotely, creating her concept art at home and flying back to the studio regularly to share her ideas.

While Mary cherished her new freedoms, other women at the studio were clinging uncertainly to their positions. World War II had opened new doors for women in the animation, camera, background, and editorial departments. Walt's training program for Ink and Paint employees had broken women out of the Nunnery, their separate building, and allowed them to be employed throughout the lot. With the layoffs of 1946, some of these opportunities were swept away, but other doors were unsealed. Young men might be returning to work, but the women who'd held on to their positions of creative influence had no intention of letting their jobs go, especially with the new opportunities before them. International markets were slowly reopening, and feature-length animation was ready to bounce back.

Walt was painfully aware that the studio could not bear another massive loss. Convincing the banks to underwrite even a single feature-length animated film was challenging. Should the movie fail, his business would likely never be given another opportunity. He had to manage expenses more vigilantly and choose the next project with tremendous care.

The story department had developed many ideas over the years, and perhaps it was a safe choice to pick another princess — after all, their first stab at such a tale had been far more profitable than any of their subsequent films. Walt chose *Cinderella,* pinning the hopes of his entire business on it. The simplicity of the story was appealing, and it would allow the studio's full artistic expression while minimizing costs.

At story meetings for *Cinderella,* Walt seemed like his old self, expounding on his ideas endlessly. Mary seldom spoke up in these, and it would have been difficult even if she'd wanted to. There was hardly a chance for anyone but Walt to talk, which he did exuberantly, crowding the room with the expanse of his vision.

Even with Walt's concepts before them, the team faced difficulty. They simply could not afford a film with the intricate backgrounds they had crafted in the past. The level of detail they had brought to *Snow White, Pinocchio, Fantasia,* and *Bambi* had required an enormous investment in terms of both the number of artists and the hours necessary for the features' creation. It took intense effort to create twenty to thirty drawings for every second of screen time, and every line drawn represented dollars. Now the artists faced a new challenge: How could they give *Cinderella* a sumptuous look at a budget price? To solve this riddle, Walt turned to Mary.

Mary carefully considered how to take advantage of color when addressing the film's economic limitations. It would have to be used in place of the detailed lines the studio usually relied on to add richness to its films. Mary was uniquely positioned to carry out this task, given her own minimalistic artistic style. She embraced modern midcentury graphic design, a movement popular from the 1940s to the 1960s and exemplified by Paul Rand, Alexander Girard, and Lucienne Day, whose work frequently depicted flat visuals in bright colors. Her goal was to use these techniques to trick audiences into thinking they were seeing a film as decadently animated as those of the prewar years.

For *Cinderella,* she chose unusual palettes not merely for her own pleasure but to help shape the narrative. Each sequence she designed was basic in its use of lines — the key to cutting costs — but full of unexpected bursts of color that distracted the eye and saturated the scenes with a sense of opulence.

In some ways, Mary created Cinderella in her own image. She drew the young woman up in her tower room looking out onto a majestic castle in the distance, the sky pink with the rising sun, while the only color in Cinderella's immediate surroundings was a cheerless gray. The scene matched a self-portrait Mary had drawn early in her career in which she gazed into the distance, disregarding the troubles around her.

Mary also brought an interpretation of modern fashion into her sketches that had previously been missing from Disney films. She drew gowns that Snow White could never have worn: calf-skimming and cinched at the waist, revealing the character's hourglass figure, and confections covered in bows and ribbons. The designs celebrated the new postwar fashion era. It was a response to years of utilitarian military uniforms, Rosie the Riveter denim coveralls, and clothing rationing in Europe, where details such as cuffs, pockets, and ruffles had been tightly restricted. French designer Christian Dior's postwar New Look used ten times the fabric of a typical wartime dress to create a full-skirted silhouette that accentuated the hips, sometimes including extra padding. The top of each dress featured a tight, fitted bodice and rounded, soft shoulders. The resulting look was an embrace of femininity that was soon found on fashionable women across the globe. Even the glass slipper Mary drew was reminiscent of the popular postwar pump, a shoe with a stacked heel and blunt toe.

There was hardly a scene of *Cinderella* that Mary did not influence. Her touch was everywhere, from the stepsisters' singing lesson at the harpsichord to the squat and balding king dwarfed by the grandeur of his palace, from the gothic staircase that leads to Cinderella's tower to the birds and mice uniting to complete a pink gown with ribbons. She even designed a visually fantastic dream sequence complete with seven housemaids, although eventually, much to her disappointment, it would be discarded.

Perhaps nowhere was her influence more keenly felt than during the dance sequence in which Cinderella and the prince waltz to the love song "So This Is Love." Mary worked closely with the songwriting team — Mack David, Jerry Livingston, and Al Hoffman — to ensure that this duet, the first between a heroine and her prince in a Walt Disney production, would suitably advance the plot. Mary painted the romantic scene in dark, vivid blues so that the sky and earth seemed to merge and send the couple dancing among the stars. She placed sumptuous touches in the scene — a white Grecian-style gazebo and urns, flowers sprinkled here and there. The result perfectly conveyed the mood of falling in love and contrasted sharply with the rising action of the chase scene that followed. Here, Mary created a fleet of king's men racing after Cinderella, their horses seemingly sprinting on shadows, the men's dark red capes flowing behind their bodies, creating an intensely dramatic turning point.

Mary's concept art made its way to nearly every department of the studio, including animation, Ink and Paint — where colors were selected — and layout and editing. But the artists working on her vision were starting to fear not only for their jobs but for the longevity of the studio itself.

"This is it. We're in a bad way. If this picture doesn't make money, we're going to be finished. The studio's going to be kaput!" said Walt to a group of artists working on *Cinderella.*

Thelma Witmer, one of the artists feeling the pressure of Walt's dire warning, was working on background art for the film. She'd been born in Nebraska, but her father, a shoe salesman, moved the whole family to Northern California during the Great Depression. She'd come to Los Angeles for art school and worked odd jobs until she was hired in 1942 by the Walt Disney Studios. By this time, she was in her forties and, like Sylvia, older than most of her female coworkers. She was brought directly into the background department, and unlike many women hired at the time, she managed to hold on to her job even after the war ended.

Thelma was finding a way to use Mary's concept art to saturate *Cinderella* with the lavish look audiences expected from a Walt Disney production. It wasn't the first time Thelma had worked with Mary's paintings as inspiration, having created backgrounds for *Song of the South* and the package film *Melody Time.* Though Thelma hadn't gotten screen credit for either film or for the shorts she had worked on, she was being given new responsibilities, and her talent in the background department was on the verge of being recognized.

Background artists created the scenery

and backdrops used throughout the film. In some ways they had an easier task than the character animators. Background artists didn't have to produce the massive number of drawings needed to depict action on-screen. Yet in other ways, the job was more challenging, as they had to bring detail and realism to the animated set design. The work required intense creativity; the artist had to invent a world that was believable for the characters while still advancing the narrative.

Given her experience, Thelma knew the task ahead of her would not be easy. Translating Mary's scenes into the film was one complexity, utilizing her distinctive color scheme another, but a far greater challenge was incorporating her style. The look of Mary's paintings was exceedingly difficult to reconcile with their animation techniques. This was because midcentury modernism lacked perspective. While the graphic elements were easy to incorporate in textiles and logos, in animation, the lack of dimension made the character, foreground, and background indistinguishable. Yet Walt was insistent they find a way to bring Mary's style into the film.

The demands for "More Mary" from Walt brought anger and jealousy from many men at the studio. When she flew in from the East Coast, Walt would immediately heap compliments on her paintings. Embittered, a group of story men and animators complained about the chosen artist and spread rumors accusing her of exploiting her gender to take advantage of Walt. "It's just because she's a woman that she gets away with it," they said.

The discontent spurred this group of artists to veer away from Mary's work, leaving aside some of her best ideas just when the studio needed them most. The character animators in particular were unwilling to adopt her designs, as they feared any change to their standard methods. Fortunately, Thelma harbored none of these petty resentments. She incorporated the look Mary envisioned into as many details as she could, including the paintbrush style of the title cards, the staircase and tower room, the royal castle interior, and especially the backgrounds for "So This Is Love." The men who worked on the character animation may have dismissed Mary's talent, creating characters that looked much like those they had styled previously, but Thelma was unafraid to wholeheartedly embrace Mary's artistic vision.

Sometimes Mary's concept art was challenging to the artists working on *Cinderella* not because of their resentment and envy but for technical reasons. One scene in particular required an unprecedented marriage of sophistication and technique: the fairy godmother's enchanted transformations. In Mary's paintings, as the fairy godmother waves her wand, sparks of magical dust fly, enveloping a pumpkin and transforming it into a magnificent carriage whose rounded shape and spiraling wheels retain its vegetable heritage. She then turns her wand on Cinderella and transforms her rags into a magical silvery ball gown.

Working on the scene was veteran animator Marc Davis. Marc had first applied to the studio after seeing a newspaper ad announcing "Walt Disney Wants Artists," but he was immediately rejected. The letter sent to him began "Dear Miss Davis" and went on to explain that "at the present time we are not hiring women artists." Marc was puzzled and then figured that someone must have mistaken his name for a feminine one, perhaps reading Marc as Marge. As soon as he corrected this misconception, he was hired, yet this brush with gender discrimination would stay with him, forever influencing the consideration he gave the female artists he worked with.

Marc had started at the studio in 1935 and was one of Walt's "Nine Old Men," a group of gifted animators; the others were Les Clark, Ollie Johnston, Milt Kahl, Ward Kimball, Eric Larson, John Lounsbery, Woolie Reitherman, and Frank Thomas. Walt gave them their nickname not based on their ages, as they were all in their twenties when they were hired, but in jest after President Franklin D. Roosevelt called the members of the 1937 U.S. Supreme Court the "nine old men." Roosevelt had meant this to be derogatory, as at the time he was pushing to increase the number of justices to fifteen, but Walt felt the talents of his core animators were truly superior. As part of the group, Marc had considerable influence. He was also, unlike many of his fellow animators, unafraid to openly admire Mary's talent.

The soundtrack for the fairy-godmother scene was "The Magic Song," the lyrics of which were almost complete gibberish; it was later renamed "Bibbidi-Bobbidi-Boo." The effects animation was overwhelming, requiring a dynamic sense of timing and the technique to float magic dust across the scene using thousands of minuscule pencil marks. Marc oversaw every part of the sequence, bringing Mary's magical vision to life. When Walt saw what they had accomplished, he stood in silent awe. It would remain, over the years, his favorite piece of animation.

Yet it was still unclear whether anyone else would like it. After all, Walt had been enthusiastically predicting success for all his projects over the past thirteen years, and yet none had even come close to the commercial phenomenon of *Snow White and the Seven Dwarfs.* Their future hung on the fate of a teenage girl named Cinderella, and with the clock about to strike midnight, they were nearly out of time.

CHAPTER 11
IN A WORLD OF MY OWN

There was paper everywhere — lining the walls, covering the floor, and even hanging from the ceiling. This was what it was like to work as an artist in Walt's studio in 1950; you felt as though an ocean of drawings was swallowing you whole. The women working as assistant animators were riding the rough seas of *Cinderella.* They kept their fingers and thumbs lightly pressed together around their pencils, their palms relaxed, as they drew a host of helpful mice, a loyal dog, and a villainous cat. They flipped the top edge of the pages as they worked to follow the flow of the action from one moment to the next while the bottom edge of the paper was held down by pegs fixed to the desk.

The characters they were creating were faithful representations of the animal cast that Bianca had proposed a decade earlier. The drawings piled up on their desks, but still they needed more. Every second of the final film necessitated twenty-four drawings. The pressure to produce was intense, especially as financial worries had limited hiring to the story and animation departments. With the studio starved of profit, a tidal wave of work was sweeping over them, and every animator needed to work at full capacity.

The competition to get a job in the animation department was intense, regardless of one's gender. But female applicants had to be better than good; they had to be exceptional. Their portfolios had to overcome the belief, ingrained in the minds of many of their colleagues, that women had no place in the animators' room. Of the more than two hundred animators employed by the studio, twenty were women. The animators were working on not just one but two features at once. Even as they put the final touches on *Cinderella,* they also were drawing white rabbits and tea parties.

Their next feature was an adaptation of the 1865 novel *Alice's Adventures in Wonderland* and its 1871 sequel, *Through the Looking Glass,* both volumes featuring detailed illustrations by the English artist John Tenniel. Like *Cinderella,* it was a relatively safe choice. Walt had conceived of both films at Laugh-O-Gram, the first animation studio he incorporated in Kansas City in 1921 when he was twenty years old. Walt ran the business, directed the shorts, and also worked as an animator alongside a host of impressive artists, including Ub Iwerks; Hugh Harman, who went on to cofound the Warner Brothers and Metro-Goldwyn-Mayer animation studios; and Friz Freleng, who later developed Bugs Bunny and other iconic characters for Warner Brothers. *Cinderella* was released by Laugh-O-Gram as a silent short in 1922, and the studio began the first of *The Alice Comedies,* a series of fifty-seven silent shorts that combined a live-action Alice with an animated world, which ran from 1923 to 1927. With so much uncertainty in Walt's professional life thirty years later, perhaps it was natural that he would return to the simple story lines of his youth. He now had the resources to give the animation everything it had previously lacked.

The project was not new to those at the studio. Story meetings had been held for *Alice in Wonderland* on and off since 1938, when Walt purchased the rights to the story and the original Tenniel illustrations. In the late 1940s Walt struggled to decide whether to make *Alice in Wonderland* or *Cinderella* first, going so far as to hold meetings with noncreative employees at his studio where he showed them storyboards and polled them on which film they preferred. While these opinions were informative, it was the challenge of bringing *Alice* to the screen that ultimately caused her delay.

Aldous Huxley, the writer most famous for his 1932 novel *Brave New World,* wrote an early script for *Alice in Wonderland.* Walt hired him not for his dystopian vision of the future but because the writer was, by all accounts, "an *Alice in Wonderland* fiend." It was a project Huxley loved far more than the other screenplays he had worked on, such as adaptations of *Jane Eyre* and *Pride and Prejudice.* Part of the appeal was the challenge inherent in the text; there was no clear structure to build on. Instead, Huxley dived into nonfiction, focusing on the real-life relationship between the author and Alice Liddell, the girl who'd served as his inspiration. This concept didn't last long. Walt disliked it and tossed the script aside.

With no script or storyboard decided on, Mary had little besides the novels and Sir John Tenniel's original illustrations to guide her. She soon realized that translating Tenniel's intricate designs, originally engraved onto wood blocks, into concept art was impossible and that having the animators hand-draw such a high level of detail over and over for each scene would be impractical. She had to find a way to connect with the whimsy of the text itself and create her own personal representation of Wonderland.

Mary tackled these challenges in her studio space in the home she and Lee had moved into on the North Shore of Long Island, an hour's drive from New York City. Lee's gamble on television advertising was paying off, and his income was enormous, fifty-two thousand dollars a year. Mary's salary from Walt, while a fraction of Lee's, was among the highest paid to artists at the studio: three hundred dollars per week. With their combined wealth, the couple could afford a spacious home for their growing family, which included Donovan, born February 12, 1947, and Kevin Lee, born August 15, 1950.

Walt and Lillian came to visit Mary on Long Island, and Walt found his darling artist apparently unchanged by motherhood — her hair was perfectly coiffed, her clothes and makeup elegant. The only difference was that she had a three-year-old toddler playing at her feet and a baby bundled in her arms. She cooed over the infant sweetly, saying his name over and over again until it sounded like he was called "Heavenly." Walt was more than Mary's employer, however; he was intimately tied to the growing Blair family. Mary thought so highly of Walt that she named him godfather to both her boys.

The scene was tender, and Walt and Lillian sat contentedly on the porch as the breeze floated off the sound. The visit was social, but as Walt examined Mary's latest sketches for *Alice in Wonderland,* he turned quiet. Mary's work was highly experimental. She had used aspects of the original Tenniel illustrations as a backdrop, their black-and-white composition contrasting with the brightly colored characters. The dreaded eyebrow rose sky-high, Walt's signal that he wasn't pleased. No words were spoken but a clear message was conveyed — Mary would have to try again. Walt easily controlled the story and animation departments and felt comfortable giving criticism to his employees, yet he found it nearly impossible to direct an artist like Mary. She would have to find the path for herself.

The fact that Mary had a job at all was something wonderful. Even four months earlier, the future of Walt Disney Studios had still been uncertain. When *Cinderella* premiered, on February 15, 1950, the studio employees held their breath. Box-office success on this film was their only hope for salvation.

The reviews came in swiftly and were generally full of praise. The *Chicago Tribune* gushed, "The film not only is handsome, with imaginative art and glowing colors to bedeck the old fairy tale, but it also is told in a gentle fashion." Other reviews were mixed, with some touching on the lack of character development, such as one in *Variety* that described both Cinderella and her Prince Charming as "colorless."

The handful of lackluster reviews did not seem to deter audiences. Lines to see the film wrapped around the block in New York City. It was one of the top-grossing films in 1950, pulling in eight million dollars at the box office. The studio had finally produced another blockbuster success after thirteen years of struggle. But it wasn't just ticket sales that turned the economic tide for Walt. He had learned the power of a new deity in film production, and its name was merchandise.

In Washington, DC, Retta was happy to be stationed with her navy officer husband, but she missed Mary's loving presence in her life. After leaving California, she had joined Benjamin in Key West before he was transferred to DC. Both Mary and Retta were on the East Coast now, which made it easier to keep in touch, but it wasn't the same as the years they had spent sharing a house. Retta was bouncing between animation studios, trying to keep her hand in while balancing the demands of being married to a military officer and, at age thirty-four, thinking about starting a family. Then came a welcome opportunity: Golden Books and the Walt Disney Studios signed a licensing agreement in 1944; the publishing company would now create books based on the feature films, and with Retta's background, she was only too qualified to work as an illustrator.

One of Retta's early projects was a Golden Book to accompany *Cinderella.* To create her illustrations, she turned to Mary's concept art. The result is a warm amalgam of the two artists' work, integrating Mary's colors and designs and Retta's powerful and dynamic style. Her illustrations were not mere replicas of the film — in fact, they possess only a passing resemblance to the final animation art. Instead, they capture the feel of the film, thanks to their embrace of Mary's vision. They stand as a tribute to amity, uniting the talents of two of the strongest female artists ever to work at the

Walt Disney Studios.

When the final book was printed, Retta gazed at the slim volume and then opened its cover. Beneath *Walt Disney's Cinderella*, she found *Illustrations by the Walt Disney Studio, adapted by Retta Scott Worcester.* It was the kind of clear credit that she had often struggled to obtain on-screen. She might no longer be working directly for the studio, but her fortunes were still linked to Walt's.

For the first time, Walt released new merchandise in advance of the movie's premiere, with products hitting the market in time for the holiday-shopping season in 1949. There were *Cinderella*-themed clothes, dolls, even a pair of women's transparent, jeweled "glass" slippers that came in a Lucite box tied with a ribbon. The push was made possible thanks to the brand-new character-merchandising department, formed in 1949, and the Walt Disney Music Company, incorporated in 1947, whose first undertaking was *Cinderella.* The company was no stranger to the power of licensing. Previous deals, notably the Mickey Mouse watch in 1933, had been bringing in revenue for years. Now, however, the company took full advantage of branded products by expanding their reach and availability.

A copy of the Cinderella *Golden Book that Retta inscribed to Mary as a tribute to their friendship* *(Courtesy the estate of Mary Blair)*

Together with RCA, Disney released a multi-disc soundtrack album of *Cinderella* that reached number one on the *Billboard* music charts just two months after the film opened. Similarly, the accompanying Golden Books picture book full of Retta's brightly colored illustrations was massively popular.

The artists had little time to bask in their success. *Alice in Wonderland* was waiting. Mary tackled the concept art afresh, but she struggled with the scenes. As an early member of the story department once said of the book, "It doesn't have any plot at all." Mary realized that to faithfully render the novel's literary absurdity, she needed to create images that mirrored Carroll's whimsy.

Working on Long Island, Mary let her painting flow into realms of unadulterated imagination. She wasn't relaxed — on the contrary, she sat tense before her easel, the brush gripped tightly in her hand as she worked. She painted Alice upside down on the canvas, her blond hair flowing beneath her, her blue dress curved like a parachute as she falls down the rabbit hole. Behind Alice, Mary designed a detailed backdrop, with red and gold wallpaper, lamps, and a rocking chair. A mirror floats opposite Alice, and her reflection shines in the glass, one girl upside down, one right side up, each with a startled expression on her face. While not a literal illustration of Carroll's prose, the painting seamlessly captured the impression of Alice's long fall down the rabbit hole in chapter 1.

Mary soon became lost in her work, oblivious to everything around her, as she created hundreds of paintings. The scenes were undeniably striking; for example, the March of the Cards sequence, where Alice is chased by the Queen of Hearts' army of playing cards, is exhilarating, with unexpected angles, long shadows, and rich colors.

Mary visually rendered every part of the books. She interpreted one scene in which Alice gets lost by showing a dark wood with signs pointing in different directions reading UP, BACK, THIS WAY DOWN, TULGEY WOOD, and YONDER. Suddenly, the Cheshire Cat's bright smile appeared. It was Dorothy Ann Blank in a story meeting in 1939 who expounded on the possibilities of this imagery, insisting they keep this part of the script true to the book and reminding them of Carroll's line from chapter 6: " 'Well! I've often seen a cat without a grin,' thought Alice; 'but a grin without a cat! It's the most curious thing I ever saw in my life!' "

In Mary's hands, Wonderland became a shadowy dreamscape. She sketched a surreal living flower garden where live crabs grow from the crabgrass, butterflies flutter with buttered toast for wings, and tiger lilies have orange-striped faces and whiskers. Mary put all of herself into her art, so even when she was with her children and husband, her mind stayed with Alice. The desire to pour herself into her work became stronger as her home life grew more volatile. In the evenings, her husband, Lee, was often in an alcohol-fueled fury, characterized by verbal and physical abuse. But inside the quiet of her in-home art studio, surrounded by her concept art, she felt safe.

At the studio, the executives had deeper worries than how their next feature film would look. The landscape of entertainment was shifting, and television, once the quiet little sibling that no one paid any attention to, was now pushing and shoving to get a seat at the table. At the end of World War II, few Americans had known what a television was, but now, in 1950, there were three million sets across the country. The price of the product was dropping too, from six hundred dollars to close to two hundred, about the cost of a full set of living-room furniture. Those in the film industry watched the change with concern. If people could merely flick on their televisions in their living rooms when they wanted amusement, would they ever bother going to a movie theater? Their worries were justified, as audiences in movie houses across the country were declining. In 1930, 65 percent of all Americans went to the movies on a weekly basis. By 1950, the number had dropped to 20 percent. And the changes were becoming more precipitous. In 1952, fifty-one million people per week bought movie tickets, down from ninety million in 1948.

Walt appraised the situation carefully and decided to take on the menace of television by advancing on three fronts. First, he'd make the experience of the movie house more awe-inspiring by investing in new technology so people would want to go to the cinema again. Second, he'd try his hand at television, including a venture in live action, in the spirit of the old adage "If you can't beat 'em, join 'em." Third, he'd start thinking outside the confining boxes of cinemas and television sets when it came to popular entertainment.

These expensive undertakings were made possible thanks to *Cinderella,* whose popularity was soaring and whose profits were lifting the fortunes of the group in Burbank. The film was the sixth-highest-grossing film in the United States in 1950. Internationally, particularly in England and France, the

343

film was also highly popular. The studio that had been on the threshold of bankruptcy was now swimming in cash, having been rescued once again by a demure princess.

A twelve-year-old girl hung upside down, her face contorted in an expression of disbelief while the blood rushed to her face. It was a scene Mary had drawn down to the last detail, and it was now coming alive on a soundstage at the studio in Burbank. The animators had used live-action footage as a reference for their drawings many times before, even as early as the development of *Snow White,* when they watched an actress dance around the room in a long flowing dress in order to get the movement as true to life as possible.

The use of live action to inform animation was immensely popular, not just at the Walt Disney Studios but all over Hollywood. Yet some, especially those animators working for Walt, felt that the technique had gone too far. In 1917, Max Fleischer, whose animation studio brought Betty Boop and Popeye the Sailor into the world, had patented a technique called rotoscoping. Animators at his studio and others who used the invention projected the live-action reference footage onto the back of an easel holding a glass pane. Paper was placed over the glass, and every frame was traced methodically, creating a near-perfect ink copy of the photographic image. The result was realistic character movement made in a fraction of the time it took an animator to sit down at a table and create a similar image from scratch. Detractors, however, complained that the final product was stilted and dull, drained of its artistic essence.

A number of these critics were animators at the Walt Disney Studios, many of whom had gone to art school. They were striving to elevate the cartoon medium, which could be crass, into a beautiful, albeit imperfect, imitation of life. While the animation department respected the role live-action reference material could play, they refrained from tracing the images created. Instead, they studied the movement itself, incorporating not just how it looked but how it felt to a viewer. For *Cinderella,* they had filmed the majority of the feature using live actors and actresses. For *Alice in Wonderland,* they filmed it all.

This meant that every vision Mary had for *Alice in Wonderland* was jumping out of her paintings and coming to life. After Mary drew Alice trapped in a bottle riding the waves of an eerily green sea, Kathryn

Beaumont, the young actress who would perform Alice's voice, found herself trapped in a real glass container. The curved edges deformed her view of the people and movie cameras capturing her likeness, while the wobbly platform beneath her sent her rocking back and forth, as if she were bobbing in a real ocean. When Mary drew a giant Alice trapped in the White Rabbit's house, her arms wedged in the windows and her eyes framed by the fringe of a thick thatched roof, Kathryn was similarly stuck inside a miniature wooden house frame. The chilly soundstage and awkward mechanics were doubtless uncomfortable for the actors, but thanks to Mary's artistic interpretation, the studio was creating a faithful representation of Carroll's text, a feat that many writers had once deemed impossible.

In the background department, Thelma Witmer was once again using Mary's art as her muse to paint settings that defied reality. She incorporated elaborately decorated rabbit holes, dark forests, and contrasting colors that stretched boldly behind the Queen of Hearts. Though many women had worked in the department over the years, Thelma was the first to receive on-screen credit for her work, on *Cinderella*.

But many others were continuing to work with little acknowledgment. In the layout and camera departments, there was a strong contingent of women, promoted during World War II, including Ruthie Thompson, Katherine Kerwin, and Mimi Thornton. These women were responsible for planning each scene of the film, breaking down the shots and camera angles, and determining the position and movement of the characters. Their task was formidable, as they had to create perspective and build action in a film that resisted convention. They spent hours with the scenes of playing cards alone, keeping the perspective constant even as the rectangular soldiers stretched in long lines far into the distance. The work was intense, but the artists were happy to have the studio humming again, full of creativity and purpose.

Walt was traveling more frequently than he had a decade earlier but his employees still kept an eye out for him, conscious of his path as he walked along the hallways or wandered into offices. His criticism was as feared as ever. But they no longer yelled out lines of their script as a secret signal when they saw Walt coming. Instead, a dry, hacking cough announced Walt's presence wherever he went.

■ ■ ■

Walt was making his own incursions into the world of television. In 1950 he filmed a television special called *One Hour in Wonderland* that aired on Christmas Day. Walt hosted what was essentially a long advertisement for the studio featuring Kathryn Beaumont in her *Alice in Wonderland* costume as well as other stars of his live-action footage. The program was a success, getting exposure for the film that would be released the following year while also teaching Walt the value of corporate patronage. Because Coca-Cola sponsored the show, he hadn't paid a cent to make it.

Even with *Alice in Wonderland* still in production, Walt was beginning to think beyond screen-based entertainment. Other studios were offering back-lot tours to their fans, a venture that not only brought in extra money but also promoted their films. But Walt didn't like the idea of his young fans, eager to meet their hero Mickey Mouse in the flesh, learning the sad truth that the cartoon character they idolized was as thin as the paper and plastic he was drawn on. Walt began dreaming of something else — a park, perhaps, where families could picnic surrounded by cheerful statues of his cartoon characters. Accustomed to sharing his daydreams with his staff, he mentioned the idea to several people and then started appraising the empty lot across the street from the studio with an eye to its acquisition.

At the time, amusement parks were generally seen as poor investment choices. Their rising popularity in the 1920s had come to a quick end during the Great Depression, with many of the parks falling into disrepair and frequented by pickpockets. By the end of World War II, fewer than fifty amusement parks remained in the United States. These bleak odds did not deter Walt, of course, and he began outlining his ideas in earnest.

On July 26, 1951, Kathryn Beaumont's car pulled up in front of the Leicester Square Theater in London. The Mad Hatter held out his hand and helped her out of the vehicle. Dressed in a bright blue dress paired with a simple white apron, Beaumont had recently been transformed from a regular girl into a celebrity. The past few weeks had been a blur of appearances, all culminating in this important day: the world premiere of *Alice in Wonderland*. It was the first time since *Saludos Amigos* in 1942 that the studio had debuted a film overseas. The event was held in London, Kathryn's hometown, as a nod to the author's English roots. As she posed for pictures next to Walt, she felt giddy with excitement and proclaimed to anyone who asked how much she loved the film.

Walt did not feel the same way. He smiled for the cameras and waved at his fans, but the movie had not matched his vision. He would later call it a "terrible disappointment" and explain that "we just didn't feel a thing, but we were forcing ourselves to do it." After more than seven hundred drawings and three million dollars, his regrets were severe. It wasn't Mary's work that he blamed — he continued to admire her concept art for the feature — nor was he displeased with the young actress next to him, whom he had already hired to work for the studio's next venture. The problem was with Alice herself. Walt regarded her character as aloof and "entirely too passive."

Critics didn't think much of her either. The *New York Times* complained that Alice "is not the modest and plain-faced little English girl of Mr. Carroll's suggestion and of Sir John Tenniel's illustrations for the books. She is a rosy-cheeked, ruby-lipped darling right off Mr. Disney's drawing-board, a sister of Snow White, Cinderella, and all the fairy-tale princesses he has drawn." The inevitable backlash against Disney princesses had started. Other critics found the film an odd mishmash of the Carroll books that was missing many characters and had lost the essence of caprice and cleverness that distinguished the original text. Still others protested the "Americanization" of literature, the idea that books in the United States were stripped of their cultural nuance and retold with a uniformity that obliterated their significance. The result was felt hard at the box office, where the film made just half the profits of *Cinderella* the year before despite a nearly identical budget. Yet fate had been kind. If Walt had chosen to release *Alice* first, the company might well have gone bankrupt before *Cinderella* made its appearance.

After *Alice*'s release, no one at the studio even wanted to mention the feature, speaking of it in hushed tones if it had to be talked about at all. Everyone felt the sting of failure, including Mary. Unlike Walt, she had become attached to Alice. It wasn't simply that she loved the books; it was that she saw in Alice a heroine who seemed to have developed a personality of her own. She was unlike their other princesses — she wasn't a hero, she didn't grow emotionally during the film, and there was no moral at the end of her story. After the flawless Cinderella, there was something refreshing about Alice in all her imperfection.

Fortunately Mary had a new project to sink her teeth into. Before the ink was even dry on her concept art for *Alice in Wonderland,* she was working on their next feature. In the seclusion of her studio, she painted pirate ships and hauntingly colored islands and struggled with one of their most difficult characters yet: a small fairy, covered in sparkling pixie dust, named Tinker Bell.

CHAPTER 12
YOU CAN FLY!

Occasionally the plane caught a tailwind that pushed it across the country faster; traffic on the highway toward her house mysteriously evaporated, and even her heels clicked more quickly across the pavement. For a woman who traveled as frequently as Mary did, regularly commuting between New York and Los Angeles, the joy of getting back early was keenly felt. It was wonderful to turn your key in the door, drop your bags, and embrace the comforts of home. But that was not what happened today.

Mary opened the front door and heard voices coming from the adjoining room. Walking in, she saw her husband sitting with a pad of paper and pencil. In front of him was a woman posing with not a stitch of clothing on. A terrible silence hung around them. It was clear to all what Mary had just stumbled upon. The atmosphere was nothing like the innocent life-drawing classes the couple had enjoyed at the studio. All her suspicions of Lee's unfaithfulness were instantly confirmed. Mary turned to the young woman who had been sleeping with her husband and said, "You must model for me sometime." Then, without a word to Lee, she spun on her heel and left the house — albeit temporarily.

She was walking out of her dream home. The sprawling four-bedroom mansion the couple had built in Great Neck was close to the sparkling waters of the Long Island Sound, where the family frequently went sailing on their boat. Such an excess of luxury was something Mary could never have dreamed of as a child in Oklahoma.

An art studio with its ceiling and three of its walls made entirely of glass sat perched in an elevated wing of the home. A real estate agent might call it a "jewel box," but it felt to Mary like a glass cage. It was undeniably a beautiful place to live and work, but it did not offer her shelter from the increasing abuse of her husband.

As Lee was not inclined to share in the labors of married life, Mary was raising their boys essentially on her own and keeping house herself while putting in long hours on her artwork. They had some hired help,

Mary's glass studio at her home in Long Island, New York **(Courtesy the estate of Mary Blair)**

particularly necessary during Mary's travels, but not nearly enough. Mary was overwhelmed. It seemed that the burdens of their family were hers to bear alone. Lee was often out, working or, possibly, sleeping with other women — until the incident with the model, Mary hadn't been sure. When he was home, he sometimes drank so much that his conversation devolved into cruel barbs at Mary before he finally, mercifully, passed out.

Mary did not know what to do. She was becoming like the Alice of her brightly colored paintings. In California she spoke cheerfully to her colleagues about her home life, devoted husband, and sweet boys. In her letters to and conversations with Walt, she was always circumspect, never giving a hint of the difficulty she faced at home. But on the plane back to New York, she felt she was falling down the rabbit hole, returning to a life that was as bewildering as Wonderland and much more miserable.

Divorce was an ugly word in 1951. Many women felt immense shame in leaving their husbands and were often told that a broken covenant was their own personal failure. The stigma that persisted could tarnish even a reputation as brilliant as Mary's. Approximately 25 percent of all marriages of the era ended in divorce, a rate that would stay constant throughout the 1950s, due in part to laws governing how couples could legally separate. It was not yet possible to cite irreconcilable differences — one member of the couple had to show evidence of adultery or cruelty. Faced with these options, Mary chose to stay, despite this latest incident. She had always loved drinking martinis with friends, but now when she reached for her glass, she was drinking not in the spirit of the occasion but to drown out the pain that was screaming within her.

Two hundred miles to the northeast, a

group of engineers in Cambridge, Massachusetts, were working on a machine with roughly the same square footage as Mary's grand house on Long Island. Jay Forrester was determined to build the fastest computer in the world using more vacuum tubes — thin-walled cylinders that conduct electrical charges — than any other computer anywhere. The project had started in 1943, when, under the pressures of war, the government tasked the servomechanisms lab cofounded by Forrester at MIT with designing and building a flight simulator to train pilots.

The war ended before they finished their research on Project Whirlwind, yet the engineers could not leave the challenge behind. So the group shifted focus; they were no longer interested in training pilots but in building a computer that no other lab could even dream of.

World War II provided the spark of interest and military funding that resulted in the first modern computers. There were not many of them in the world; the few that existed were almost exclusively housed in academic and military centers, and they were severely limited in function. One of the most prominent was the ENIAC, the Electronic Numerical Integrator and Computer, typically referred to by the popular press in the late 1940s as the "Brain." It was the first all-electronic programmable computer and, compared to human computational time, blazingly fast at calculating the accuracy of ballistic weapons, including hydrogen bombs. The machine, like all computers at the time, was massive, weighing in at more than sixty thousand pounds.

The machine Forrester and his team of men and women built weighed in at twenty thousand pounds and necessitated five thousand vacuum tubes. It cost only a third of *Alice in Wonderland*'s production budget, one million dollars, and utilized a far smaller staff, just a hundred and seventy-five people. These engineers were so clever that they were nicknamed the "Bright Boys," although women were included in their ranks.

The first model, Whirlwind I, was completed on April 20, 1951, and it was sixteen times faster than any other computer then in existence. Forrester and his team had revolutionized the internal architecture of computers, so instead of using bit-serial mode, where the machine solves a single problem at a time, the Whirlwind worked on multiple inputs at once, thus calculating results more quickly. It was the forerunner of a new type of computer that used parallel computation and that would take over the industry in the years ahead.

The Whirlwind wasn't just fast, it was also groundbreaking. The engineers built a display console, a primitive type of computer monitor, on which the calculations could be viewed in real time. Even more impressive, the technology included a light pen that, to outsiders, resembled a magic wand. When it was raised to the display console, it could point and draw directly on the screen using a photo sensor, lighting up individual pixels that were so small they were not visible to the human eye. In Burbank, Walt Disney Studios continued their work unawares, having no inkling that the technology being unveiled across the country was poised to radically alter their work and art.

While light pens worked their magic in Cambridge, Massachusetts, Mary was creating pixie dust back at the studio. *Peter Pan,* like *Alice in Wonderland* and *Cinderella,* was a recycled idea. The studio had worked on the adaptation more than a decade earlier, poring through J. M. Barrie's text and sketching concepts for the large cast of characters, including Peter Pan, "the boy who wouldn't grow up," the Darling family, and a fairy named Tinker Bell.

Barrie introduced the character Peter Pan in his 1902 novel *The Little White Bird.* In the book Peter Pan flies out his nursery window when he's only seven days old. He plays happily with the fairies at Kensington Gardens but ultimately plans to come home to his mother. However, when he returns at the end of the chapter, he finds his nursery window closed, with iron bars preventing his entry. When he looks through them he sees "his mother sleeping peacefully with her arm around another little boy."

The themes of childhood innocence and painful rejection continue in Barrie's 1904 play *Peter Pan; or, The Boy Who Wouldn't Grow Up,* later published as a novel in 1911. In this story, the character Peter Pan is no longer a baby but a child who, although old, has never become an adult. He listens outside the bedroom window of the Darling children as their mother tells bedtime stories. Peter wants Wendy, the eldest, to act as his mother and tell him stories, and so he invites the children to fly with him to Neverland. Here they have numerous adventures, meeting the Lost Boys, Peter's gang of feral children; rescuing a princess named Tiger Lily, of the "pickaninny tribe";

and battling Captain Hook and his band of pirates.

Peter is not a particularly likable character in the novel. He despises adults so completely that he increases his respiratory rate because "every time you breathe, a grown-up dies; and Peter was killing them off vindictively as fast as possible." He also murders Lost Boys: "The boys on the island vary, of course, in numbers, according as they get killed and so on; and when they seem to be growing up, which is against the rules, Peter thins them out." Peter's perspective on death is revealed in a scene where he confronts his own mortality; he says, "To die will be an awfully big adventure."

At the end, Wendy, her brothers, and even the remaining Lost Boys all go home to the Darling parents. The book leaves Peter alone, befuddled and fulfilling the promise made in the first line of the story: "All children, except one, grow up."

Designing the characters was a fairly straightforward proposition, with the exception of Tinker Bell. In the play, the fairy was represented merely as a glowing orb dancing around the stage. She had no human form and could not talk. To the artists at Walt Disney Studios, Tinker Bell was a blank slate, full of possibilities. In the early days of the feature's development at the studio, numerous artists had tried their hands at depicting the fairy.

Dorothy Ann Blank, one of the early women of the story department, was the first to imagine the possibilities of Tinker Bell drawn as a fully formed woman. Dorothy had just completed work on *Snow White,* and so the fairy became an antidote to the princess. Whereas Snow White was meek and unassuming, Tinker Bell was saucy. "Tinker Bell is a surefire sensation," Dorothy wrote to Walt, "for the animation medium can now, at last, do justice to her tiny, winged form and fanciful character."

Bianca saw the fairy much the same way. She was the first to go to the studio library and check out *Peter Pan,* and in her sketches she depicted a sweet pixie with her golden hair in an updo, her body curved and womanly. In the original sketches made by the female artists of the studio, Tinker Bell strikes a balance between stereotypical extremes. She is neither the girl-child of Snow White nor the sexual fantasy of *Fantasia*'s centaurettes. Instead, she is a fully formed woman in miniature. Each female artist gave the fairy a gift; in Bianca's hands, she became overtly sensual, in Mary's sweetly feminine, and in Sylvia's divinely colorful.

Tinker Bell's impish yet sweet attitude is clear in Bianca's sketches, where the fairy has a silly smile as she poses in front of a mirror while playing dress-up with Wendy's belongings, or looks frightened by the children's toys, or glows irresistibly above the three Darling children, who sit on clouds in a night sky. Bianca's male colleagues at the time talked about Tinker Bell's character in their story meetings, but most of them refrained from drawing her.

Bianca, unburdened by their hang-ups, was free to create, and at first Walt seemed to be listening. "Bianca has been working on some very colorful sequences in which Pan shows how he can call the fairies from their seclusion by blowing upon his pipes," he said in a story meeting in 1939. In Barrie's book, Tinker Bell is just one of a large community of fairies who live in Neverland. Inspired by the text, Bianca drew many different sprites, envisioning a complete world for the delicate creatures. She created imaginative sequences such as one in which Tinker Bell leads the Darling children underwater, and, with the help of pixie dust, they transform into merpeople and explore a sunken pirate ship.

Sylvia also worked on early concept art

for the film, her paintings starkly different from Bianca's and relying more on color than form to convey mood. She drew Wendy being crowned the Queen of the Fairy Ball by Tinker Bell, the girl's eyes wide in wonder as the golden crown is lowered onto her head. Bianca worked on the sequence with her, imagining the fairies glowing like firecrackers around Wendy as they dance late into the night. Soon, however, the women who created fairies so successfully for *Fantasia* lost all hope for *Peter Pan.* The feature had been intended to follow *Bambi,* but with the overwhelming difficulties the studio faced in the 1940s it seemed unlikely ever to be made.

While Bianca, Sylvia, and Dorothy had all been dismissed, the studio retained their artwork. Unused concept art was stored in what Walt nicknamed "the morgue," a term borrowed from police departments and newspapers for rooms where old materials, such as notes, evidence, or clippings, were stored. At the Walt Disney Studios, this room was underground, down a concrete corridor beneath the Ink and Paint building and behind a wooden door with MORGUE written in fancy gold lettering on it. Inside, bookshelves and file cabinets housed every scrap of material connected to the studio's past work. Artists were free to wander in and out, doing research and gathering the material they needed for their projects.

When Mary began her work on *Peter Pan,* which Walt had finally green-lighted, she spent many hours in the morgue. She was reaching back in time to concepts and story lines that had been shaped by other female artists. Inspired by the bold vision of so many women before her, Mary began to chart her own passage. She painted a bright gold pirate ship sailing through the night sky, indigo clouds lapping like waves at its hull. Under her brush, green rolling hills flattened into the sandy beaches of Neverland, the entire island surrounded by a pink and purple aura. The darkness of the night sky overhead is punctuated by colorful nebulae. In Mary's lagoons, mermaids feel the cool touch of a waterfall while resting on sunny rocks. Her imagination was unstoppable, and she also designed forest settings, a cozy grotto home for the Lost Boys, and, most unsettling, Skull Rock.

Captain Hook's hideout is untouched by her usually whimsical color palette and instead stands gray and forbidding, the jaw of the skull opening into the cave within. The image would become iconic, forever tied not only to the original *Peter Pan* but also to the many future movies set in Neverland. Confronted with the products of Mary's talent, the restrained Walt was unusually effusive, gushing over her seemingly ceaseless stream of ideas. Her work was almost too beautiful to be concept art, which was destined for the exclusive use of the studio's artists and not meant for the public eye.

Mary's paintings of indigenous peoples, however, did not deserve as much praise as they received. It was unfortunate that Retta Scott was no longer working as an artist at the studio. If she had been, she likely could have helped Mary refine her depictions.

One of the last projects Retta worked on there was a later-abandoned feature called *On the Trail.* Retta always took her research for a film seriously, and for this project she had spent long hours studying the Hopi tribe of northeastern Arizona. Committed to accurately portraying indigenous populations, Retta studied many texts, particularly a book called *Hopi Katcinas Drawn by Native Artists.* Her sensitivity is reflected in her concept art for the project, which is inspired by the original artists rather than coarse stereotypes.

In contrast, Mary's paintings of the "Indian Camp of NeverLand" lack the refinement that study and application would have given them. They pull imagery from a mishmash of native cultures and have no fidelity to any real tribe. Nearly every stereotype of indigenous peoples is represented in the final film, including halting speech, tepees, feathered headdresses, and totem poles. Although Mary's art alone would not have rescued the film from its racial caricatures, which are a central feature of the original play and book and were soon made even more pronounced by the animators, her edification might have at least softened their crudeness.

In 1951, in the midst of production on *Peter Pan,* a man named Eyvind Earle began work at the studio. The place was new and intimidating to the thirty-five-year-old artist whose background was in the fine arts and who had never worked in animation. As he wandered around his new workplace, he came upon a wall covered with small paintings. Over a hundred diminutive images filled the space, as exquisite in their squares as the truffles in a box of chocolates. Every single one had been done by Mary — she was already a legend at the studio, her name known to all. Earle stood before the images and felt deeply envious. Here was a woman who seemingly did everything: designed characters, fixed plots, selected color palettes, created scenery, and shaped the feel of an entire film. Studying the paintings, he thought, *That's the job I want at Disney.*

Mary's talent, advantages, and gender had always sparked strong reactions among her colleagues. Many seethed with resentment and jealousy, but for those artists able to appreciate her skill and work alongside her, the rewards were great. Marc Davis was among those who collaborated closely and successfully with Mary. Davis was sometimes known around the studio as a ladies' man, not for his propensity to flirt with women, but for his mastery of the female form. Mary had worked with Davis on the title characters in *Cinderella* and *Alice in Wonderland.* Now they were brought together again for *Peter Pan.*

As an art director, Mary was designing every scene of the movie, although some would not make the final cut. Her work was wide ranging — in one scene she heightened the tension between Peter Pan and Captain Hook, while in another, she created the fantasy of a mermaid lagoon. Davis, as a character animator, had a more focused role. Mary experimented with color and concepts, but he was responsible for creating the final animation that would bring Tinker Bell and Mrs. Darling to life. It was the challenge of Tinker Bell that had brought Mary and Davis together, with Mary's art informing Davis's drawings. Neither was content with Tinker Bell's superficial depiction in the book, and they resolved to make her more independent than any female character they had previously developed.

That representation, however, conflicted with the wholesome portrayal of women that was typical in the 1950s. At a story meeting, one of the men shook his head in disgust and then blurted out, "But why does she have to be so naughty?" Other story artists complained that her hips were too curvy and her personality too bold, the opposite of the demure and sweet Wendy Darling. Building on the work of so many artists before him, Davis infused Tinker Bell's look with attitude, giving the playful fairy a loose bun with swooped blond bangs, green slippers with puffy white pom-poms, and a green leaf dress hugging her curves.

The one thing the artists didn't have to worry about was Tinker Bell's dialogue — she didn't utter a single line. The only sound that came from her mouth was that of a tinkling bell. Since the fairy was denied words, Tinker Bell's body language in the film was especially important. Davis called in Ginni Mack, a young artist working in the Ink and Paint department. Davis and the other animators crowded around Mack to sketch her lovely face and figure while she sat perched on a stool, posing and gesturing as directed. Professional actors, including Kathryn Beaumont, the woman who had modeled for Alice, were also brought in to film the movie in live action.

Male story artists and animators had long shunned drawing fairies, but Tinker Bell was turning the tide. Animating her represented an irresistible challenge, and her charming and impish nature was more interesting than the many docile female characters previously crafted at the studio. She quickly became a favorite.

Giving Tinker Bell the magical glow that Mary had painted on canvas seemed at first impossible on the acrylic cels. The solution lay in an unlikely source: the bile of an Asian ox. The studio employed multiple chemists whose role was highly creative. They experimented with various materials, becoming general problem solvers for the artists and creating paints that were completely unique to the Walt Disney Studio. By mixing gouache paints, a type of opaque watercolor, with ox bile, head in-house chemist Emilio Bianchi invented a sparkling glaze that would become essential to *Peter Pan.*

The foul-smelling paint was kept refrigerated, and the artists had to work fast when they used it, as the chemical could not be exposed to the air for long. Carmen Sanderson, an artist in the Ink and Paint department, spent long hours working on the three-and-a-half-inch sprite. To make Tinker Bell's wings and body glow, she flipped the cel over and brushed the bile solution across the plastic. She used only a small amount and it had to be applied in a very thin layer. It was so delicate that if not glazed on properly, it pooled and formed ugly dark spots. When it was finished, however, Sanderson could admire its iridescent effect around the fairy's body, the way it made her wings look radiant. The glow would combine with twinkling grains of pixie dust, each dot hand-drawn by the female artists, to make the fairy look utterly magical.

While the team concentrated on *Peter Pan,* it often seemed that Walt was somewhere else entirely. At story meetings, he frequently broke into discussions about plot and dialogue to discuss his favorite topic: the Mickey Mouse Village. He loved to talk about the train that would wind its way around the park, stopping at Main Street, a replica of a small town's center that would be a relaxing place for people to sit and rest and that would have a string of stores selling company merchandise, a large movie theater, and a hot dog and ice cream stand. There would be rides too, carriages pulled by Shetland ponies, and even an old-fashioned riverboat. It was designed to be a trip back in time to an America that had never actually existed. Yet the nostalgia was intoxicating, not only for Walt but also for the many artists he was pulling in to work on the project, including Marc Davis. By 1952, the park that lived in Walt's imagination had a new name: Disneyland. But as the park of his dreams slowly materialized, his animation studio started to falter again.

CHAPTER 13
ONCE UPON A DREAM

Each lens fit perfectly in a human hand. They were heavy, square, and trimmed in gold and silver alloys, and they were considered so valuable that they traveled only under the protection of guards. As the technicians at the studio physically mounted the precious lenses on their movie cameras, it was hard to understand what all the fuss was about. Walt had paid a substantial sum to be one of the first to license the anamorphic lenses known as CinemaScope from the Twentieth Century Fox film studio.

The technology, although valuable, was not new. In 1926, Henri Chrétien, a French astronomer and inventor, patented a technique using a distorted lens. When the lens was attached to a camera, it created an optical illusion, an image far wider than that of a standard lens. This was because his anamorphic lens compressed the image along its longest edge, improving image quality while widening scope. Chrétien had originally developed the lens cylinders for tank periscopes during World War I as a way for French soldiers to get a wider look at what was occurring outside. Despite the French inventor's attempts to get the film industry to notice his lenses, they went largely unappreciated until the 1950s, when the threat of television forced filmmakers to pursue novel approaches.

In the early 1950s executives from Twentieth Century Fox flew all the way to Paris to see the lenses for themselves. There were only a handful remaining — the inventor's laboratory had been bombed during World War II, destroying much of his work. The film executives were impressed with what they saw and decided to purchase the system and rename it CinemaScope. They described their wide-screen film format by urging consumers to "imagine Lauren Bacall on a couch — and sixty-four feet long!"

They weren't the only ones who wanted to get their hands on new lenses. Considerable interest in the wide-screen format was building at studios all over Hollywood, and different technologies were emerging. Warner Brothers had their own anamorphic lens system that they called WarnerSuperScope, and Paramount was speedily working on a new wide-screen projector mechanism that improved definition called VistaVision.

Walt became eager to use the French lenses and quickly licensed them from Twentieth Century Fox. The anamorphic lenses attached directly to a standard camera lens and gave a "big screen" experience to an audience jaded by entertainment in their living rooms. CinemaScope, however, was imperfect — it produced an image that was stretched sideways, resulting in blurriness. Walt decided to trust in a company he had long been associated with, Technicolor, which was merging the technologies, combining the anamorphic lenses of Cinema-Scope with the sharp quality produced by VistaVision. Not to be outdone by others' flashy trademarked names, the company called it Technirama. In addition to the standard 35 mm format, they could also create a higher-resolution 70 mm film in a stunning 2.35:1 aspect ratio. The aspect ratio is the width of the screen compared to its height. In comparison, the Academy ratio, created by the Academy of Motion Picture Arts and Sciences in 1932, is 1.37:1. The first film to be made in Super Technirama 70 was *Sleeping Beauty.*

When the wide-screen lenses first arrived

at the studio's motion picture laboratory, located off D wing next to the Ink and Paint building, they were hardly inspiring on their own. It wasn't until the artists got involved with the process, testing their pencil sketches under the new lens, that it became clear how the technology would change the aesthetic of moviemaking. A main character could no longer dominate a scene — there was too much room left over on either side. The animators needed to develop more action scenes to take advantage of the added space.

The studio had always prided itself on cleverly detailed backgrounds, but now it had to emphasize them even more, as audiences would be seeing more of them. Thelma Witmer, with her extensive experience, was now absolutely essential to the making of their next picture.

Alice in Wonderland had flopped at the box office, and *Peter Pan* did not fare much better. After premiering in New York City on February 5, 1953, the film got a largely positive critical reception, with several reviewers commenting on the innovative use of color and lush backdrops. Once again, the only two female artists to receive on-screen credit — Mary as color director and

Thelma on backgrounds — could not have been insensible to the compliment to their work.

But criticism was leveled at the film as well. The *New York Times* labeled Tinker Bell a "vulgarity," while other reviewers were taken aback that Peter Pan, always played by female actresses onstage, was now unabashedly male. Oddly, the same *New York Times* critic who had bashed *Song of the South* seven years earlier for its racist depiction of the "master-and-slave relation" now praised scenes in the "Indian village" as having "gleeful vitality."

The reviews were generally favorable, and moviegoing audiences, such as they were, were heading to the box office. The film grossed $7 million, far more than flops like *Alice in Wonderland,* which had grossed $5.6 million, but not as much as *Cinderella,* which had grossed $8 million with a much smaller production budget. Live-action movies, however, could generate similar profits and cost much less to make. With a budget of $2 million, the romance *From Here to Eternity,* released by Columbia Pictures in 1953, earned $12.5 million.

It seemed to some executives at the studio, including Walt's brother Roy, that the artistry and detail-oriented-ness that defined

Walt Disney Productions was financially untenable. The profits made from each film were sunk right back into the business, where investment in production, along with new technology, was swallowing them whole. Hand-drawn animation combined with years of story development and refinement was slowly killing the studio.

Walt's was not the only studio under financial strain; other animation studios were similarly struggling. In response, many adopted what was called the UPA style. UPA was an acronym for the United Productions of America, a studio formed in the wake of the Walt Disney Studios 1941 strike, and the style was a form of limited animation that reused drawings, kept character movement to a minimum, and generally cut costs by reducing artwork. When Walt charged one executive with finding a way to "produce better pictures at a lower cost," these were the tactics that the manager came back with. Walt immediately rejected them, yet concerns over the long-term viability of the work remained. Faced with obsolescence, the studio returned to what it had succeeded with in the past: a princess fairy tale.

Like *Snow White* and *Cinderella,* the story

of a young maiden in an enchanted sleep who can be awoken only by a kiss has been told and retold over centuries. Its origins trace back to a gothic romance titled "The History of Troylus and Zelladine" in a collection called *Perceforest,* believed to have been produced in France in the 1300s. In it, Princess Zelladine falls asleep after pricking her finger on a piece of flax that she was about to spin into linen. In the original tale, this sleeping beauty is not kissed by her true love but raped. She wakes up to discover that she has given birth to a baby boy, who is suckling her finger. A hundred years later, Giambattista Basile published an Italian version of the story. His adaptation is even more brutal: A married king comes across the sleeping beauty's lifeless body and rapes her. The princess awakens only after she has given birth to twins. In this version, the malevolent character is the betrayed queen, who takes her revenge by ordering the babies to be killed and served to the king for dinner and by attempting to throw the princess into a bonfire. Subsequent adaptations by Perrault ("The Sleeping Beauty in the Wood") and the Brothers Grimm ("Little Briar Rose") would eliminate the themes of adultery, rape, and cannibalism and substitute an evil fairy and the prick of a spindle.

As the story department studied the different versions of the sleeping-beauty folktale, it became clear that the plot itself was troublesome. In neither the Perrault nor the Grimm brothers' version does the villain play any significant role. She merely appears, casts her evil spell, and leaves. And Sleeping Beauty was not inspiring as a character, being merely a girl who spends most of the story slumbering.

Story meetings were no longer the traumatic proceedings that had once caused Bianca to flee the room like a wounded animal. For one thing, there were far fewer gatherings where ideas were bounced around; for another, the boss was rarely present. Whereas Walt had previously spent countless hours in the meetings, wanting to be involved in nearly every detail of plot development, he now rarely participated, instead brainstorming on his own and approving storyboards between his many other pursuits. The writers' room, once the scene of so much excitement and competition, was now in danger of extinction.

Walt wasn't the only one absent from the story department. The hiring of story artists remained stagnant following the massive layoffs of 1941 and so the department was slowly shrinking. Women in particular were vanishing from its ranks. The rooms once crowded with female talent that had taken Walt years to recruit — Bianca, Grace, Dorothy, Mary, Sylvia, Ethel, and Retta — were now devoid of their ingenuity. They had all left, and very few voluntarily.

Mary's art had turned improbably dark. She had already finished concept art for their next feature, *Lady and the Tramp,* which was one of the first projects she had worked on at the studio and which, like so many before it, had lingered in production. She was now focusing on *Sleeping Beauty.* As she sketched the villain, the evil fairy, each shadow was a reflection of the growing darkness in her own life. Her misery informed the spectral world the "mistress of all evil" waded in. In contrast were the light scenes she painted of the Princess Aurora and Prince Philip. Rendered in her fresh, bright style, the couple shine in the warm glow of the sun.

Whereas the studio's last three films arrived after many years of development, *Sleeping Beauty* was a mere adolescent, its plot raw and unrefined. Some in the story department believed there wasn't enough time to create a script and wished that Walt had chosen the other fairy tale the studio had been seriously considering, one that had been in development for far longer: "Beauty and the Beast," based on the 1740 French story by Gabrielle-Suzanne Barbot. But there was no going back now, and so, to hurry along the film, the writers started to sift through their previously used or discarded ideas.

Many of the evil fairy's facial features could be borrowed from *Snow White*'s wicked queen, who had in turn originally been modeled on writer Dorothy Ann Blank. Mary borrowed a dance sequence she'd developed for *Cinderella* in which Cinderella and the prince dance among the clouds, unbounded by gravity, and took out old concept art to design the villain's clothing. Other artists similarly rescued their rejected story ideas. In meetings, they pondered a deleted sequence from *Snow White* in which the prince was kidnapped and held captive in the evil queen's castle. *Surely that scene could work here,* they told one another. They had never recycled material to such an extent, and the practice was eating away at their self-confidence.

Another challenge in adapting *Sleeping*

Beauty was that the characters, particularly the princess, were so bland and lifeless that the entire plot felt heavy and dull. The writers needed to bring conflict into the script and create far more compelling action.

As the months progressed, Princess Aurora lay passive, with no writer able to give her deficient character a push. They wrote her just eighteen lines of dialogue, barely enough for her to be considered a supporting character, although she was presumably the heroine. The evil fairy, however, was growing stronger. Her appeal was similar to that of the rule-defying Tinker Bell — her character had potency and resolve. But the group had little to work with, as the villain of Perrault's and the Grimm brothers' fairy tales was as unformed as she was unnamed. At last, the group decided to name her Maleficent.

The story group turned to Tchaikovsky's 1890 ballet *The Sleeping Beauty,* with its malevolent Carabosse, the wicked fairy godmother. It wasn't just the music of the ballet they decided to incorporate into the film but also the look of its characters. In the original performance, the female Carabosse was played by a man, but later the part would be played by both sexes, one of the few roles in ballet to maintain such fluidity. The Sadler's Wells Ballet, later known as the Royal Ballet, premiered *Sleeping Beauty* in 1946 in London, a city trying to recover its arts and culture after World War II. The Royal Opera House's lights dimmed, and with the royal family seated in their box, the theater came alive with dancers arrayed in costumes, tights, and shoes that had all been purchased with ration coupons.

That night, the role of the villain Carabosse was played by Robert Helpmann, and his costume could not fail to make an impression. His dress was exquisite, covered in black velvet with dragon-like wings protruding from the arms. Most memorable of all was his headdress, capped by two stylized, pointed horns. It was this feature that Mary noted in 1953 when the ballet company made its third tour of the United States, performing in twenty-one cities, including New York and Los Angeles.

As Mary developed concept art for Maleficent, the ballet costuming inspired her. It was reminiscent of a sketch she had made, but never used, for *Cinderella*. In that drawing, the fairy godmother is dressed in long flowing black robes lined in pink with a single long, twisted horn on her head. She is not a grandmotherly old lady; she is young and vital. When designing Maleficent, Mary combined the ideas, putting the head-dress with two horns atop the youthful head of Cinderella's would-be godmother. A smile spreads across her face, and in her hand she holds a magic wand.

At the same time, the group was aging three of their female characters. Since 1952, the story department had been developing the team of good fairies who confer gifts on Aurora and ultimately come to her rescue. Once regarded with abhorrence by the male artists, fairies were now bringing the group together as its members debated their portrayal. They were originally envisioned as nature sprites with the ability to control, respectively, the plants (Flora), the animals (Fauna), and the climate (Merryweather). Their roles were not minor in the story — it was their skill and bravery that, with some assistance from Prince Philip, would ulti-mately bring Maleficent to her knees.

While the fairies' part in the plot was becoming fixed in the story department, their appearance was still a source of debate. This is where the animation department came in. Walt considered making the three identical, but the animators rebelled against this homogeneity. Frank Thomas and Ollie Johnston, two of Walt's Nine Old Men (and now in their forties), began studying how women several decades their senior moved through the grocery store. They paid close attention to the wardrobe and hairstyles of seventy-year-old women. In the story department, the fairies had been labeled "positive and aggressive," but it was only under the animators' pencils that each was given her own body type and personality. The result was a trio of women who seemed ripped from real life, each one grandmotherly in appearance but with a unique height, weight, and way of carrying herself. Although the feature's title character might be dull and sleepy, the new host of female characters were charismatic and powerful.

Mary was traveling so frequently that she became a member of TWA's elite million-miler program. As much as she tried to keep her work and home life distinct, her worlds were collapsing. She was drinking more; some days she drank herself into a stupor to blunt the pain of Lee's frequent verbal and sometimes physical attacks. Yet the emotional toll could not be so easily dampened. At night, as she lay in bed beside her husband, the effects of his words lingered. She couldn't bear to tell anyone about it, not even her closest family and friends, so she kept the suffering in until it seemed she would burst with it. Mary decided to resign. Someone had to hold the pieces of their lives together before the vicious discontent that defined her marriage ripped them all apart.

Walt was careful not to show his displeasure when she told him. His letters remained full of affection, and every Christmas he sent boxes of toys to the children. Perhaps even then he was thinking of how he might lure Mary back to the studio one day, and so he was careful not to betray even an ounce of bitterness to the artist who got away.

Letters from Walt and other friends at the studio kept Mary abreast of their progress. Walt shared his excitement about the development of Disneyland, especially when he and Roy finally purchased 160 acres of orange groves and walnut orchards in the sleepy town of Anaheim, southeast of Los Angeles. And now Walt was about to share his plans with the country. Buoyed by his experience with *One Hour in Wonderland,* he signed a deal with the ABC television network on March 29, 1954, to produce a weekly hour-long series called *Disneyland* that would promote the park by showing off its future attractions. In addition, each episode would tell a story, either live action or animated, that would take place in one of the park's four regions: Adventureland, Fantasyland, Frontierland, or Tomorrowland.

Thanks to investment from ABC, construction progressed at a rapid pace. The builders broke ground in July 1954, and by that December the park was already taking shape. In a letter to his sister, Ruth, Walt shared his happiness. He took particular delight in the Christmas decorations, describing the frosted windows of Main Street, the white and green trees, and the thousands of twinkling lights.

The decorations were ready but it would be six months and many millions of dollars before Disneyland would be open to the public. Yet Walt was already eagerly sharing his joy about it with everyone who would listen.

Disneyland was built swiftly and opened in 1955 while the asphalt was still soft enough to take impressions of the high-heeled shoes that strolled the "happiest place on Earth." In its first seven weeks, the park had more than one million visitors, each paying one dollar a ticket. By contrast with the theme park, the studio's next feature was barely crawling along. Mary was gone and so was her inimitable perspective on not just color and styling but also character development.

Marc Davis began working with her early concepts and then added significant research of his own as he animated a large cast of characters: Aurora, Maleficent, Diablo the raven, King Stefan, and Queen Leah.

Yet it was Maleficent who grabbed his attention. He studied medieval history books and old religious texts from Czechoslovakia, noting the long flowing robes and dark colors that filled paintings of the era. He soon became preoccupied with the sorceress, giving her the power to hypnotize, teleport, and turn herself into an enormous green — later, black and purple — dragon. He sculpted her head from dark clay in life-size, realistic proportions, her chin jutting out and her horns regally twisted. To appear truly menacing, he decided, she would move very little. Her stillness would make her especially chilling, as would her sinister dialogue spoken to her pet raven Diablo. He wasn't afraid to confer with Mary about his ideas when he saw her during her social trips out west or his out east. She might be gone from the studio but she was hardly absent from his professional life.

One evening in 1956, Marc visited Mary's home in Long Island, his new bride, Alice, joining him. Alice was a graduate of the Chouinard Art Institute, which she'd attended on scholarship. She'd taken classes from Gyo Fujikawa and had originally wanted to become an animator but was convinced to push those daydreams aside by her teachers, who viewed the field as the domain of men. They encouraged her to pursue costume design, which ultimately proved profitable advice. A few years after graduation, she received a call from Marc, a former teacher of hers at Chouinard, asking if she'd like to work on wardrobe for *Sleeping Beauty.* It wasn't long before he started calling her for other reasons, and the pair fell in love and married.

On their honeymoon, Alice entered the Blair home in Long Island for the first time and was instantly drawn to Mary. She had heard so much about the artist, not only from Marc but also from people at Chouinard, where Mary's paintings were frequently exhibited. In her playful manner, Mary pointed to a tray sitting on a table by the window that held a pitcher and two martini glasses. She handed a glass, a piece of ribbon tied around its delicate stem, to Alice. Alice was puzzled at first but then understood that it was a game, and she was instructed to follow the ribbon through the house. She moved from room to room, looping the slack around her hands, and finally made her way into the kitchen. The ribbon went straight to the refrigerator. When she opened the door, she was stunned to see a candle burning on a shelf of the fridge, obviously placed there but a minute earlier. She'd never seen such a thing before: a burning flame contained within the cold walls. With a smile, Mary announced, "I'll always leave a martini in the window for you, and a candle in the fridge." Marc and Lee started laughing and soon Alice joined in, entranced. "It's a wedding present," Mary explained, indicating the handsome tray, pitcher, and glasses, all covered in etched flowers and the words *His, Hers,* and *Ours.* "Anyway, it's better than giftwrap, don't you think?" As she drank the icy gin and vermouth, Alice nodded in agreement.

At the studio, Marc Davis became fanatical about Maleficent, his interest leading him to develop her character in compensation for everything else that was lacking in the plot. The feature was progressing slowly, particularly without Walt driving it. The boss rarely participated in regular story meetings, as he had far too much else to interest him with his new amusement park and his *Disneyland* television show.

Yet even with these distractions, Walt was showing the film's new color director support. With Mary gone, Eyvind Earle's dream of getting her job had come true, and at a salary twice what she had commanded. It wasn't enough for him merely to occupy her role, however — he was also emulating her style. Earle took inspiration from Mary's graphic, flat, thoroughly modern look that had become as distinctive as her signature on the bottom of each painting. His *Sleeping Beauty* artwork was occasionally indistinguishable from hers, although some critics would later note the difference between the two, saying, "You wouldn't call Earle endlessly inventive like Mary Blair, who was like an explosion."

Although his work imitated Mary's, Earle rarely named her among his inspirations. Instead, he cited the vast research he had performed for the film, and when asked about the artists who stimulated him, he invoked "Van Eyck, and Peter Bruegel, and

Albrecht Dürer, and Botticelli." Then he added, "On top of all that I injected a little piece of Eyvind Earle."

Armed with his research and Mary's concept art, Earle began to show the animators his work. Walt insisted they incorporate Earle's style, but this in itself was nothing new. He had been similarly insisting on "more Mary" for years. If she were at the studio, Mary might have told Earle that he was on a fool's errand — most of the artists were highly critical of modernism and believed it had no place in informing the look of their characters. Yet instead of struggling to have his art represented, as Mary had done, Earle was listened to. The animators grumbled over the stylistic differences that added hours to their work, but they accepted the changes.

With all the challenges and delays to production on *Sleeping Beauty,* perhaps none presented more difficulties than the technical aspects of making the picture in the new wide-screen format. Wide-screen gave a panoramic view of the backgrounds, shifting attention away from the character animation on the cels. This presented both opportunity and challenge. On the one hand, the lavish detail of the backgrounds would draw viewers into the scene; on the other, there was far more to draw. Whereas a background for a particular scene had once taken a day for an artist to complete, it now took ten. Assistant animators accustomed to producing tens of drawings a day were now able to complete only a few. There was so much to do that the studio instituted a quota system, insisting that the artists complete eight girls, thirty-two birds, and twenty-two squirrels a day.

To meet such high demand, the studio once again began advertising in the papers for new artists.

Elizabeth Case Zwicker, known as Liz, was twenty-six years old when she started scanning the want ads in the *Los Angeles Times.* There were two separate sections, one for women and one for men, but Liz was never one to follow rules blindly, so she perused the men's section too.

Liz was an artist and poet. She was born in Long Beach, California, to an artist/writer mother and a radio-announcer father. The family soon moved to New York, where Liz grew up a sickly child, confined to her home for months at a time. She suffered from severe ear infections that made her too weak to attend school or even hold up a book. In the 1930s, without the benefit of

394

antibiotics, middle ear infections were a leading cause of childhood mortality. Eventually, Elizabeth grew stronger, and around the age of eight, she was able to resume normal schooling. She graduated from Elmira College in New York and then attended the Art Students League, a school in Manhattan that offered studio art classes.

It was in New York that she met Walter Zwicker, an engineer with the air force. The two married there in 1951 but with Walter's position in the military, they knew they were not likely to stay in one place for long. Sure enough, Walter was transferred to Texas, and soon afterward, in 1953, Liz gave birth to a boy. The young family moved to Glendora, California, where Walter took a job at Aerojet General and Liz had their second child, another boy. On the surface they were a quintessential family of the 1950s, but in truth, their five-year marriage was crumbling. Liz was deeply unhappy, and so the couple made a decision unusual for the era: they split up.

As the divorce proceedings began, Liz knew that she needed an income to support herself and her children, so she decided to respond to an advertisement in the men's section of the classifieds that read "Fine Artists Wanted." Elizabeth was told to report to the studio with her portfolio. She had little idea what a portfolio should contain, so she went out to the art store, bought a leather case, and did her best to fill it with her work. Armed with drawings, most of which she considered only "cute," she entered the studio at Burbank. The interviewer immediately took note of her divorced status and asked, "Do you have any other source of income? We don't pay very much." The salary they were offering, thirty-five dollars a week, certainly wasn't enough to live on, but Liz was desperate for the position. She told them not to worry, that she received child support from her ex-husband.

Salaries at Walt Disney Studios had fallen dramatically. When Ethel Kulsar, also a single mother of two children, was working as an assistant to Sylvia a decade earlier, in 1946, she had made $67.50 per week. Now Liz, hired as an assistant animator, was making half that. Part of the reason for the discrepancy was the soaring cost of the *Sleeping Beauty* feature, which was rapidly becoming the most expensive film they had ever produced. The fact that Liz was a woman also hurt her salary. Many employers justified lower pay for women by noting that the ones who were married shared in their husbands' income, the ones who were divorced received alimony, and ones who were unmarried had no family to support and therefore should be paid less. A woman simply couldn't win.

Although Liz was disappointed by her paycheck, her children would later find the benefits of her new job priceless. When the family visited Disneyland, her boys delighted in the live mermaids who swam in the lagoon and loved waving to them through the portholes in the Submarine Voyage attraction. Unbelievably, the teenage girls the children admired, with their long flowing hair and custom-fit neoprene tails, made forty-five dollars a week, more than their mother earned in animation.

The work at the studio was not easy. Liz found the pressure of CinemaScope tremendous. The process doubled the width of the projected image and then optically enlarged the format from 35 mm to 70 mm film. Each panorama required countless drawings done in the most exquisite detail. Liz was put in charge of birds, and she took the task seriously, spending hours with research material in the studio library and drawing them meticulously. She was disappointed to learn there was no possibility of advancement. The Nine Old Men occupied every senior animator position, and so the most a

new hire could hope for was to work alongside the masters, cleaning up the action of
their animation by tracing over their lines
and removing stray pencil marks. Occasionally the assistant animators would be offered smaller scenes and minor characters
to work on. Even saying hello to one of the
Nine Old Men in the hallways might get
you in trouble, and inbetweeners learned to
avoid them.

At work Liz was playful. She quickly made
friends with the fresh group of hires, and
they teased and played pranks on each other
in the same spirit that had prevailed among
young artists at the studio for decades. At
six foot one and with a fondness for heels,
she soon became known among her friends
as "Big Liz."

There were women too — many more
than Liz had expected to see. While the
story department had been drained of many
of its female writers and the ranks of senior
animators had closed, the number of women
working as assistant animators, in layout,
and in backgrounds was expanding. As she
looked around the studio, Liz wondered if
they were all like her, immersed in their art,
struggling to make a decent wage, and full
of gratitude to be within Walt Disney's walls.

■ ■ ■ ■

Mary was reveling in life outside the borders of her native country. In 1956, as the studio continued to struggle with *Sleeping Beauty,* she, Retta, and a friend from art school named Virginia toured Europe. It wasn't yet common for women to travel without men, especially abroad, but the three relished the time they spent together without husbands or children. They rented a car and drove around Spain, France, and Italy, visiting museums, eating delicious food, sketching, and drinking wine on wrought-iron terraces. As Mary sat in the sunshine of southern France with her friends, she felt the darkness of the past few years lifting. Nothing could take away the hardship she had experienced or the pain that might still be to come, but with Retta and Virginia, she felt she could finally breathe.

CHAPTER 14
DALMATIAN PLANTATION

All day, Liz had been getting calls to bring her drawings down to the camera room. The requests had gone from urgent to insistent to desperate, and Liz was working as fast as she could. As *Sleeping Beauty* neared completion, she wasn't concentrating only on birds and animals but also animating Prince Philip's horse and the jester character. There was much to do, she was under heightened pressure, and Liz could feel the stress radiating off her hand as it gripped the pencil.

When she was done, she gathered up her heavy load of artwork to rush it over to the camera room for filming. Frustrated to find the elevator busy, she decided to use the stairs in order not to lose another minute. Women's fashion in the 1950s was not well suited to dashing up and down stairwells at top speed. Liz had embraced the clothing of the era, as she believed that dressing like a stereotypical secretary would help her fit in and perhaps soften the impact of her silly antics at the studio. That day, she was wearing three-and-a-half-inch heels, a wide-skirted dress over layers of petticoats, and a belt that cinched her waist tight. She ran up the stairs, her hands so full of drawings that she could barely see what was in front of her. Just as she stepped out of the stairwell, Fess Parker Jr., the actor playing Davy Crockett for the *Disneyland* television series, came out of the makeup department and started rushing down the stairs to the back lot where the show was filmed.

The six-foot-seven actor and the six-foot-one animator collided and went tumbling. Liz's skirts flew into the air while Parker's coonskin cap soared down the stairs. With a ding, the elevator doors opened in the middle of the chaos and there was Walt, at first shocked by the scene. He stepped out of the elevator and saw three hundred drawings scattered about the open stairwell. It was too much for him; he started laughing uproariously. Liz looked up at him with apprehension — this was the first time she was meeting the boss — but she soon overcame her embarrassment and started chuckling too while they scouted the stairs to retrieve her drawings.

■ ■ ■ ■

The women of Ink and Paint put the finishing touches on *Sleeping Beauty,* curling Princess Aurora's eyelashes with expert, delicate strokes of their pens. Yet all the artistry of the department was about to disappear. This would be the last feature film at the studio to be graced by their work. Three intruders had entered their midst, and the women in the building eyed their robotic competitors uneasily. It was clear that everything was about to change.

In 1958, three Xerox machines were introduced to the Ink and Paint building. The technology was based on the electrophotography technique that inventor Chester Carlson had nearly given up on in 1942 after he was rejected by every corporation he applied to.

The technology took advantage of the fact that negatively and positively charged objects attract each other and that some objects conduct electricity when exposed to light. The machine works by exposing a document to be copied to a bright light, which casts a kind of electric shadow onto a charged cylindrical drum; the shadowed areas on the drum — the text of the document — are positively charged. Negatively charged toner, which adheres only to the dark, positively charged parts of the shadow, is then added. The negatively charged toner is transferred to a blank piece of paper and then heated so that the toner fuses to the page, creating a copy.

In 1946, the Haloid Photographic Company saw promise in Carlson's patent and decided to refine the technology for commercial use. They invented the term *xerography,* the Latin roots of which loosely translate to "dry writing." The Xerox photocopier was born and was ready to radically alter workplaces everywhere.

The challenge at the Walt Disney Studios was to find a way to photocopy not onto paper but onto plastic cels. Ub Iwerks traveled to the East Coast and began working directly with the Haloid Photographic Company on a way to alter its commercial copiers so the studio could use them. It was clear that the quality of the reproductions would worsen with Xerox machines, but significant financial savings balanced this loss.

While the earliest machines could copy only in black and white, the studio was already betting that in the future they would be able to copy in color. The technology could potentially eliminate the need for the Ink and Paint department by copying the animators' drawings directly onto the cels. A single machine could churn out a thousand cels per day, easily putting an inker, who could produce only fifty cels a day, out of work. Ken Anderson, a longtime employee who bounced around from writing to animation to directing, brought Walt the financial verdict: if they eliminated Ink and Paint, they would save over half the cost of their pictures.

The copiers got their first try at making movie magic at the end of *Sleeping Beauty,* where a crowd of people walk across a bridge toward the castle. It was the sort of scene that required long hours of work, with each face needing detailed outlining. The machines did their job, and because the scene was shown from a wide angle, no difference in detail could be detected. The animators challenged the Xerox again, this time on the drawings of Maleficent as a dragon in the film's climax. Once again the machines performed well, with the dark shading that characterizes the scene mostly unhampered by the mechanical process, although the animators noted that the black lines produced by the Xerox were not as smooth as those drawn by hand. The copiers hummed with activity, working far more hours a day than a single person ever could, and their human operators came and went in shifts. While a portion of the women of Ink and Paint copied on the Xerox, most continued their work as they always had, but now with the premonition that their days at the studio were coming to a close.

After nearly eight years in production, *Sleeping Beauty* premiered at the Fox Wilshire Theater in Los Angeles on January 29, 1959. The film was the most expensive animated feature of its time, costing roughly six million dollars to make, twice as much as either *Peter Pan* or *Alice in Wonderland.* The Sleeping Beauty Castle, built from brick and mortar at the center of Disneyland, had been completed four years earlier and was still awaiting its princess.

The critical response to the film was mostly positive, although some reviewers noted the elements borrowed from previous films, particularly *Snow White.* Yet, with the film's modern midcentury look, it could not help but stand out as significantly different from anything the studio had made previously. That wasn't enough to sell tickets, however, and the film earned just $5.3 million at the box office, far short of *Cinder-*

ella's $8 million. By the end of its first run, the film had lost over a million dollars.

In contrast was Disney's *The Shaggy Dog,* a movie loosely based on the 1923 novel *The Hound of Florence* by Felix Salten, author of *Bambi.* It tells the story of a teenage boy who is transformed into a dog and was the first live-action comedy film produced by Walt Disney Studios. It cost a mere one million dollars to make, and it was one of the top-grossing films of 1959, pulling in over eight million dollars. The lesson to studio executives was clear: Handdrawn animation could not sustain itself. The studio needed to clean house.

The letters went out alphabetically; if your last name began with an A, then you were one of the first to find out you were cut. Liz, with the last name Zwicker, knew the envelope was coming long before the words were typed. As she waited for her letter to arrive, she watched as artists who had worked for the studio for decades were fired. It was a hopeless feeling, as if you were standing on the bow of a ship about to sink into the ocean and could only watch your torturously slow progress into the waters below. In the winter of 1959, Liz received the news she dreaded: she was being laid off as an animator. The studio offered her a job in layout, this time for more money, but she turned it down. If she wasn't in animation, she'd rather not work on movies at all.

Liz certainly wasn't alone; the studio fired all but seventy-five of its five hundred and fifty artists and animators. Even the jobs of those select few men and women who remained were under threat. Walt's brother Roy suggested that they do away with the animation department altogether, as both their animated feature films and animated shorts were losing money. He implored Walt to focus his efforts where the profits were: on live-action television and feature films.

Walt wasn't ready to let go, so the animation department survived, but at a fraction of its previous size. It was the Nine Old Men who went through the records of the animation department and decided which lucky artists could stay and which had to leave. While Liz turned down the opportunity to work in layout, other women were not so fastidious. Men had dominated that department since its inception, as it played a coveted role in production. The layout artists were responsible for staging every shot and plotting the action of the characters in each scene.

Two of the women advancing into openings in layout from their positions in Ink and Paint and animation were Sylvia Roemer and Sammie June Lanham. A benefit of the massive layoffs, if one wanted to look on the bright side, was all the extra space. No longer were they crammed into small offices and meeting rooms. The women spread out their pencils and paper in the capacious 2C wing, previously used only by directing animators.

Along with the exodus of talented animators was the near dissolution of the Ink and Paint department at the studio. Ink and Paint, the division that hired more women than any other, was slowly being stripped clean. Painters held on to their jobs for the moment, as the studio's copiers were not yet able to reproduce in color, but they all knew their time was coming. The company line was that people weren't losing their jobs; they were merely being retrained as Xerox technicians. The reality was more painful. A small number worked with the machines, and some found their way into other departments, but many left altogether. Of the once vital crew of inkers, at one time totaling more than forty, just two members remained. In the departed workers' place stood massive hunks of plastic, glass, and metal. Many women from all over the studio watched the rooms empty with tears in their eyes.

As if brought in on purpose to cheer the forlorn staff, the studio was suddenly full of black-and-white-spotted puppies. They ran around the studio wildly, played in the halls, and sometimes just napped quietly under the animators' desks. There were adult dogs too for the artists to admire, their coats shiny and their tongues hanging out in pure canine contentment. Walt was smitten with a book called *The Hundred and One Dalmatians* by Dodie Smith. This time the studio was not adapting a fairy tale that had been retold over thousands of years but a novel published in 1956. It included modern elements they had never incorporated into their movies before, such as television, neon lights, and contemporary music. The story felt refreshing to the artists; it was just the change they needed and ideal for adaptation.

There was a reason the book felt tailored to them. Dodie Smith had written the text with animation in mind, hoping the Walt Disney Studios might pick it up. She made the plot tight, in a slim volume of just 199 pages full of personality, animals, and a villain that was suitably horrible. Yet despite the story's advantages, the studio could not even have contemplated making the film just five years earlier. It would have been astronomically expensive for animators to draw ninety-nine puppies over and over again, each one carefully inked. Now the new Xerox machines made such concerns vanish; nothing could be simpler than making copies of drawings of black-and-white puppies.

The story department no longer housed rooms of writers and artists eager to debate the merits and faults of each scene. Where forty men and women had once ripped into a book eagerly, this time the manuscript was handed to a single artist who had worked at the studio since 1937, Bill Peet. Without the collaborative story meetings that had previously characterized script development, Peet had only himself to consult. He did it all, constructing storyboards and writing the script without either harsh criticism or the stimulation of new ideas. Wisely, Peet stayed close to the book's narrative; he recognized the power of its simplicity and made few changes.

In animation, the path was unusually smooth. Marc Davis, the master of female villains, was able to copy Cruella De Vil's inimitable style directly from the book, from her hair (half black and half white) to the smoke from her malodorous cigarettes to her long fur coats. Where Marc's genius shone was in the subtleties of her appearance — he made Cruella's face skeletal and her eyes wild with rage.

Those designing the look of the film were highly influenced by the Xerox technology. Eyvind Earle was not among those designers; he had left the studio a year previously, before *Sleeping Beauty* was even released. He left voluntarily, but his departure was likely encouraged due to the expense of his detailed backgrounds, and his attitude, which many coworkers felt was arrogant, probably didn't help either. Before leaving the studio, he described his work there as "not Walt Disney. It was one hundred percent me."

Instead of the lush, romantic look that defined *Sleeping Beauty* and many of the studio's earlier films, the designers were going with a rough, pencil-sketch appearance that played to the strengths of the Xerox. The machine couldn't hide the lines the animators made while drawing the film and that had previously been carefully traced and inked by female employees. With this in mind, production designer Ken Anderson decided to embrace the lines, giving the film a raggedy look in comparison to previous features. For the first time, they would show the pencil marks of the animators directly on-screen.

The look required the animators to be tidier in creating their art and to perform much of their own cleanup, getting rid of stray lines that they ordinarily would have left for the inbetweeners and Ink and Paint artists to handle. But despite the added effort, they were thrilled to see their own hand-drawn lines on a cel. Marc was happy with how his drawings looked directly under the camera lens, feeling that previously his art had always been "watered down."

Walt, however, was not so pleased. The styling, he believed, was reminiscent of what they'd made in the 1920s, when animation was in its infancy and crude lines were acceptable. For decades they had worked to get rid of any stray marks on the cel, and they'd improved their techniques until the dreaded outlines vanished into the colors around them. Inkers had used colored lines with great skill so that every feature was rendered lifelike. Now, thanks to the Xerox machines, the black lines were back and they were everywhere. Production had gone too far, and Walt had been distracted, but it was too late to start over now. Still, he had strong words for the future: "We're never gonna have another one of these god-damned things," he grumbled. "Ken's never going to be an art director again."

The women who once reigned over Ink and Paint were similarly incensed, yelling at Anderson after he gave an interview about how Xerox would save the company money. Given the contentious environment, perhaps it's not surprising that Anderson accepted Walt's offer to take a break from feature films and design rides at Disneyland.

While the studio was awash in a superfluity of photocopies, the artists who had left the company were finding new homes for their creative work. Many of them turned to children's literature. Both Mary and Retta were working for Golden Books, producing a treasury of titles that would persist across generations.

Gyo Fujikawa, who'd once lent her elegant style to *Fantasia*'s promotion and the accompanying book, was also making a name for herself in children's publishing. Unlike Mary and Retta, however, she eschewed Golden Books. "They pay the artist only two hundred fifty dollars a book," she complained. Most children's book illustrators of the time received only a lump sum for their work; they didn't get royalties. This seemed inherently unfair to Gyo, akin to giving her art away. She decided to hire a literary agent to better represent her interests. She illustrated a 1957 edition of Robert Louis Stevenson's *A Child's Garden of Verses,* and her work was so well regarded that her agent was able to insist on Gyo's receiving royalties from then on.

Emboldened by her new clout in the book world, Gyo took on a new project as both author and illustrator. It didn't seem radical at first — she was only drawing babies. She sketched infants experiencing the sweetness of everyday life, from cuddling to sleeping. The perspective was that of a child delighted with having a new baby brother or sister in the house. The babies she drew reflected the range of ethnicities Gyo came in contact with in her life in New York City; in her words it was "an international set of babies — little Black babies, Asian babies, all kinds of babies." Her images were soft, warm, and lovable, and the text was kept simple to appeal to preschoolers.

When Gyo presented her book to her publisher, however, she received an unpleasant reaction. An executive was quick to criticize the diversity of the images and insisted that the African American babies be removed for fear that their inclusion would hurt sales. It was the early 1960s and only 6.7 percent of new children's books in the United States depicted children of color, despite the social and cultural changes afoot. The Supreme Court had struck down "separate but equal" racial segregation in public schools, and the Civil Rights Act of 1964 was imminent, yet children's libraries remained so homogenous that one editor referred to "the All-White World of Children's Books."

Gyo was defiant. She would not allow the book to be published if the illustrations were not kept multicultural. Her resolve was rewarded; the book was finally published in 1963 and it became a bestseller, with more than a million and a half copies sold so far. "Children want facts," Fujikawa once said. "I include them all in the art because I know children sit and look for them when the stories are read." Gyo revealed sensitivity in her texts, an understanding that the images we present to children and the stories we tell them influence their perception in later years. It was an appreciation of the principles of inclusivity and individuality that the Walt Disney Studios desperately needed and that Mary Blair was about to bring back to them.

Despite Walt's displeasure and the discord among employees, *One Hundred and One Dalmatians* met with praise following its premiere on January 25, 1961. *Time* magazine said, "It is the wittiest, most charming, least pretentious cartoon feature Walt Disney has ever made," while *Variety* was more modest in its compliments, writing, "While not as indelibly enchanting or inspired as some of the studio's most unforgettable animated endeavors, this is nonetheless a painstaking creative effort." Yet there was a distinct difference in how the film was assessed in comparison to Walt's previous features. He was no longer the avant-garde artist making movies that defied expectations and crossed generations. The artist who once said, "We don't actually make films for children, but we make films that children can enjoy along with their parents," seemed to have lost his own pleasure in animated film. *One Hundred and One Dalmatians* was produced as children's entertainment and made with profit in mind.

On-screen credits may never have fully reflected the efforts of those working on the films, but in *One Hundred and One Dalmatians* the acknowledgments were unusually concise. Given that the studio now housed so few artists, the ones who remained had put in very long hours. Although many female assistant animators worked on the movie, none of them saw their names on-screen. They hadn't expected to — they knew how the system worked. The only two women to receive credit for the movie were Sammie June Lanham on layout and Evelyn Kennedy as music editor.

The appreciation for xerography, however, was clear. *One Hundred and One Dalmatians* had been made in record time, going from start to finish in a mere three years. Even more impressive, with a budget of $3.6 million, the movie made $6.2 million on its release. Xerox technology effectively saved animation at the Walt Disney Studios, whose future had been teetering since *Sleeping Beauty.* Yet the cost to the female workforce was unprecedented.

Whereas women had once reigned in Ink and Paint, desks now sat empty. In story and animation, careers were stagnant, and there were few opportunities for women to advance. The departments might have survived, but Walt's interest in future cartoon features had faded along with the demise of traditional hand-drawn animation. In order for women to strengthen their

417

position within the studio, they would have
to find a project outside its walls.

CHAPTER 15
IT'S A SMALL WORLD

At the dinner table Mary was thinking about her boys. They were teenagers now and as different from one another as could be. Her elder boy, Donovan, seemed much like her and Lee with his interest in art and animation. Yet at times he displayed a wild streak that made her heart beat frantically in her chest. He was out with friends tonight and Mary told herself not to worry, he was fine. She looked over at Kevin, who was quiet, like her, but with very different interests. He loved talking about rockets, engineering, and space exploration. Tonight, though, no one seemed to be in the mood for conversation. With Donovan out, the little family of three sat quietly. Kevin was picking at his food with the finickiness of a child. He refused to even touch his salad, maintaining a strict space between it and the rest of the food on his plate.

Mary noticed that her husband had been

drinking, but this was not unusual — he did so every day. In her youth she had scanned her father's face looking for signs that the drink had carried him away. Now she watched her husband with the same careful eye, trying to assess how inebriated he was. The alcohol gave Lee not an ounce of pleasure, but it had become a necessity. It seemed he could not function anymore unless he had a few drinks in him. A couple of vodkas led to a couple more, and by the end of the day Lee was frequently so drunk that he passed out in a stupor.

Tonight, Lee was still hours from this state of blissful (for Mary) unconsciousness and in fact seemed unusually alert to those at the dinner table. He watched his son with increasing anger. "Eat your dinner," he said, and then added, "Eat your salad." Kevin looked at his salad, then at his father. He didn't want to touch the greens. He looked back down at his plate and stayed silent, hoping the moment would pass. But it didn't. The tension at the table was building, and although Mary gently tried to calm him, Lee was soon yelling.

Drunk and overflowing with anger, Lee picked up one of the dining-room chairs and smashed it over his son's head. Kevin tried to catch the wooden rungs but was unable to protect himself from the blow. Mary's mind spun in shock, and she began yelling unintelligibly as she hurled her body in front of the chair just as it came down for a second time. There was no curbing Lee's rage and he struck his wife with the force intended for his son. When Mary looked up, her son was hunched over with deep wounds across his head, and what had once been a chair was shattered pieces of wood on the floor. She was so stunned that it took her minutes to realize that blood was running down her own face as well.

Lee fell into a pattern of alcoholism and abuse that was punctuated by his inevitable apologies. Mary couldn't bear to talk with anyone about what was happening. The idea of revealing her secrets to her extended family or friends was painful. Instead, she hid her anguish, being especially careful during her visits to California when she knew Walt was watching.

During one such visit in 1963, designer Rolly Crump was sitting on top of a stepladder at a soundstage on the studio lot when he caught a glimpse of an elegant woman with cropped blond hair. *Oh my God,* he thought, *I'm gonna meet Mary Blair.* For him, being near Mary was like being in the presence of a movie star; her renown in the company was second only to Walt's. Rolly smiled at her and she smiled back. He thought he might die of happiness.

Rolly had started as an inbetweener at the studio in 1952. During *Sleeping Beauty* production, he moved up to the position of assistant animator, cleaning up the senior animators' drawings. After the massive layoffs of 1959, he went over to WED Enterprises — a private company Walt had started in 1952 to manage Disneyland — to design attractions for the theme park. (WED came from Walt's initials: Walter Elias Disney.)

Rolly had just finished the Enchanted Tiki Room at Disneyland, the first attraction to include audio-animatronics. Animatronics were human or animal figures that could talk and move, using mechanisms hidden inside them to make them lifelike. On vacation with his family in 1949, Walt had been fascinated by the wide variety of wind-up toys he'd seen in Paris. As he watched the toys move, he marveled at the simple mechanism that propelled their action.

With these toys in mind, in 1951 he asked several of his employees, including a machinist and a sculptor, to work on an assignment called Project Little Man. The goal was to make a nine-inch-tall mechanical person who could dance and talk. While it was never completed, Walt was intrigued by the idea of incorporating mechanical figures into Disneyland and decided to go bigger. He envisioned a life-size model of Confucius that offered words of wisdom and would be housed in a Chinese restaurant he had planned. Before the head of Confucius was finished, however, Walt changed his mind and proposed the group build a talking and gesturing Abraham Lincoln whom they could place in a proposed Hall of Presidents. In 1961 they started calling the moving and talking figures "audio-animatronics," a term the studio trademarked in 1964. The technology required an intimate knowledge of movement and language. While Lincoln lingered in development, requiring a significant amount of time and money, in 1963 the animatronic birds of the Enchanted Tiki Room made their debut.

The mechanical birds weren't confined to the Enchanted Tiki Room; they spread throughout the studio. In 1964, a realistic-looking audio-animatronic robin landed in the studio's newest feature, *Mary Poppins*. That film, like so many others, had been conceived in the late 1930s, but getting permission to produce it had proved challenging. P. L. Travers, author of the 1934 novel of the same title and its seven sequels, was resolutely against giving Walt the rights to make it into a film. It wasn't until 1961, when Walt flew Travers to Los Angeles and offered her a hundred thousand dollars, 5 percent of the profits, and script approval, that she finally gave in to Walt's persistence.

Production started immediately. The film was planned as a live-action/animation crossover. The live-action format would considerably reduce costs, while the group could add in segments of animation to boost the whimsical nature of the story. To accomplish this, Walt hired Petro Vlahos, an engineer skilled in Hollywood special effects.

Vlahos was known in Hollywood for his work on blue-screen technology, a technique similar to the modern green screen popular among television meteorologists. It involved filming a scene in front of a specific color screen, then removing the color, using a filter in the negative processing, in order to isolate the actors from the background. The result was a negative that showed the actors in front of a transparent background, ideal for Walt to fill in with animation using the optical printer. Blue was originally chosen as the background color because that hue is generally absent from skin tone. However, this meant that all clothing and set items had to be devoid of the color blue.

Vlahos thought they could do better. He developed a new process in which the actors were filmed in front of a white background and the set was lit with strong sodium-vapor lights. Sodium gas emits light at a specific wavelength — 589 nanometers — so Vlahos created a prism that filtered light only at that wavelength. Unlike blue-screen technology, where the color had to be filtered from the negatives, the prism was placed inside the camera itself, simplifying the process. The system also meant that the scenes could incorporate any color, as only a single wavelength was being removed. It was a stunning advance in special effects and would later earn Vlahos an Academy Award in the field. For now, it was technology that the studio owned exclusively. Vlahos had made only a single prism and Walt had it.

The new technology was complex, but the script seemed simple. Unlike books such as *Alice in Wonderland,* which had been a challenge to adapt, *Mary Poppins* and its 1935 sequel, *Mary Poppins Comes Back,* lent themselves to adaptation.

As in his dealings with Roald Dahl, however, Walt would find that Travers's requirement for script approval complicated matters. A 1963 letter from the author to the studio head began with "Dear Walt, Don't be frightened by the size of the enclosed letter . . ." What followed were pages of detailed criticism and demands for character and dialogue revisions punctuated by occasional pleading. When discussing Mrs. Banks, the children's mother, Travers wrote, "I beg, beg, BEG you to give her a more sympathetic, more Edwardian name . . ." Travers would win that battle, and the character's name was changed from Cynthia to Winifred, although much of the script would ultimately go against her wishes.

Walt wrestled with Travers's letters, but a songwriting duo known as the Sherman brothers would deal with the author in person. Walt had hired Richard and Robert Sherman in 1960 after one of their songs, "Tall Paul," became a chart-topping hit for former Mouseketeer Annette Funicello. For *Mary Poppins,* the songwriters embedded themselves in the story department, working closely with the writers to create a host of songs that advanced the narrative arc with memorable musical themes. Yet while Walt and the department gushed over their original creations, from "A Spoonful of Sugar" to "Supercalifragilisticexpialidocious," Travers remained unimpressed, repeating, "No, no, no."

One decision Travers approved of was the casting of Julie Andrews in the role of Mary Poppins. In the early 1960s Andrews was well known for her work onstage in plays such as *My Fair Lady* and *Camelot,* but she had never been in a feature film. After seeing her on Broadway in 1962, Walt decided Andrews was perfect for the lead role and offered it to her. Andrews declined, explaining that she was three months pregnant. This wasn't a problem for Walt, who told her, "We'll wait for you." Six months after the birth of Andrews's daughter, production started up, with the live-action portions filming during the summer of 1963.

Julie Andrews also entranced Retta. Working from her Washington, DC, home, Retta was drawing the actress every day from photographs of the nearly finished film. She was now working at a small animation studio while continuing to freelance as a children's book illustrator. She had just signed with Walt to complete illustrations for a promotional item called *The Story and*

Songs of Mary Poppins, which included an illustrated picture book packaged with a vinyl record of the soundtrack.

Retta was drawing scenes of the upcoming movie in her bold style, sending Mary Poppins, the chimney sweep Bert, and the children flying through the air on brightly colored carousel horses. Not all of her paintings would make it into the book, and the face of Julie Andrews would later be altered due to a legal permissions issue, but each scene captured the adventure and excitement of the film. As she replicated the magical joy of childhood in gouache paint, Retta was also witnessing it in real life. With two young boys, Retta, now forty-eight, was often the oldest mother at the elementary-school playground, but she had a distinct advantage the other parents lacked. Her drawings could give the children a peek at the upcoming Walt Disney movie.

Mary Poppins premiered on August 27, 1964, at Grauman's Chinese Theatre in Hollywood. The theater, with a façade reminiscent of tiered East Asian pagodas, had opened in 1927 and was famous for its handprints of celebrities cast in the concrete sidewalk out front. Walking over the handprints that evening was a host of celebrities, including the stars of the film, Julie Andrews and Dick Van Dyke, and a variety of Disney characters, such as the Seven Dwarfs and Mickey Mouse.

The premiere was a fund-raiser for the California Institute of the Arts, known as CalArts. Walt and his brother Roy formed the school in a 1961 merger between the Chouinard Art Institute and the Los Angeles Conservatory of Music. To promote it, Walt had made a short documentary film, *The CalArts Story,* that would be screened before *Mary Poppins* began. Walt was proud of their work, saying, "CalArts is the principal thing I hope to leave when I move on to greener pastures. If I can help provide a place to develop the talent of the future, I think I will have accomplished something."

It was the studio's first gala Hollywood premiere since the spectacle of *Snow White and the Seven Dwarfs* back in 1937. The grand celebration was fitting for the fantasy film that was already drawing near universal acclaim. "Disney has gone all-out in his dream-world rendition," declared *Variety.* Audiences seemed to agree, as the movie grossed thirty-one million dollars during its first run. For a film that had cost approximately five million dollars to make, less than *Sleeping Beauty* five years earlier, the profits were enormous. The film would go on to be nominated for thirteen Academy Awards, including Best Picture, the only film created in Walt's lifetime to be considered in this category.

The lesson to studio executives was clear: animation was a bloated dinosaur. They could never expect a film like *Bambi* or *Peter Pan* to pull in significant profits. After the release of *The Sword in the Stone* in 1963, a film that had made only one million dollars, the animation department of the studio slowed down its feature work, and it was unclear when, or if, it would ever pick up again.

Walt had previously pushed feature production at the studio, but his attention was now divided. The same audio-animatronic bird that sat on Mary Poppins's hand during filming in 1963 was making its way to Walt's newest project. This time the exhibit wasn't in Disneyland; instead, it was destined for the 1964 World's Fair, to be held in New York City. The fair's theme that year was "Peace Through Understanding," and Walt was in charge of designing four separate exhibits: Great Moments with Mr. Lincoln, Carousel of Progress, Magic Skyway, and It's a Small World.

It was this last project that had Walt turning his thoughts to Mary Blair. He was envisioning a boat ride celebrating the children of the world, as the exhibit would be located in the United Nations Children's Pavilion and proceeds from its ticket sales would benefit UNICEF. As part of the ride, they would need to create models of hundreds of children of different nationalities, reflecting the individual characters of the countries but also communicating a message of peace and unity. It was a delicate task for any artist, but after Walt looked over his staff and heard their proposals, he had only one question: "What is Mary doing?"

Mary, still living on the East Coast, was incredibly busy. She was not only illustrating Golden Books but working on a wide range of freelance projects, including fashion design for Lord and Taylor; advertising for national brands such as Nabisco, Johnson and Johnson, and Maxwell House Coffee; window-dressing for storefronts on Fifth Avenue; and designing sets for Radio City Music Hall. Yet as soon as she received the call from Walt, she dropped everything and got on a flight to Los Angeles.

Walt and Mary had a similar perspective. They both looked at life with the excited, curious gaze of a child. They were not childish or immature, but the feeling that the world was full of wonder waiting for them to discover it had never left them. It was this feature of their personalities that Mary captured in her paintings, a sense of pure childhood joy unspoiled by years of painful adulthood. When Walt viewed Mary's art, he recognized this sensation in himself. For the boat ride, he wanted to seize that feeling and impart it to others.

Immediately Mary threw herself into the "most interesting job I've ever had," as she called it. She began to send collages to her colleagues in Burbank full of her vision for the ride, and they were astounded at what they contained. Her ideas burst with color and texture, the patterns colliding unexpectedly. The packages just kept coming. Although she had been given very little direction, her artwork for the ride was unstoppable, and she produced it at a remarkable pace.

She was drawing from multiple inspirations, chief among them her visit to Mexico City in 1942, when she had witnessed the tradition of Las Posadas. Her memories of the children she met were so happy that she couldn't help but see their sweet, round faces as she crafted the ride. Yet no one seeing the joyful spirit of the lead designer's plans for It's a Small World could imagine the personal pain she was enduring.

Two of those ignorant of her struggles were Alice Davis, Marc's wife, even though she and Mary had become as close as sisters; and Rolly Crump, who had been smitten with her at first sight and was quickly becoming a close friend. The ride was built at a large soundstage in Los Angeles, although it would ultimately be shipped to New York for the fair. During breaks, Mary sat outside with Rolly, enjoying the California sunshine as she smoked or drank coffee. In those moments she felt light and happy, and New York seemed far away. As she chatted, she painted an idyllic picture of her family life that she wished were true: A warm and loving husband who threw her an inner tube from their boat as she dived into the bay. A snowy afternoon spent building snowmen with her family before retreating for hot cocoa by the fireplace of their grand home. It all sounded perfect, but the more Rolly heard, the less he believed. Even Mary was aware that she sounded like a child describing a dream rather than an adult sharing her life experiences. Yet how could she reveal the disturbing truth?

Mary's colleagues got their first sense that all might not be right in the Blair marriage when Lee accompanied Mary on one of her trips west. He bristled at the widespread acknowledgment of her talent and even grumbled to Walt, "I could have done this," painfully conscious that he hadn't been asked. Mary said nothing.

The project was coming to fruition, and they were ready to test the movement of their animatronic children. To do so, the team made a mock-up of It's a Small World on a spare soundstage. Each section was positioned as it would be on the ride, the set was lit up, and the melody played so incessantly that it soon grated on the nerves of every member of their group. Alice Davis, who was working as a costume designer for the ride, felt that the song followed them wherever they went, later saying, "We hated it."

Alice was walking a fine line on this project, with her husband on one side and her best friend on the other. Mary and Marc sometimes disagreed on how the costumes should be styled. On one occasion, Mary directed Alice to decorate the queens of the ride with jewels to set them apart from the other dolls. Alice obliged but then was told by her husband, who disliked the adornment, to remove them. Alice did. When Mary saw her friend squirm, she felt terrible. She said, "I'm sorry you're in this uncomfortable position," then added, "but put the jewels back on." Ultimately, Mary was in charge.

At the California dry run — quite literally dry, with no river in the soundstage for the boat to float in — they showed the final design to Walt for his approval. Then, so that he could get the full experience, they seated the boss on a boat equipped with wheels and slowly pushed him through the attraction. The scene must have looked comical from afar, but to Walt, the soundstage had turned wondrous. The ride featured Mary's art magnified. It was a celebration of her style, never fully appreciated in his films. Yet he did have one complaint. "Why," he asked Alice, "did you put pantaloons on the French cancan dancers?" Alice faltered, as in truth the costume had been added because of a complicated technical hurdle they faced in getting the audio-animatronic dancers to move naturally. Preferring a jest instead of the truth, she quipped, "You told me you wanted a family show."

New York City was ready for the Disney group, although not in the way they were expecting. As President Johnson gave the

435

keynote address and crowds gathered to see what future delights the space age would hold for them, voices were rising in the U.S. Federal Pavilion. The protesters chanted "Jim Crow must go!" and "Freedom now!" so loudly that the president's voice became inaudible. Some held signs that read A WORLD'S FAIR IS A LUXURY BUT A FAIR WORLD IS A NECESSITY and SEE NEW YORK'S WORSE FAIR — SEGREGATED SCHOOLS FOR NEGROES, PUERTO RICANS AND RATS.

The activists were part of an effort aimed at bringing attention to the neglected boroughs of New York City, which had been untouched by the extensive preparations for the World's Fair and were suffering from dilapidated schools, high levels of crime and unemployment, and police brutality. It was the beginning of massive protests and riots that would rattle New York and other major cities across the United States in the summer of 1964. The World's Fair demonstration was originally supposed to be a larger "stall-in," in which thousands of cars would surround the fairgrounds and block the visitors expected to arrive. While this level of civil disobedience didn't occur, the protesters gained significant attention for these issues, forcing President Johnson to discuss their demands the next day when questioned by the press.

Amid social upheaval, technology was sparking new innovation. In 1964 a doctoral student at MIT was poised to transform how humans interacted with machines. Ivan Sutherland had always considered himself a visual thinker, understanding best what he could see and touch. As a student, Sutherland was captivated by a 1945 article published in *The Atlantic* by the legendary engineer and MIT alumnus Vannevar Bush. In his piece, titled "As We May Think," Bush dreamed of a machine called a memex, a device capable of storing "books, records, and communications" and acting like a supplement to a person's memory; it would come complete with a stylus that allowed writing directly on the screen. Sutherland recognized that there was something intimate about the interaction Bush described, and with Bush's article in mind, he designed a new computer program called Sketchpad.

The program took advantage of the light pen, a precursor to today's mouse, conceived and developed at MIT's Project Whirlwind a decade earlier. Sutherland's program used the light pen to draw directly on the screen of a Lincoln TX-2 computer, creating the first visual communication between computer and user. It was just the beginning of what computer graphics would one day accomplish. The program was like an outstretched hand, reaching to pull artists without experience in engineering into the world of computers. Despite the open invitation, computing was a domain that those at the Walt Disney Studio weren't yet ready to enter.

It's a Small World proved such a popular attraction at the World's Fair that Walt decided he had to have a lasting version of the experience in Anaheim. As the lead designer, Mary began adapting the ride for the park. Her friendships with Alice and Rolly deepened, as the three were spending long hours together. Their time was not just confined to California — both Alice and Rolly visited Mary in Long Island as well.

Sometimes their trips revealed more than Mary had anticipated. On a visit east while Lee was out of town, Rolly played with Mary's teenage sons out on the veranda of their house. He boisterously performed magic tricks, his hands riffling the cards in the deck with ease. They sat for hours, the boys laughing with Rolly until the sun began

438

to set. When Rolly turned to look at Mary, he saw her standing quietly apart and watching them. She was crying. "What's wrong?" he asked. It had been a happy day and he couldn't imagine what had upset her. Her eyes still wet, she replied, "I've never seen Lee play like that with the boys before."

The opposing sensations of pleasure and pain were pervading all aspects of Mary's life. As she looked at the finished It's a Small World ride in Disneyland, she felt both exultant and uneasy. The ride was bursting with her art, the pinnacle of a career spent experimenting with color and form. It also communicated a message she believed in and offered children a glimpse of the many languages, landscapes, and cultures of the world. And yet it was imperfect in her eyes. Given her unhappiness at home, it seemed worthwhile to pursue perfection in the one arena she could control. She found it nearly impossible to consider the job complete. If she had had her way, she would have tweaked and changed the design forever. But for all its flaws, whether in Mary's perception or in the criticism of a subsequent generation, who noted the presence of ethnic and racial stereotypes, the ride lives on, carrying with it a vision of peaceful human connection.

As difficult as it was for Mary to let go of It's a Small World, her distress was mitigated by Walt's plans for her. He delighted in the resurgence of their working relationship and had no intention of letting her escape this time. He proposed a number of projects: a large ceramic mural for the new children's wing in the Jules Stein Eye Institute; a massive fifty-four-foot-long mural in the Tomorrowland section of Disneyland; a mural in what Walt referred to as "the Florida project," later to become Disney World and still under construction; and the promise of even more to come. Mary had more artistic freedom and commanded a larger salary than she ever had in the past.

Mary had barely made a start on the wealth of projects before her when she received horrible news. Walt was sick. He had been diagnosed with lung cancer in November 1966, and by the end of the month he had to be rushed back to St. Joseph's Hospital, just across the street from the studio in Burbank. There was little for any doctor to do — the cancer was too advanced, likely caused by his five decades of smoking cigarettes. On December 15, he died. There had been little warning, and Mary did not have a chance to say goodbye. She was heartbroken. At the studio, whose halls had been kept alight so that Walt might see their glow as he lay dying across the street, there was a distinct feeling that nothing would ever be the same.

Lee became so intoxicated one night at dinner that he passed out in his salad. The boys were alarmed, crying out for their father in voices filled with fear. Mary, however, had run out of anxiety for him. She merely picked up his head, then dragged him off to bed. The life they had built together, once full of artistic ambition and inspiration, had flattened into horror and dread.

When Gyo visited Mary, she saw how miserable her former coworker had become. Mary cried over Walt's death, which had devastated her, and Gyo comforted her as best she could. Yet Gyo suspected that Mary's dejection was not due to Walt's passing alone.

With Walt gone, Mary found that all the happy prospects for her future at WED Enterprises had evaporated. She still had the work Walt had assigned her, but her future as an Imagineer — a term coined to describe those in the elite group that designed the Disney parks — was stalled.

Walt's admiration of Mary had long triggered jealousy among others at the company. Perhaps if he had loved her less, she might have been more readily employed after his death.

However, there were worries greater than work pressing on Mary. Donovan, her elder son, was in trouble, and she felt she could confide in no one about it. Her sister Gussie could tell something was wrong, but Mary refused to acknowledge her misfortunes to anyone until Alice visited one evening. "Mary?" Alice said in the solitude of the kitchen. "I happen to love you very much and I think something terrible has happened in your life. Could you share it with me? Would it help you to get it off your chest?" Mary looked at her dear friend and said, "No one asks me anything," before collapsing in tears.

She told her friend the sad story. Donovan had been experimenting with drugs in college and something had gone horribly wrong with his mind. The boy had needed to be hospitalized. Mary and Lee, with no health insurance, paid the steep hospital bill of thirty thousand dollars, and yet they were no closer to having an answer for what was wrong with him.

Donovan was delusional, unable to express

himself clearly, paranoid about those around him, and listless. He couldn't take care of himself and yet had grown so aggressive that it wasn't safe for him to live at home either. He was in his late teens, the age when people who have schizophrenia often start showing symptoms, but in the 1960s, the disease was so stigmatized that there were few treatment options. Donovan would have to be institutionalized. Mary was overcome with grief. She hugged her friend and told her they'd be selling the house and moving back to California. Her life was becoming painfully contracted, and, sadly, her small world just kept shrinking.

CHAPTER 16
UP, DOWN,
TOUCH THE GROUND

"This studio will never allow a woman to be an animator," Heidi Guedel was told by a coworker on her first day in the animation department. "I'm an assistant animator and that's the farthest any woman has ever gotten here. The last girl who tried this training program left in tears." Heidi nodded her head but then promptly closed her ears. She didn't need to hear that becoming an animator at the Walt Disney Studios was difficult; she knew it already.

Heidi was familiar with the trials of Hollywood. Her father was John Guedel, a producer known for his work on radio and television shows such as *You Bet Your Life*, hosted by Groucho Marx. Guedel and his wife, Beth, had adopted Heidi as a newborn in 1948 and brought her home to their grand white colonial on a palm tree–lined street in Beverly Hills. Despite the opulence of her surroundings, Heidi grew up deeply unhappy. There was no love in her home. Her father was frequently absent and her mother displayed a cold, emotionless façade, even while beating her daughter with the back of her high-heeled shoe. Heidi frequently wished she were a boy; her older brother could at least defend himself against their mother's attacks.

After graduating from Beverly Hills High School in 1966, Heidi applied for work at multiple animation studios, but even with her father's extensive connections, she was rejected. Every letter said the same thing — she needed a degree from an art school first. So Heidi turned to the college that seemed most likely to get her the job she craved: CalArts. In 1972, with her bachelor of fine arts in hand, Heidi joined a long line of women who were hired at Walt Disney Studios after graduation.

She entered the famed D wing of the studio, where the Nine Old Men had once sketched a host of classic films and whose halls a few of them still roamed, but it was different than she'd expected. Its walls were shabbier and its occupants sometimes difficult to get along with. As an inbetweener on a probationary trial, she often found her lines erased or traced over by the more senior animators. The environment was competitive and full of jealousy. The top animator positions were just beginning to open up, and assistant animators who had worked at the studio for two decades without an opportunity for advancement eyed the jobs possessively.

While women in the 1970s were entering the workplace in unprecedented numbers elsewhere, at the Walt Disney Studios the opposite was true. In the story department, the number of women had dropped from a peak of approximately 40 percent in 1940 to roughly 10 percent in 1975. In animation, women were confined to assistant animator positions. The most precipitous drop was in the Ink and Paint department, whose ranks were almost depleted. A core group of twenty-four women remained and still hand-painted each cel and inked fine detail work onto the scenes. Altogether, there were far fewer women employed at the studio than a decade earlier, and the histories of those former female employees were rapidly fading from consciousness.

As Heidi was graduating with her bachelor of fine arts, a man named Edwin Catmull was also getting his degree. He was earning a bachelor of science in physics from the University of Utah and yet he felt like a mere beginner in the field.

As a child, awestruck by *Pinocchio* and *Peter Pan,* he had dreamed of becoming an animator at the Walt Disney Studios, but his inability to draw soon convinced him to put those aspirations aside. Instead, he decided to pursue the emerging field of computer science. Ivan Sutherland, known for his development of Sketchpad at MIT, had just started as a professor at the University of Utah, and Catmull found in him a mentor and, later, when he entered the university's graduate program, an adviser.

For a man studying computer science, Catmull seemed to be taking a strange approach to a class project in graduate school. He was making a mold of his left hand, painfully ripping out the hair on the back in the process. He filled in the mold with plaster, and then, after it was set and freed, he began to draw directly on it. Catmull and his fellow student Fred Parke drew three hundred and fifty black polygons on the plaster model of his hand, following its contours and making careful note of their dimensions.

To digitize the model, they painstakingly measured the coordinates of each polygon and entered the data into a 3-D animation program Catmull had written. Using the

447

animation program, they could get Catmull's disembodied hand to flex its fingers, point, and make a fist. Then the program dramatically panned in from the base of the hand to show the model from inside the fingers. Using a 35 mm movie camera adapted to the computer screen, they were able to make a short film of the process. Catmull and Parke also digitized an artificial heart valve and, in a fit of ambition, the face of Parke's wife. The final product was waxy and misshapen, but those at the University of Utah who saw the films were speechless — it was 1972 and they were getting their first glimpse of the potential of computer graphics. The Library of Congress would later call the film "an early landmark in the development of computer animation." The work would be a stepping-stone to the three-dimensional wonder that would later characterize the nascent field of computer-generated imagery, or CGI.

Despite Catmull's stunning achievements, the job opportunities he was hoping for didn't materialize. His adviser set up a meeting with executives at the Walt Disney Studios, persuaded that the technology could augment traditional animation, but the meetings weren't fruitful. If Walt had been alive, it seems likely from his history of investing in new and unproven technology that Catmull would have been given the opportunity. For the remaining executives, animation was a dying art that they were unwilling to put resources into.

However, they didn't turn Catmull away empty-handed. Recognizing his talent, they offered him a position as an Imagineer at Disneyland, where he could help develop a new space roller-coaster ride, later called Space Mountain. Catmull declined and returned to the University of Utah and his dissertation.

Even though he didn't take the job with the company, Catmull kept fiddling with Walt's characters. He was working on a mathematical approach to representing curved surfaces in his programming. As part of his dissertation, he figured out a way to project an image onto a curved surface, an invention called texture mapping. It allowed him to replace the waxy look of his graphics with a projection of any surface type he wanted — wood, marble, even feathers. His first selection for a curved surface to work with was the face of Mickey Mouse.

Catmull graduated in 1974 but despite his originality, there were few job prospects. Computer-animation departments were scarce, and he was turned down for a teaching position at Ohio State University. With a wife and a two-year-old daughter to support, Catmull decided to take a dull programming job in Boston. He wondered if he'd ever get to pursue his real interests in computer animation.

After Walt died, in 1966, his brother Roy became president of Walt Disney Productions. Roy was seventy-three years old and had retirement in his sights, but he felt his presence was distinctly needed on the "Florida project," later known as the Walt Disney World Resort when it opened on October 1, 1971.

One of the attractions of the new theme park was the It's a Small World ride, a near-identical twin of the California version. The ride had achieved the pinnacle of theme-park popularity: a long line snaking its way into the attraction. When the park opened, Mary was staying at the Contemporary Hotel, part of the new resort and the home of the last assignment Walt had given her. For the Grand Canyon Concourse, Mary had designed a ninety-foot-tall mural. The mural was composed of eighteen thousand hand-painted tiles shipped from California to Florida, and it had taken the artist and her staff more than eighteen months to build. The result was an eye-popping array of images of animals and children in a style that was completely Mary's own.

Mary had flown to Florida to celebrate the resort's opening with a group of friends and family. She wished Retta could be there, but, sadly, the artist was living more than four thousand miles away. Retta's husband, still in the military, had been transferred to Honolulu, Hawaii. The move had wiped out her employment opportunities; she was simply too far away to work for Walt Disney Productions or any other animation studio. Instead, she focused on her artistry, learning calligraphy, experimenting with silk-screening, and sending her friends and family the most exquisite Christmas cards they'd ever laid eyes on.

Even as Mary basked in the praise for her work at Disney World, she knew the company was changing dramatically. After Roy Disney passed away in late 1971, Esmond Cardon Walker took the helm as president of the company and Donn Tatum became chairman and CEO. The two men were already planning on expanding their successful theme parks internationally. The animation department, however, was working on far fewer feature projects than it had in any decade previously. Of the fifty-two films the studio released in the 1960s, only two were animated: *The Sword in the Stone* (1963) and *The Jungle Book* (1967). Both films were conceived and developed at the studio during Walt's lifetime. With the exception of *Mary Poppins,* the sole live-action/animation hybrid, the rest were all live-action films. Although both of the animated features made modest profits, the rewards were not large enough to tempt executives to continue them. Animation, just like Catmull's new technology, was seen as too risky.

In the 1970s, the number of women in professional fields was increasing. They made up 40 percent of the workforce in the United States and played a key role in computer programming, accounting for 28 percent of all graduates in the field. But that was not the case in animation. When Cal-Arts unveiled its character-animation program in 1975, one of the first of its kind in the country, there were only two women in the program. Without women in the pipeline, few could be hired by Walt Disney Studios to work on their newest features.

Thelma Witmer in backgrounds and Sylvia Roemer in layout had watched many changes sweep through the studio's halls over the decades, none so devastating as the passing of Walt. Although imperfect, he had frequently been an advocate for female artists. Without him, not even the exceptionally talented Mary Blair could find work.

Mary was now based in Soquel, California, a community about an hour and a half south of San Francisco. She had thought that finding jobs on the West Coast would be easier than it was in the east, but the opposite proved to be the case. The studio that had employed her for over two decades was no longer interested. Marc and Alice Davis sent her to an agent in San Francisco, but he quickly rejected her. Despite Mary's portfolio of diverse artistic endeavors, no one would hire her. Perhaps people sensed her desperation.

After getting multiple traffic tickets, Lee was caught driving while intoxicated and was sent to jail for twelve months. His arrest, along with Donovan's hospitalizations, brought Mary low. She was sixty years old but sometimes she felt much older. Now that Kevin was out of the house and in the navy, she was frequently alone. The need to anesthetize her mind from the world grew dominant. The melancholy was deepening, and Mary was desperate for relief.

■ ■ ■ ■

At the studio, Heidi replicated the animators' drawings, filling in the action between
their scenes and transforming their rough
pencil sketches into clean, crisp lines suit-
able for transfer onto cels by the Xerox
machine. Sometimes she needed to lay a
fresh piece of paper over the original work
so that the lines could be neatly traced.
Other times she could break out a kneaded
eraser and beat the graphite pencil smears
into submission. She always preferred to
erase if she could, not because it was faster
— in fact, it always took longer — but
because retaining the animator's lines
preserved the spark of life of the original
drawings.

At home, Heidi created her own animated
scenes, also bristling with life. She was
determined to be hired after her probationary period, but to accomplish this she'd
need to execute her own sequences, which
she would then turn in to a review board of
animators and directors. If they liked her
work, she would be promoted from temporary inbetweener to animation trainee.

While Heidi was prepared to dive into
their next feature, she wasn't expecting to

fall in love with the character Tigger. The studio was in the process of making the third of three short Winnie the Pooh films: *Winnie the Pooh and the Honey Tree, Winnie the Pooh and the Blustery Day,* and *Winnie the Pooh and Tigger Too,* all based on A. A. Milne's books *Winnie-the-Pooh* and *The House at Pooh Corner,* published in the 1920s. It was one of the last animation projects Walt had championed at the studio. He had bought the rights to the books in 1961 and helped develop the shorts, the first of which was released in 1966 before his death. They would repackage all three shorts, editing them together to make the two-hour feature called *The Many Adventures of Winnie the Pooh,* Walt Disney Studios' twenty-second animated film, released in 1977.

As Heidi sketched Tigger, she found that he seemed to have a life of his own. He was joyous and completely content in his own skin. As in previous decades, the animators worked closely with the story department. She chose him directly from the storyboards, tickled by a sequence in which he falls out of a tree, hits the ground below, and bellows, "Oooohhhh! Good ol' terra firma! Smmmaaack!" Heidi envisioned him splayed happily on the ground, not caring how silly he looked, and then pressing his lips to the earth in a loud kiss.

With her nerves on edge, Heidi showed the completed set of pencil sketches to a handful of animators on a Moviola, the simple projector device that had been at the studio so long that even Bianca had regularly used one for film editing. Heidi was tense for a moment afterward, perspiration building on her skin, but then the laughter started, and warm congratulations poured in. The sequence she had drawn was a hit with the group. She was not safe yet, still not past her probationary period, which would be repeatedly extended, but the euphoric feeling of making legendary animators laugh stayed with her.

The history of women at the studio was already becoming lost, buried by those who preferred to forget, and so Heidi believed that she was one of the first women there, oblivious to the many female artists and animators who had once trodden the same halls and occupied the same rooms. She was, however, about to enter a world her predecessors had never seen. On a Friday afternoon, she got in an elevator that had long been barred to women and took it to the top floor and the forbidden Penthouse Club.

Women were being permitted entry because of a momentous occasion — employees were celebrating the fortieth anniversary at the studio of animator Milt Kahl, one of Walt's Nine Old Men. As Heidi's eyes roamed around the exclusive club where Walt and his favorite animators had spent countless hours, she couldn't help but feel jealous. Female animators had no such retreat. The club was restricted to male executives, senior animators, and select assistant animators. It seemed unfair that no matter how many hours she worked or how high she rose in the ranks, she'd never gain admittance. Certainly the old tearoom in the Ink and Paint building was no substitute for all the amenities of the club, which still offered massages, haircuts, and an exclusive restaurant.

But Heidi had an advantage that previous generations of women working in animation had not: the new Equal Employment Opportunity Commission (EEOC). When Congress passed the Civil Rights Act of 1964, it barred discrimination based on race, color, religion, national origin, or gender. Unfortunately, at first the legislation was toothless, lacking a way to enforce it. It was not until the 1970s, when Congress passed a series of laws giving the EEOC the ability to sue employers, that businesses felt any pressure to comply with the law. Subsequent protections for female employees were even further delayed. It wasn't until 1986 that the Supreme Court judged that women should be protected from a "hostile or abusive work environment."

Heidi and another female trainee decided to make an official complaint to the National Organization for Women, which had been founded in 1966. The two were hoping the studio would open up the Penthouse to women or, alternatively, create a similar space for its female employees. Instead, the club was closed down, the private elevator boarded up, and resentment against female animators gained new ammunition.

Heidi had little recourse against other, more distressing behavior at the studio. Outside the doors of her animation wing was a counter where the animators would drop off their pencil drawings, which would then be transferred to the camera operators. Since assistant animators produced dozens of drawings a day, they spent considerable time at the counter. Yet Heidi and her female colleagues wished they didn't have to.

Hustler, the pornographic magazine published by Larry Flynt, had just hit the market in 1974 and its depictions of women were known, even when compared to *Playboy* and *Penthouse,* to be particularly explicit and demeaning to women. Heidi was shocked to find all three walls behind the counter plastered in pages ripped from the magazine.

The culture of pranks around the studio had not diminished with time, and as Heidi looked at the revolting images before her, she had an idea. Another magazine had recently entered the scene: *Playgirl.* Working late hours when the men who acted as messengers at the counter had left for the day, Heidi began to sneak pictures of nude men in with the women. Days passed and no one seemed to notice the change. Then one of the men caught sight of a picture and pointed it out. The man working at the counter had a fit, cursing at the image as he tore it off the wall. In retaliation, Heidi decided she had better paste up more pictures, preferably higher up, where it was harder to rip them down. The antics saved her sanity, and in 1978 Heidi finally attained the position she'd yearned for. She was no longer an assistant but a full animator. The legacy of the women who had come before her, however, remained unappreciated.

Fresh CalArts graduates kept streaming through the front doors of the studio as they had for generations. Yet there was something different about the new group of inbetween-ers that started after Heidi was promoted in the late 1970s. For some reason, they kept going down to the morgue.

The morgue still comprised a complex of rooms in the belly of the studio, beneath the old Ink and Paint building, connected by long concrete tunnels with pipes hanging from the low ceilings. It was where all the materials previously used for films, includ-ing research, scripts, and concept art, were housed. But it was not a place for art to die. Nor was it yet organized as a formal research library with museum-quality stan-dards, as it would be in the late 1980s. Instead, it served as a source of inspiration, a place where studio employees could bor-row previous artwork for months and let the style of past greats influence their pres-ent work. The historical significance of the material the morgue housed was just start-ing to be recognized. For the new genera-tion of artists, the ability to peruse the work of their heroes, the animation greats they had learned about in art school, was intoxicating.

Michael Giaimo was a recent graduate of CalArts who, along with his contemporaries, had just discovered the wonders contained in the morgue. The 1970s had seen just four fully animated films from the studio: *The Aristocats* (1970), *Robin Hood* (1973), *The Many Adventures of Winnie the Pooh,* and *The Rescuers* (both 1977). Michael was working as an assistant animator on *The Black Cauldron,* a dark piece of animation loosely based on a series of fantasy novels published in the 1960s by Lloyd Alexander.

As Michael and some of his young colleagues were searching for hidden treasures one afternoon, they came across an old cardboard box. When they opened its lid, they were stunned at its contents. The box was filled with the most astounding concept art in colors and incorporating a style completely unlike any other at the studio. The pieces were signed with the name Mary Blair.

Michael had heard of Mary Blair, of course, but he'd never realized the potency of her art. He asked a few of the senior animators what they knew about her, but the group no longer included those who'd worked alongside her. The Nine Old Men

461

were now truly old and mostly retired. The current senior animators were a kind of second-string lineup, and they swiftly brushed Mary's talents aside. They knew little of the female artist and didn't care to know more.

The bold art directors who had reigned during Walt's lifetime were gone, and the studio had moved to a more uniform style, each film looking much like the last. Yet as Michael viewed Mary's art, he felt he was receiving a graduate education in design. Clutching the box in his arms, he decided that he would live with Mary Blair's art as long as possible. He pinned her paintings up to a storyboard, a practice almost as old as the studio itself, and immersed himself in the scenes of joy and melancholy before him.

CHAPTER 17
PART OF YOUR WORLD

Retta gazed into Mary's face and saw evidence of the passage of time. It was 1978 and they were both now in their sixties, but if she looked past the wrinkles that pinched the corners of Mary's eyes, she still recognized the young woman she had once been. She was staying at Mary's house for the weekend, and the two were reminiscing about living together thirty years earlier when they had been immersed in their work at the studio; Retta had been single, and Mary's husband had been thousands of miles away.

They laughed at the reversal of fortune that the movies they had crafted at the Walt Disney Studios were experiencing. The company, now run by Walt's son-in-law Ron Miller, had started rereleasing features they had created in the 1940s and 1950s. Those films, such as *Pinocchio, Bambi, Dumbo, Fantasia, Alice in Wonderland,* and *Lady and the Tramp,* once considered financial flops, were now raking in millions at the box office.

As they gleefully contemplated the twist of fate that had brought their work back to movie theaters, Lee sat sociably with them. He was sober now. After getting out of jail, he had joined Alcoholics Anonymous. While his relationship with Mary had mellowed, and he no longer frequently erupted in violence, the repeated abuse had taken its toll on her.

Retta spent the night with her friend, and she was outwardly silly and affectionate, but privately she felt concerned. Mary appeared weaker than Retta remembered her. Retta saw reflections of her own anguish as the two drained their glasses and indulged in blissful nostalgia. The past decades had brought them both unexpected hardships.

Like Mary, Retta had been drowning her disappointments. Every day she'd drink wine at the kitchen table and try to feel like herself again. Her marriage had deteriorated and then collapsed; her husband left her as soon as their two boys were out of high school. She had lost herself these past few years, and she realized that she wanted to reconnect with the artist she had been most of her life.

With this new impetus, Retta began seeking a job in animation. She was living in Northern California and so began informing her connections in the Bay Area that she was looking for work. In 1980 she received a call from Martin Rosen, head of Nepenthe Productions in San Francisco. During the phone interview he told her that he could hire her only as an assistant animator. Retta was not deterred by the junior nature of the position. She knew from experience that she could work her way up. On her first day, she walked into the animation studio with the confidence that comes only from experience. She was sixty-five and it had been years since she'd sat at an animator's desk, but she was ready to feel the paper under her pencil again.

Rosen had already made the animated film *Watership Down,* based on the novel by Richard Adams and released to critical acclaim in 1978. He was now making *The Plague Dogs,* based on the 1977 novel by the same author that follows the lives of two dogs as they escape the perilous world of animal research in Great Britain. It was an ideal project for Retta, given her vast experience animating dogs for *Bambi* decades earlier.

Working alongside Retta was an animator

who'd just been fired from the Walt Disney Studios. Brad Bird (who would later be known for his work as a writer and director on hit films such as *The Incredibles* and *Ratatouille*), was then in his early twenties, a graduate of CalArts who was happy to be employed as an animator after his short, tumultuous career in Burbank. Bird had spent a few years at the Walt Disney Studios, but he was disappointed by the skill of the animators he worked alongside. He saw the animation studio as being in decline, devoid of the artistic talent that had once distinguished it. "These bunglers tended to play everything safe, which is a bore," he would later say of the experience. By contrast, he cherished working with Milt Kahl, one of Walt's Nine Old Men, whom Bird described as "incredibly exacting."

Not all the young people were aware of Retta's history at the Walt Disney Studios, but they were soon impressed with her work. Her lines were clean and sharp, the result of years of practice. Her work ethic was from an earlier era. She came in early, stayed focused at her desk, and created stacks of completed drawings at a rapid pace. Finally, she was back where she belonged.

As Retta found success in Northern California, Ed Catmull was moving to the region. Word of his dexterity in computer graphics had made an impression on a young director named George Lucas. His movie *Star Wars: Episode IV — A New Hope* opened in 1977 and stunned audiences with its story of adventure and heroism as well as its special effects, makeup, and costumes. Yet many of the Star Wars trilogy's stunning visual effects belonged to an earlier era. The team adapted stop-motion animation, where objects are photographed frame by frame as they are moved ever so slightly to create the illusion of motion. With this technique, first used in film in the late 1800s, Lucas's team made plastic models of alien monsters battling in a game of holographic chess between Chewbacca and R2-D2 aboard the *Millennium Falcon.* Similarly, the films relied on cel animation and optical printers to create mind-bending scenes, superimposing a light-saber fight between the villain Darth Vader and hero Luke Skywalker onto a perilous catwalk high over Cloud City. To craft the legendary duel, Lucas used the same sodium-vapor process Walt Disney

Studios had pioneered a decade earlier to make Mary Poppins fly. Walt's technology was on display throughout the Star Wars trilogy, including the use of a quad optical printer. The device incorporated four projection heads, allowing the filmmakers to assemble multiple shots at one time and thereby send TIE fighters careening through the galaxy.

In 1979, Lucas hired Catmull to lead the Lucasfilm computer division. What Catmull offered Lucas was an opportunity for the company to forge its own path in animation and special effects. It was a tantalizing concept, but the reality was complicated. Catmull was developing software and technologies that created complex three-dimensional images. One of the first projects his group worked on was *Star Trek II: The Wrath of Khan,* due to be released in 1983. They were creating a scene where a dead planet is brought back to life through the use of a "genesis device." The scene of rapid terraforming, where the dead gray surface of a planet is set ablaze and then becomes Earthlike, was a remarkable achievement in computer graphics. Yet Catmull couldn't get the quality he wanted — Lucasfilm computers simply didn't have the muscle. Catmull realized he needed to focus on the hardware before he did anything else. If he was going to be able to produce graphics with higher resolution, he needed more computational power.

Lucasfilm, however, was no longer the right home for Catmull's ambitions. The company was experiencing financial stress and could no longer pour money into developing computers. Members of the computer division decided that their best option was to stay together and form their own enterprise. Pursuing this goal, in 1986 Catmull and his team formed Pixar, with Steve Jobs, recently ousted from Apple, as a majority investor.

They weren't the only ones changing names; in Burbank, corporate restructuring had also caused a shift. The group was now the Walt Disney Company, with Walt Disney Feature Animation becoming a subsidiary of their film division, the Walt Disney Studios. In the midst of this reorganization, the company had, once again, declined to invest in Catmull's company and its enticing new technology.

No matter the name, the Walt Disney Company was in turmoil. In 1984, Walt's nephew Roy E. Disney had left the board of directors in frustration over the studio's neglect of its film division. In the eighteen years since Walt had died, none of the films released by the studio had earned as much critical acclaim or financial success as those produced prior to 1966. Many of the old-timers, including the Nine Old Men, had retired. With the dearth of talent and lack of creative freedom, droves of younger animators were also leaving the studio. This included Heidi Guedel, who, along with eleven others, left to start a new animation company headed by animator Don Bluth.

Roy E. Disney, who believed, much like his uncle Walt, that animation was the heart of the business, launched a campaign to rescue it. In a dramatic move, he rejoined the board of directors, pushed out Ron Miller, Walt's son-in-law and the current president and CEO, and brought in Michael Eisner to take charge of the operation. Eisner, coming from his position as CEO of Paramount Pictures, brought Jeffrey Katzenberg with him as chairman to reinvigorate the company's motion pictures.

In 1985, *The Black Cauldron* lost twenty-one million dollars, and Eisner was forced to consider shutting down the animation department altogether. It was an undeniable low point, akin to the desperation felt after 1959's *Sleeping Beauty*. It was clear that a major cultural shift in the company had to occur in order for animation to survive. Roy E. Disney, as the new chairman of feature animation, was ready to roll the dice and invest in innovation. For the first time in decades, a man named Disney was pushing the company to take significant risk in both artistry and technology.

Even as Roy E. Disney was plotting new investments, Eisner was looking for bold cost-cutting measures. While he decided not to shutter the animation department completely, he took away its home. The building itself was considered precious, but only because it attracted live-action filmmakers who preferred to work on the studio lot. The rooms and offices where ideas had blossomed were swept clean, and the animation department — now consisting of only one hundred and fifty artists — moved off the lot to a set of trailers surrounding an old warehouse on Flower Street in Glendale, a town four miles from Burbank. The humble setting was reminiscent of the conditions on Hyperion Avenue where Walt and his artists had started out sixty years earlier.

Meanwhile, the new studio executives were examining Pixar with fresh eyes. With Pixar's sustained focus on hardware, the company's first product was a computer. It looked much like other desk-size personal computers of the age: a gray box that held the computer's hardware, a display monitor, and a keyboard. Unlike its competitors, however, the Pixar Image Computer had an unusually powerful processing speed and the capability to produce very high-resolution images. Although advanced for its time, its price tag of $135,000 meant that it did not sell particularly well. In 1986, Pixar's first customer was Walt Disney Feature Animation. Next, Pixar would sell the product to government agencies and research labs, yet by 1988, it had sold only a little over a hundred of the machines. IBM was offering personal computers at $1,565, a more modest price point, and it was selling approximately a computer a minute. For Pixar, it was not a promising beginning.

Ellen Woodbury grew up disliking Disney movies; she found them overly sentimental. She preferred Warner Brothers cartoons, which matched her own silly sense of humor. Despite this, when she was a high school student in Corning, New York, and her best friend begged her to come see the 1972 reissue of *The Sword in the Stone,* Ellen reluctantly agreed to go. She had just finished T. H. White's tetralogy *The Once and Future King* on which the movie was loosely based, and she didn't have high expectations. The film, originally released to poor reviews and little profit, tells the story of a young King Arthur's rise to power. Although she expected little, Ellen was stunned by what she witnessed on-screen. It was overwhelming to consider that artists had hand-drawn all the beautiful scenes before her.

Attending college at Syracuse University, Ellen had limited opportunity to study animation, and so she devised her own independent program. She read as many books about animation as she could find, including *The Illusion of Life,* published in 1981 by two of Walt's Nine Old Men, Frank Thomas and Ollie Johnston. In her zeal for the subject, she wrote to Frank Thomas, and he was kind enough to reply encouragingly. She treasured the letters from the famed animator and decided to follow in his footsteps — first art school and then on to Walt Disney Feature Animation.

Ellen earned her MFA in experimental animation at CalArts, a program that allowed students to pursue innovative techniques that pushed the boundaries of current animation practice. Yet when Ellen started at the Walt Disney Studios in 1985, her work seemed stuck in time. She was an assistant animator, taking the rough sketches of the senior animators and tracing over them with her own sharp, elegant lines. In doing so, she was connected to the generations of animators who had come before her at the studio. But that thread of hand-drawn tradition, as strong as it seemed to Ellen, was about to be broken.

In 1986 the Pixar Image Computer entered the studio along with new software exclusive to the Disney group. The software was called the Computer Animation Production System, or CAPS. Integral to its assimilation was Tina Price, an employee who had started as an inbetweener and was now the head of the newly formed computer animation department. The department was so new that no one had any idea what to call it. People referred to it simply as "Tina's department."

In Tina's department, the CAPS software acted like a computerized Ink and Paint unit. Using the layers familiar to traditional animators, with the background and foreground separated, an artist wielded a computer mouse to form the lines and colors once made with india ink and gouache paint in an entirely digital format. Movement of the camera that once required a giant fifteen-foot crane could now be programmed using the "digital multiplane camera feature." It was not the computer graphics revolution that Catmull had been dreaming of, as the resulting two-dimensional scenes still could not compare to the illusion of depth in Catmull's 1972 video of his hand, but it was well suited to the more modest needs of the Walt Disney Company.

The program was so intuitive that traditional cel animators at Disney, like Ellen, were able to start using it immediately. Yet to those who had no computer experience, truly understanding the software and operating the computer hardware represented a challenge. For many of the artists, even using a computer mouse for the first time was awkward and frustrating. Ellen could see how the computers were changing the studio and so she organized classes for the animators at the new Disney computer lab. When the sessions began, Ellen was so enthusiastic that she helped design a training program specifically for newcomers.

Ellen was promoted to animator while working on their next feature, *The Little Mermaid*. The film was the studio's first princess movie in thirty years. Not since *Sleeping Beauty* had a fairy tale with a female lead captivated the Disney team's attention. It was part of a renewed vision for the animation department ushered in by Roy E. Disney, Eisner, and Katzenberg. After decades of languishing both artistically and technologically, the studio was about to enter what many would later call its renaissance era.

For the first time since Walt's death, significant money and resources were put into an animated feature. The film's budget initially was forty million dollars, considerably higher than any of the other four animated films made by the studio in the 1980s: *The Fox and the Hound, The Black Cauldron, The Great Mouse Detective,* and *Oliver and Company.* However, with the added cost of the new CAPS, the film seemed likely to outstrip that already high price tag.

In addition to money and technology, the studio was also bringing back the central place of music. While films made during Walt's lifetime frequently relied on the soundtrack to play an integral role in storytelling, from "Whistle While You Work" in *Snow White* to "A Spoonful of Sugar" in *Mary Poppins,* music had played a lesser role in recent years. Some films, such as *The Great Mouse Detective,* had been released without any soundtrack at all.

Now Jeffrey Katzenberg, the new chairman of the studio, hired Alan Menken and Howard Ashman to write the score and lyrics, respectively. The duo had worked on numerous musicals together, including the off-Broadway play *Little Shop of Horrors,* later adapted into a 1986 film. While they had never written a movie score, they were inspired by their experiences in theater and intent on creating a work worthy to stand beside the soundtracks of classic Walt Disney films they remembered from their own childhoods, particularly *Pinocchio* and *Peter Pan.*

Menken and Ashman embedded themselves in the animation department in its new off-lot location and sat in on all the script discussions in the story department. These meetings had become vibrant again, a return to the collaborative environment that had pervaded the studio in prior decades.

In order to introduce his storytelling style to the group, one afternoon Ashman gathered the entire animation staff into the small theater in the warehouse on Flower Street. It was a moment as pivotal as when Walt collected his employees in the auditorium of the Hyperion studio in 1934 and acted out his vision for *Snow White.* Sitting on the stage in front of the full staff of artists, Ashman described both the evolution of the American musical and the progression of Walt Disney films. "It's called the girl's 'I want' song," Ashman explained when he discussed a key tenet of both American musicals and the classic animated features. "You're not going to miss what the film's about. That's the central issue of the entire film. By having her sing it, it makes that point indelible." By connecting musicals such as *My Fair Lady* with animation classics such as *Snow White,* he clearly laid out a case for merging the storytelling mediums.

The Little Mermaid had initially been developed back in the 1940s, when Sylvia Holland and Ethel Kulsar wrote treatments and scripts for the Hans Christian Andersen story. It was their extensive work, brought up from the morgue, that some of the team were now reviewing.

In many ways the story department of Walt Disney Feature Animation in 1987 was not very different from its counterpart in 1940. The group still hand-sketched drawings and pinned them up on corkboards with pushpins. They still stood up in front of one another and acted out the scenes, pointing at each drawing as they sang and sometimes danced. They still criticized one another, often harshly, in an effort to improve the story. But a component was missing — there were almost no women. The story department of nearly fifty years earlier had benefited from the brains of Bianca Majolie, Grace Huntington, Mary Blair, Retta Scott, Mary Goodrich, and Ethel Kulsar, among others, but in 1987, one woman stood alone. Her name was Brenda Chapman.

Brenda grew up in rural Illinois, the youngest of five children. Her brothers and sisters were all much older; her closest sibling was eight years her senior. Brenda sometimes felt like an only child growing up in the middle of her farming community. There wasn't much to do — the nearest movie theater was ten miles away — and so from an early age, Brenda loved to read and draw. Her family was supportive, and after studying art at Lincoln College in Illinois, she moved to California to attend CalArts.

Brenda graduated in May 1987 and applied to Walt Disney Feature Animation. The man interviewing her was not enthusiastic about her future at the studio, telling her, "If you don't work out after six weeks we'll just hire another trainee." He grudgingly explained that the studio's new executive leadership, which included Eisner and Katzenberg, wanted more women hired in animation, particularly in the story department.

Brenda was embarrassed by the tenuous nature of her employment and was determined to prove her capacity for hard work. As she sorted through scenes created in the 1940s of a glittering undersea palace, she was inspired by the work of the female pioneers who preceded her, although their names had already faded from the studio's consciousness.

Much of what the story and animation departments were producing now was new. The story department played with different ideas for the villain of the film, Ursula the sea witch. In one sketch they made her into a manta ray with sharp facial features, in another she was a lionfish, and in yet another, she was an attractive, albeit evil, swordfish. But it was a sketch from animator Rob Minkoff that caught Ashman's eye. This Ursula wore jewelry and heavy makeup and had a stout frame. She looked familiar to Ashman; he declared that she was the spitting image of Divine, the legendary drag queen known for her performances in the John Waters movies *Pink Flamingos* and *Hairspray.* Ashman, a gay Jewish man, felt a connection with Divine, who'd grown up in the same neighborhood in Baltimore as himself. The staff decided to embrace the inspiration and created an Ursula with the body of a squid who not only resembled Divine superficially but swung her hips and sang like her too.

The film perfectly embodied the transformation occurring in animation as it merged the old with the new. It was the first Disney film to use computer software and the last to use the multiplane camera, the 1937 technology that had been so critical to the company's success.

Working on *The Little Mermaid,* Ellen Woodbury became skilled at blending colors and generating shadows, rendering the shade created by objects and animals in a way that seemed impossibly real. Unlike hand-drawing, computer animation could depict transparency, allowing layers and colors to blend together in a style completely new to the studio. As much as she enjoyed seeing what the computer program could do, Ellen was intensely frustrated by the two-and-a-half-second lag time between her movement of the mouse and the cursor's movement on-screen. It seemed that the computer should make their work go faster, but the opposite was often true. When she attended the Disney life-drawing class during her lunch hour — the same class that Bianca, Retta, Sylvia, and Mary had enjoyed decades earlier — she reveled in the ease of putting pencil to paper again.

The animators played with CAPS during various sequences of the movie, but it was the second-to-last scene of *The Little Mermaid* that put the software to its critical test. As Ariel and Prince Eric sail away after their wedding, a crowd of merpeople wave goodbye and a rainbow appears on the horizon. The scene created by CAPS generated a rainbow that was bright and yet had just the right level of transparency. No hand-drawing could have created such perfect translucency; it blended into the sky almost like the real thing. It was clear that computer animation was superior. Xerox and cel animation were done for.

The studio did not expect the movie to do particularly well at the box office despite the new technology and catchy score. "It's a girl's film," said Jeffrey Katzenberg to the directors, perhaps forgetting the power of princess movies in the studio's history. As the movie neared completion, however, his attitude shifted. It was clear to all that they had something special here.

When the film opened on November 17,

1989, the critics were ebullient, with *Variety* specifically praising the character Ursula, whom the reviewer called "a visual feast." Roger Ebert, then a film critic for the *Chicago Sun-Times,* favored Ariel, whom he described as "a fully realized female character." The film would go on to win two Academy Awards: Best Original Song ("Under the Sea") and Best Score. In addition to winning awards, the movie was a hit at the box office, pulling in $84.4 million in its first run.

It was a complete turnaround for animation at the studio. With their new success, the executives decided to expand the department and opened Walt Disney Feature Animation Florida, a small group of forty artists digging into new story lines. While the profits made from *The Little Mermaid* had clear consequences for the future of animation and technology at the studio, the fate of female characters was far murkier.

"Belle is not baking a cake!" Linda Woolverton yelled during a story meeting about the studio's next feature, *Beauty and the Beast.* Woolverton was on her way to becoming the studio's first credited female screenwriter, and she was increasingly frustrated with many of the male writers she worked with. She stared disbelievingly at the story-boards in front of her. In her script she had written a scene where Belle puts pushpins in a map to signify all the areas of the world she wants to explore. The writers adapting her scene into storyboards had changed the setting and action, placing Belle in a kitchen decorating a cake. It was the kind of editorial change that made Linda lean over and literally bang her head on the wooden table before her in exasperation.

Woolverton had grown up just an hour outside Disneyland, in Long Beach, California. She'd earned a bachelor of fine arts in theater in 1973 and then a master's in children's theater. By the 1980s she was working as a writer on children's television shows such as *My Little Pony* and simultaneously writing young adult novels. In 1987 she took a copy of her second novel, *Running with the Wind,* and walked into Walt Disney Feature Animation at its modest quarters on Flower Street. There were, to her surprise, no guards or gates or anything to stop her. When she reached the front desk, she handed the book to the receptionist and said, "Maybe someone here wants to read this."

It turns out someone did. Shortly afterward, Woolverton was hired by the story department. There she caught the attention of Jeffrey Katzenberg, who promoted her to be one of the lead writers for *Beauty and the Beast.* "They didn't know what they were dealing with when they brought me on," she later said, referring to her ambition to push boundaries and create female characters that didn't need to be saved. Woolverton was working closely with Menken and Ashman, who had become instant legends at the studio for their roles in *The Little Mermaid.* Roy E. Disney was so impressed by Ashman's talent that he called the lyricist "another Walt."

Ashman, too, had a vision for the future of animation at the studio. In 1988, before *The Little Mermaid* was even released, he proposed a new feature project. The movie treatment he wrote was *Aladdin,* based on "Aladdin and the Magic Lamp" from *One Thousand and One Nights,* a collection of Middle Eastern folk stories compiled by a European translator in the eighteenth century. As a teenager, Ashman had played the role of Aladdin in a production at a community theater. With this inspiration, his story treatment stayed close to the original tale about a boy who finds a magic oil lamp containing a genie who can grant wishes. Ashman began working in earnest on the project, writing three songs with Menken and drawing concept art, but the studio soon shelved it. This was a disappointment, but the team hoped it might resurface in the future. However, even without *Aladdin,* there was plenty to keep Ashman and Menken busy. Katzenberg urgently needed their help on the studio's foundering next feature.

Beauty and the Beast, like so many other projects, was initiated during the studio's creative overflow of the 1940s. This time, however, no story treatments or concept art remained to guide the later artists, so they turned to the original text, "La Belle et la Bête," the 1740 French fairy tale. The adaptation at the studio was not going well. In 1989, Katzenberg scrapped their entire script and storyboards, feeling that the film required an entirely new direction. He decided to make it a musical and knew that he needed the Ashman/Menken magic.

Unfortunately, Howard Ashman was ill. In 1988, while working on *The Little Mermaid,* he had been diagnosed with HIV. It would be seven more years before highly active antiretroviral therapy was developed, drug cocktails that would save the lives of millions living with the virus. While the drug AZT had been approved in 1987, the virus was becoming resistant to it. Patients with

HIV had very few options.

When Ashman's immune system weakened critically and his illness progressed to AIDS, the lyricist became unable to travel to the West Coast, so Woolverton, the other writers and animators, and even some executives traveled to Ashman's home in Fishkill, New York, frequently staying at the town's Residence Inn. They also spent time in New York City, where Woolverton and Ashman slowly strolled the streets as they discussed ideas.

Woolverton had invented an endearing character, a little teacup named Chip, who added humor and sweetness to the plot. She was also holding fast to her image of Belle — she wouldn't let them turn the heroine into a baker. The story department agreed to make Belle a voracious reader, and to address concerns among the writers that the activity was too slow-paced, they had Belle walk around town while keeping her nose in her book.

Woolverton did have one ally in the story department who embraced her vision for Belle wholeheartedly. Brenda Chapman, fresh from *The Little Mermaid,* was now working on *Beauty and the Beast.* As they created storyboards for one scene in which Belle cleans and bandages the Beast's paw and he growls menacingly at her in pain, Brenda cringed at Belle's passive dialogue. *If someone yells at me when I'm trying to help them,* Brenda thought, *I would yell back at them.* She decided to bring out Belle's anger and had her shout at the Beast, "If you'd hold still, it wouldn't hurt as much!" It was the first time a Disney princess had ever yelled at her prince.

For his part, Ashman was infusing his personal experiences into the songs that would help tell Belle's story. Nowhere is this more apparent than in "Kill the Beast," which is sung when the villagers decide to arm themselves and destroy the creature whose hope of breaking the curse is withering with each petal that falls from an enchanted rose. Ashman poured his hatred for the disease and the stigma surrounding it into the lyrics. "We don't like what we don't understand and in fact it scares us," the villain Gaston sings. The words could just as easily apply to AIDS and the fear it caused in the 1980s and 1990s, a time when many Americans were afraid to even hug people infected with the virus. AIDS had already stolen the lives of many of Ashman's friends, and now he was entering the final stages of the disease himself.

At St. Vincent's Hospital in New York

City, a group of animators came to visit Ashman. He weighed eighty pounds and was suffering from AIDS-related dementia. He could no longer see and could barely speak above a whisper. He was just forty years old.

The animators told Ashman that the first screening for *Beauty and the Beast* had been a success. It was just the beginning of the near universal acclaim the movie would receive, with Janet Maslin of the *New York Times* describing Ashman in her glowing review as "an outstandingly nimble lyricist." Ashman would never have the opportunity to read her words. He died eight months before the film's release, one of 29,850 people in the United States to succumb to AIDS in 1991. When the screen fades to black at the end of *Beauty and the Beast,* these words appear: *To our friend Howard, who gave a mermaid her voice and a beast his soul, we will be forever grateful. Howard Ashman 1950–1991.*

Just one month after Ashman's death, Katzenberg resurrected the lyricist's work on *Aladdin.* Katzenberg had decided to release the film in a mere twenty months, and so the script needed a speedy rewrite. Linda Woolverton pitched in, making some story additions based on the 1940 film *The Thief of Bagdad* and including a villain named Jafar.

Some elements didn't need to change. Menken and Ashman had written multiple songs for the film, and three made the final cut: "Arabian Nights," "Friend Like Me," and "Prince Ali." But they still needed a few more songs. Katzenberg brought in Tim Rice, the celebrated English lyricist, to work with Menken in completing the score. *Aladdin* was released on November 25, 1992. The film did exceptionally well financially, becoming one of the top-grossing films of the year and pulling in over two hundred million dollars at the box office. The critical reaction to the movie was also highly favorable, with many reviewers mentioning Robin Williams's exceptional performance as the genie.

Not long after the film's release, however, part of the soundtrack was criticized as racist, specifically lyrics in the Menken/Ashman song "Arabian Nights": "Where they cut off your ear / if they don't like your face. / It's barbaric, but hey, it's home." In response to criticism from the Los Angeles chapter of the American-Arab Anti-Discrimination Committee, the studio changed the line in 1993 to "Where it's flat and immense / and the heat is intense. / It's barbaric, but hey, it's home."

With their recent string of hit movies, the team at Walt Disney Feature Animation began gearing up for their next project, originally called *King of the Jungle* but now titled *The Lion King.* Ellen Woodbury had played a key role in the studio's past four films, working as a character animator for both *The Little Mermaid* and the following year's *The Rescuers Down Under* as well as animating Belle's father, Maurice, in *Beauty and the Beast* and the monkey Abu in *Aladdin.* Now she was ready for her next challenge.

So was Brenda Chapman. Just four years after she was told she was being hired on a six-week trial basis, she was now in a momentous position. Roger Allers, director of their next feature, asked if she wanted to be head of the story department. It was a job that no woman had ever previously held. Brenda hesitated — she wasn't certain that she wanted the position, though it wasn't for lack of affection for the department. Unlike Bianca, who'd experienced exclusion as the only female story artist, Brenda felt listened to among her male coworkers and she cherished the creative freedom their group was afforded. No one was violently breaking down her door. In fact, they worked comfortably together creating dialogue and storyboards, with one of the men occasionally leaning over and saying, "Hey, do you realize you're the only woman in the room?" Brenda would shrug and they would all laugh.

Still, Brenda knew the kind of movies she wanted to make: fairy tales with strong female characters. She had hoped their next film would be a retelling of Tchaikovsky's 1877 ballet *Swan Lake.* It was the sort of project that the women of Walt Disney's past, particularly Bianca and Sylvia, would have drooled over. Unfortunately, this film was stuck in "development hell," the period of prolonged limbo before a project went into production. The studio executives decided to move ahead with *The Lion King.* The plot was inspired by Shakespeare's *Hamlet,* the story of an uncle's betrayal and a young prince's pursuit of revenge and the throne that is rightfully his. The studio's version was set in the African savanna with lions as the main characters.

Brenda had no affection for talking animals, but she knew that she couldn't say no to the job. She might never get this chance again. The only woman in the story department was now running the show. She wouldn't be alone for long. As had happened so many years earlier, the promotion of one woman was poised to draw in many others.

There were women outside the story department as well. In the animation department, 37 percent of the staff working on the film were now women. Yet most of these female employees were working as assistant animators. For *The Lion King,* Ellen was initially offered the job of animating Sarabi, mother of the lion cub Simba. It was a coveted position and many animators would have jumped at the opportunity to completely shape a critical character in the film. However, Ellen wasn't so sure. She didn't have any children herself and didn't particularly want any. As she considered the character, she felt she would have difficulty connecting with the motivations of a mother. She turned it down.

The decision was a tough one, especially since she didn't know if she'd be offered another character. As the weeks passed, she wondered if she'd made the right call. Then the animation director offered her the bird Zazu, a red-billed hornbill and adviser to the king. She was delighted. Here was a character she could do justice to. Ellen was soon consumed with researching hornbills, understanding their anatomy, their behavior, and how they fly through the sky. She spent hours researching Rowan Atkinson, the voice actor for the character. She watched every episode of *Mr. Bean* and *Black Adder* to get a sense of his acting style and mannerisms. The sassy character was starting to take shape.

Yet his form wouldn't really come together until she brought her hand-drawn sketches into CAPS. Only on the computer could she create the fluffy texture of Zazu's feathers, the airbrush-style color pattern of his beak, and the crisp blues of his body. When she saw the final creation on-screen, despite the maddening lag-time effect, the result was as satisfying as any hand-drawn animation she had ever done.

Something else could be found on-screen: Ellen's name. Unlike so many of the women before her, Ellen was properly credited. With her work in the 1980s and 1990s, she became the first credited supervising animator and character animator in the studio's history. Yet even with these stellar accomplishments, Ellen felt there were elements missing from her work.

The female characters the studio created, delightful as they were, were sometimes lacking in agency or personality. Ellen had

had trouble connecting with Ariel; she couldn't imagine choosing her for a friend. Perhaps some of the difficulty lay in the limitations of her dialogue. In *Snow White, Cinderella,* and *Sleeping Beauty,* roughly half the dialogue is spoken by female characters. In *The Little Mermaid,* featuring an often silenced albeit spunky Ariel, 68 percent of the dialogue is from male characters. In *Beauty and the Beast,* that number reaches 71 percent, and in *Aladdin* and *The Lion King,* it's an unbelievable 90 percent. Only the return of female writers in the story department would right this one-sidedness.

Rita Hsiao held the greeting card in her hands, an image of the character Mulan surrounded by soft, pink cherry blossoms, a radiant smile on her face, on its cover. It was a birthday card from her mother, and printed inside were the words *The greatest honor is having you for a daughter.* It was a line Rita had written for the film *Mulan,* released in 1998, and one that held personal meaning for her. She could hardly believe that her dialogue was in a greeting card that had been handed to her by her own mother.

The moment was precious to Rita, especially as her parents had not always been pleased with her choices. Rita grew up in Poughkeepsie, New York, the daughter of Chinese immigrants. Her parents were not often outwardly affectionate, although she knew they loved her. They pushed her to excel in school and made their expectations for her future clear. The area was a hub for

IBM, where Rita's father worked as an engineer, and it was obvious that this industry was the field they envisioned for their daughter.

With these sentiments in mind, Rita enrolled at the University of California, San Diego, where she majored in artificial intelligence, a subject that seemed to combine her parents' zeal for computers and her own interest in psychology. But the coursework did not captivate her, and she toiled through her classes for her family's sake while wishing she could pursue her own passions.

After graduation, she revealed to her mother and father that she wanted to become a screenwriter and announced that she'd taken a job answering phones at a television production company to get started in the field. Her parents' faces fell and they couldn't hide their fierce disappointment. Here was their daughter turning her back on a college education to take a low-level job. Her mother's first question was "Will you have health insurance?"

There might not have been benefits, but the position was just a springboard for Rita. She moved into television writing, working on the series *The Wonder Years* and then *All-American Girl,* an ABC sitcom starring Margaret Cho. After the series ended, she was hired at Walt Disney Feature Animation, where the group had already started on their next feature, *Mulan.*

The screenplay for *Mulan* is based on the Chinese legend of Hua Mulan. It is unknown when the poem "The Ballad of Mulan" was written or who its author was, although its first documentation can be traced back to the sixth-century Chinese text *Musical Records of Old and New.* Over the centuries the poem grew in popularity, being passed along as a folk song. It tells the story of a daughter who takes her elderly father's place when he is summoned to war, disguising her gender and bringing honor to her family. The short poem, less than a thousand words, is full of powerful imagery: "She gallops ten thousand miles for the war she has to honor . . . With wintry glow of icy hue, light glimmers on her armor."

Even with this beautiful language to guide them, the story department was struggling with Mulan's character. Robert San Souci, a children's book author with an avid interest in folktales, had originally brought the project to the studio. But the first story treatment for *Mulan* was wildly inconsistent with the poem. In the early adaptation, Mulan is an unhappy Chinese woman who leaves her native country after eloping with

498

a British prince. She is gloomy and despondent over her future and there is no sense of the purpose of her journey — the theme of rescuing her father and protecting her family's dignity is absent. Story meetings for the film were often disorganized. For the first time, pitches were made in both California and the animation studio in Florida. As ideas were passed back and forth across the country, it seemed the feature as a whole was losing its character. Missing was the brave warrior and in her place was a young woman tired of the traditions that trapped her and who required rescuing by a prince. The character the story team had created — self-serving and occasionally egotistical — was one the artists themselves sometimes didn't like.

Mulan was following on the heels of two recent female characters: Princess Jasmine from *Aladdin* and Pocahontas from the eponymous film. While Jasmine had raised the ire of some critics due to her Westernized appearance and harem-style clothing, the criticism of Pocahontas had little to do with her styling. She was the animation studio's first American Indian character and the first woman of color to be given a lead role in a Walt Disney animated feature.

Pocahontas got its start at a story meeting

in 1991 when Mike Gabriel, director on the studio's 1990 film *The Rescuers Down Under,* held up a picture of Tiger Lily, the American Indian woman in *Peter Pan.* Gabriel had drawn a buckskin dress over a copy of the drawing and above her head he'd written *Walt Disney's Pocahontas.* The idea had come to him as he researched historic figures for inspiration, including Annie Oakley and Buffalo Bill. His pitch was succinct; he described the plot as "an Indian princess who is torn between her father's wishes to destroy the English settlers and her wishes to help them." The project moved at an unheard-of pace; the pitch was accepted following the meeting and development began.

Part of the enthusiasm from executives was due to the fact that the film echoed themes from *Romeo and Juliet,* a project already under consideration at the studio. However, those in the story department were wary. This was the first time they were creating a character based on a real person, one whose real-life narrative did not resemble a fairy tale in the slightest.

Creatively, the film benefited from Michael Giaimo, who served as art director. Working with lyricist Stephen Schwartz and composer Alan Menken, he developed dramatic sequences for the musical pieces of the film. With his research in the studio's morgue, Giaimo was able to bring inspiration from the women of Disney's past. He sorted through concept art from discarded features depicting American Indians, including *On the Trail* and *The Song of Hiawatha,* both of which Retta had worked on in the 1940s. Most of all, though, he kept Mary Blair close, especially as he selected a palette that revealed emotional resonance for the song "Colors of the Wind." "I always carry her in my heart," he explained, "even though I've never met her."

Released in 1995 just as Rita was starting at the studio, *Pocahontas* told a fictionalized account of the meeting between the Powhatan woman and an Englishman named John Smith in seventeenth-century colonial Virginia. The film made a profit at the box office, but a relatively modest one, especially in comparison to *The Lion King,* released a year earlier, which earned $763 million in its first run and was ranked as the second-highest-grossing movie of all time. While many reviewers praised *Pocahontas* for its animation and story line promoting racial tolerance and environmental stewardship, others harshly criticized the work as "generic," and one reviewer called the main character "Poca-Barbie." The most damning criticism, however, did not come from a newspaper or magazine but from the Powhatan Renape Nation, whose leaders wrote in a statement, "The film distorts history beyond recognition . . . and perpetuates a dishonest and self-serving myth at the expense of the Powhatan Nation."

Certainly, no writer at Walt Disney Feature Animation could claim the screenplay was historically accurate. Rather than falling in love with John Smith, as the heroine does in the movie, the seventeen-year-old Pocahontas was taken prisoner by Jamestown colonists and forced to marry a man named John Rolfe. She died in London at twenty-one years old. The story department didn't feel these facts would be appropriate for children, and yet, in stripping away reality, they left the character Pocahontas bland, without a driving passion or personality.

With *Pocahontas* still under scrutiny and *Mulan* stumbling in the storyboards, Rita was brought into the story department. She immediately felt that she could draw on her own experiences as a young woman to make Mulan's character more sympathetic. She could relate to the conflict Mulan feels between wanting to forge her own identity and honoring her family. It was a perspective that the story department was sorely missing. Brenda Chapman had left the studio for DreamWorks Animation, a new venture formed by Jeffrey Katzenberg, Steven Spielberg, and David Geffen. Not a single woman of color had worked on *Pocahontas,* and of the more than fifteen people in the story department, there was only one female writer.

The *Mulan* team began spending long hours together both in and out of the studio, taking trips and hanging out on weekends and obsessively talking about their characters. While development was initiated on both coasts, this was the first film to be written and animated primarily in Florida. In many ways they were functioning at the level of intensity and passion that the story department had enjoyed decades previously. The Mulan who began to emerge was a young woman who considered what was expected of her and came to the realization that her life as a soldier was not only about rescuing her father but also about discovering her true self. When someone pitched the idea that the film should end with Mulan kissing her love interest, the team pushed back hard, not wanting the character to be reliant on the tropes that defined previous female protagonists. "Let's not end it on that," Rita said. She pointed out that Mulan had just saved China. "The kissing can come later."

While Rita and her team were creating an unprecedented Disney female protagonist in an innovative story line, the technology they were working with was woefully inferior to that of their competition. This was immediately clear to Rita as she watched *Toy Story,* the first feature-length computer-animated film, created by Pixar and released in 1995. Four years earlier, Peter Schneider, president of Walt Disney Feature Animation, had called Ed Catmull at Pixar and offered to finance and distribute Pixar's first three feature films. It was the first time the Walt Disney Company had ever done such a thing, and the proposal was a powerful compliment to the promise of both Pixar's technology and its artistic vision. While the offer was for three feature films, it was also contingent on the first being a success.

For Walt Disney Feature Animation, it was a gamble worth taking. The studio had a string of recent box-office triumphs but substandard technology. The group was still using CAPS, which was nearly ten years old and all but archaic, at least in comparison to the three-dimensional computer animation that was being developed at Pixar.

It had been a long road. Ed Catmull had been working doggedly toward this goal for two decades. His tireless engineers at Pixar had built the hardware for it and then refined the graphics language needed to execute it. In 1987 they called one of their programs RenderMan, a nod to a favorite product of the era, the Sony Walkman.

RenderMan was the latest product in a long line of invention. Its great-grandfather was Sketchpad, the 1963 software created by Catmull's graduate adviser that drew shapes on a computer screen, the first interactive animation. Next came the first 3-D computer graphics on film — Catmull's digitized human hand created in 1972 — and then CAPS, the digital ink-and-paint system.

Just as Catmull had been able to cover his animated hand with realistic-looking skin, RenderMan could create photorealistic images on top of either two-dimensional or three-dimensional models. Called "bump and texture mapping," the program could create green, scaly skin for Rex, the toy dinosaur in *Toy Story,* while giving Buzz Light-year, the figurine space ranger, a retractable transparent helmet. It worked like a pastry chef decorating a dessert: the artist still had to bake the cake, but the program would apply the frosting.

The frosting was proving a beautiful, if burdensome, confection. Pixar's animation projects had started out small, with animated shorts and commercials for other companies. Yet even these modest endeavors were challenging, as the time it took to render each scene was painfully long. Their computer hardware simply couldn't power through the animators' software needs. The group was so hampered by their lack of computing power that when creating a two-minute animated short called *Luxo Jr.,* about a playful desk lamp (which would later form the corporate logo), they couldn't even give the sequence a background. John Lasseter, a former animator at Walt Disney Feature Animation and an early member of Pixar, spent five days animating twelve and a half seconds of film using their computer system, twice as long as it would have taken him with hand-drawn animation. It wasn't until the early 1990s that processing speed, memory, and hard-drive space began to catch up with the animators' ambitions.

Now it was Walt Disney Feature Animation that was plugging along with decade-old Pixar Image Computers while computer engineers at Pixar were creating *Toy Story* on silicon graphics workstations and then rendering — generating the images automatically — in an area known as the sunroom because it contained racks of SPARCstation 20 computers that ran twenty-four hours a day. It took four years to make *Toy Story*. The seventy-seven-minute film needed no inkers, painters, inbetweeners, or traditional animators. It relied on a staff of just a hundred and ten people, including twenty-eight animators and thirty technical directors, and eight hundred thousand machine hours.

Toy Story was an immediate success, and not only because of the innovative technology it used. With a budget of only $30 million, the film earned $191.8 million in its first domestic run and was the top-grossing film of 1995, far outstripping *Pocahontas*. It was also nominated for three Academy Awards, including Best Original Screenplay, the first animated film to be so honored. The simplicity of the film's story resonated with audiences, who found a movie told from a toy's point of view refreshing. But in the tender connection between a boy and his toys that the film represented, there was one element missing: significant female characters.

The same could not be said for Walt

Disney Feature Animation. In 1998, the studio released *Mulan.* It was an exciting moment for Rita, who had played a crucial role in crafting the studio's first Chinese princess. Although the reviews were mostly positive, the film did suffer some criticism; *Time* magazine said, "Its lure is the image of girls kicking ass, being boylike. But how well does it prepare them to be adults in a complex world?" The film did moderately well at the box office, earning $120 million in its first domestic run. Yet Rita could see that the future of animation lay not at the studio in Florida but in the revolutionary technology at Pixar. She eventually moved to that company to begin work on *Toy Story 3.*

Filmmaker Brenda Chapman carried a business card that jokingly listed her title as "Token Female Pixar Story Artist" when she moved to that company in 2003. She explained the discrepancy between the two studios. "At the start of my career, I was the only woman in the story department at Disney, but at that time we were working on 'princess movies' with strong female leads, so at the time there didn't seem to be any need to strengthen other female roles . . . Most of the funny characters were guys," she said. "But now I'm at Pixar, and their films are very much for the boys. I don't think it's a conscious thing, I just think they're making films they want to see . . . Joe Ranft asked me to come up to Pixar to work on the female character in *Cars* to make her ring more 'true.' Pixar is something of a 'boys' club,' and little thought seems to have been given to female characters, even when it would have fit naturally. For example, why couldn't the Slinky or the T-Rex in *Toy Story* have been women?"

The differences Brenda noticed between Pixar and Walt Disney Feature Animation were about to shift considerably. In 2006, the company that had spurned Ed Catmull on numerous occasions finally bought Pixar, an acquisition worth $7.4 billion. The move was made possible by Roy E. Disney, who once again had decided to shake up leadership at the Walt Disney Company, resulting in Michael Eisner leaving and Robert Iger taking the helm as CEO in 2005. The animation studios, although now merged financially, were still separate creatively, with Pixar headquartered in Emeryville and the Walt Disney animation studios remaining in Glendale. Yet with the merging of the two companies, Brenda Chapman found herself once again under the roof of the House of Mouse, nearly twenty years after she first began at the Walt Disney Company.

The role of female characters in film had new importance for Brenda. She saw the princesses of the Disney renaissance era — Ariel, Belle, Pocahontas, and Jasmine — as stepping-stones between the heroines of the 1940s and 1950s and the future animated women she wanted to create. The women of Pixar's present — Boo in *Monsters, Inc.,* Dory in *Finding Nemo,* Colette in *Ratatouille,* the robot Eve in *WALL·E,* and Atta in *A Bug's Life* — were lovely but lacking in dimension. Brenda was now making movies not just for herself and her employers but also for her daughter.

Motherhood was a whirlwind of responsibility and fatigue, especially during the morning rush when Brenda was trying to drop her three-year-old, Emma, off at preschool before heading to work. It seemed her toddler was a mini-teenager, unwilling to eat breakfast, get dressed, and put on shoes no matter how insistently Brenda urged her. Every day, when Brenda arrived at Pixar, her head was still full of the morning's tussle, and she wondered what the years to come would look like. How would her relationship with Emma change when her daughter actually became a teenager? From these questions, a movie began to take shape.

The film was called *Brave* and told the story of Merida, a strong-willed Scottish teenager. Her appearance was different from that of previous princesses; she had a strong, athletic body and unruly red hair. Her story was different too. Here was a princess who did not rely on a single male character. Shockingly, unlike Snow White, Cinderella, Ariel, Belle, Jasmine, and Pocahontas, this female heroine had a mother who was still alive. In fact, the story focuses on the complex mother-daughter relationship and how a magical curse ultimately heals it. Brenda made up a new business card: "Token Female Director." Unfortunately, she did not last as long in the position as she should have. Before the film was released, Brenda left the studio due to creative differences. The experience was infuriating. "Sometimes women express an idea and are shot down," she explained, "only to have a man express essentially the same idea and have it broadly embraced. Until there is a sufficient number of women executives in high places, this will continue to happen."

Brave faced other challenges. Many forecasters did not believe the movie would do well. Part of their cynicism was based on the reception to the studio's last two princess movies, *The Princess and the Frog* (2009), which featured Tiana, the studio's first African American princess, and *Tangled* (2010), which told the tale of Rapunzel and was loosely based on the German fairy tale published by the Brothers Grimm in 1812. Both films did moderately well at the box office. *The Princess and the Frog* earned $104.4 million in its first domestic run, but it also drew reproach for its portrayal of race; as the *New York Times* noted, "We finally get a black princess and she spends the majority of her time on screen as a frog?"

Tangled fared somewhat better, receiving largely positive reviews and earning more than $200 million domestically in its first run. However, its success was dampened by its exorbitantly high production budget, a reported $260 million, making it the most expensive animated film of all time. Neither of the princess movies could compare with the string of Pixar hits that dominated the landscape, such as *Finding Nemo* (2003), which made $334 million in its first run, and *Cars* (2006), which brought in $244 million.

With these precedents, some in the movie industry were ready to write off *Brave* as a "pretty standard princess movie," likely to appeal only to female audiences. So it was a surprise when *Brave,* released on June 10, 2012, fiercely broke these boundaries. The film garnered largely glowing reviews and earned $237.3 million at the box office in its first domestic run.

At the eighty-fifth Academy Awards, *Brave* was considered an underdog in the category of Best Animated Feature Film, so it shocked many in the industry when it won the Oscar. Brenda was the first woman to ever win the award. When she took the stage, she was quick to thank her inspiration: "My wonderful, strong, beautiful daughter, Emma."

As Brenda stood proudly with her golden statue, a torrent of women artists were coming to Burbank from all over the world, poised to transform moviemaking. Their triumphs would rest on the shoulders of Bianca, Sylvia, Retta, Mary, and all the other women of Disney's golden age.

CHAPTER 19
FOR THE FIRST TIME
IN FOREVER

It was an ordinary afternoon in 2011 when Jennifer Lee received the phone call that would alter the course of her life. From the other side of the country, Phil Johnston, her good friend and former Columbia University classmate, asked, "Any chance you want to up and move to California . . . like . . . tomorrow?" Johnston, now a writer and producer at Walt Disney Feature Animation, wanted Lee to come out to Los Angeles for eight weeks to help on the studio's feature *Wreck-It Ralph.*

Johnston admired Jennifer as a brilliant writer, but she herself sometimes struggled to recognize her own self-worth. After graduating with a degree in English from the University of New Hampshire in 1992, she moved to New York City, where she found work as a graphic artist for Random House. It was just the beginning of her career in storytelling. At age thirty she sat staring at the Columbia Film School website. She was afraid to apply, yet she desperately wanted to attend. She summoned the courage and soon became one of the older students in the program. Seven years after graduation, she had won several awards and had two of her scripts optioned, but the projects lingered without the funding needed to bring them to fruition. Being hired as a cowriter on *Wreck-It Ralph* was exactly what her career needed next.

The movie is a love sonnet to the arcade, telling the story of a video-game villain who wants to become the good guy and the friendship he forms with a young girl who is being kept from pursuing her ambitions. Jennifer adored the "beautifully damaged, lovable, original characters," and she immersed herself in the project. The weeks passed quickly, and Phil asked Jennifer to stay a bit longer, just until the film wrapped up. While she was hanging around the studio, a new project caught her interest. The script and concept art she was looking at, however, needed a lot of work.

The story of "The Snow Queen," like so many projects before it, had long been in development at the studio. Mary Goodrich, the story artist who also worked on *Fantasia* and *Dumbo,* wrote the first treatment in

1938. The original tale, written in the 1840s by Hans Christian Andersen, was not an easy one to adapt, as it consisted of seven fragmented stories and lacked a clear narrative. Yet it was impossible not to be entranced by its repeated themes of the redemptive power of love and the triumph of vulnerable children over destructive adults. At the end of the story, the children escape the ice palace where they were being held captive, and the evocative last line reads "And they both sat there, grown up, yet children at heart; and it was summer, — warm, beautiful summer."

In 1939, the project went into development as part of a planned biography of Hans Christian Andersen that would combine live action with animation. Ultimately, the hybrid film got no traction, but it remained in the studio's consciousness. Andersen's fairy tales were a favorite among the story artists, who often retold and reimagined them as they developed feature-film ideas. Few would make it to production anytime soon, as Sylvia learned while passionately promoting *The Little Mermaid* in 1940, yet the possibility that they had a future was a powerful motivation for the artists to keep working on them.

In 1977, Marc Davis picked up "The

Snow Queen" again. He had moved over in the company from animator to Imagineer and was helping design rides such as the Jungle Cruise, the Haunted Mansion, and the Pirates of the Caribbean. Now Marc was working on a new project. He imagined a chilly attraction, perfect for hot summer days at Disneyland. The ride would feature a snow princess with a long sideswept blond braid and a flowing, glittery gown. He sketched snowflake decorations and the aurora borealis lighting up the night sky. His enchanted snow palace was built of simulated ice with a long flight of steps and a wide balcony. Though his vision was beautiful, momentum to carry out the project was lacking, and the ride would never be made.

However, good ideas have a way of resurfacing. In the mid-1990s, "The Snow Queen" was reimagined as an animated action-adventure film, one in which the villain, Elsa, freezes the heart of a poor peasant named Anna. The concept art showed an evil queen with blue skin, spiky hair, and a coat made from living weasels — an icy Cruella De Vil. Elsa's motivations came from being stood up at the altar, after which she froze her own heart so that she would never have to feel the pain of unrequited love again.

Jennifer, like many others at the studio, found the story tiresome; the women had scarcely any distinguishing characteristics. She sat watching an animatic, the filmed storyboards, which were open for any employee to view and give notes on. The practice had been in place for decades, with Walt frequently asking for feedback on proposed films. As she viewed the storyboards, Jennifer envisioned the film differently, as a musical in the vein of *The Little Mermaid.* Jennifer's notes impressed the team, and even though she wasn't yet finished with *Wreck-It Ralph,* Chris Buck, the director of the Snow Queen film, asked her to join them as a writer.

Jennifer was soon working closely with the husband-and-wife song-writing team brought in for the film, Robert Lopez and Kristen Anderson-Lopez. The partnership deepened, resembling the immersive relationship the studio had with its musical team during the tenure of Menken and Ashman in the 1980s and with the Sherman brothers on *Mary Poppins* in the 1960s.

As Jennifer wrestled with the villain, Elsa, the group began to have discussions about who she was as a character and how it felt to be alone with her powers. Lopez and

Anderson-Lopez played a demo of a song they had written for her that explored these emotions. As the story team listened to the song "Let It Go," Jennifer looked around the room. Tears were pricking her eyes and she realized that half the staff was crying. The song, which powerfully captured Elsa's desire to truly be herself, needed not a single revision. Elsa's character, however, required sweeping changes. "I have to rewrite the whole movie," Jennifer said aloud.

She didn't have much time to do so, as she had been brought in with a strict seventeen-month deadline. The team already knew they wanted the film to end with Anna sacrificing her life for Elsa's, yet they had no idea how to get to this point. Ed Catmull was giving the new hire complete freedom. In 2006, after the Pixar acquisition, Catmull was made president of both Walt Disney Feature Animation and Pixar Animation Studios. As the studios were separated by over three hundred miles, Catmull flew back and forth, usually spending two days a week to help guide the group in Glendale. Accordingly, he told Jennifer, "You can do whatever you need to do on the film, anything you want, but you're earning that moment," a reference to the proposed ending. Then he added, "And if you do, it will be fantastic. And if you don't, the movie will suck."

The film's direction was still up in the air when someone said the magic word: *sisters.* Up until that instant, Elsa and Anna were not related in any way. For Jennifer, it was a singular moment, and suddenly the film meant everything to her. She began to work harder than ever to bring an emotional connection into the script. As she contemplated how it felt to be shut out by a sibling, she drew on her own relationship with her older sister.

Jennifer had grown up in East Providence, Rhode Island, in a houseful of women. From an early age she adored reading and drawing. As a child she was infatuated with *Cinderella,* watching the 1950 classic on VHS some fifty times until every second of the film was permanently etched in her memory. Back then, as she listened to the song "So This Is Love," Jennifer had no inkling that the woman who served as art director on the film, Mary Blair, would one day influence her own career.

The theme of "happily ever after" presented in the fairy tale was blatantly missing from the reality she witnessed between her own mother and father. Following her parents' divorce, Jennifer and her older sister, Amy, were close, yet as they grew up, the two drifted apart. For Jennifer, it felt as though their connection had been lost. It wasn't until she was a twenty-year-old college student studying English at the University of New Hampshire that tragedy brought the sisters back together. Jennifer's boyfriend died in an accidental drowning, and Amy was uncompromisingly there for her in the difficult period afterward. As adults, the two were able to forge a new relationship. "And then from that moment on," Jennifer would later say, "she was like my champion."

It was these experiences that Jennifer now infused into her work. Acknowledging her passionate devotion to the project and with only a year left for the team to finish the movie, producer Peter Del Vecho asked Jennifer to become the studio's first feature-length female director, a position she would share with director Chris Buck.

Now as co-director, Jennifer felt strongly that she and the team needed to bring authenticity to the familial relationship that was central to the film. With this in mind, they did something that had never been done before — they organized a "sister summit." The idea was retro in some ways, a throwback to the large story meetings that had once dominated the studio, although never had so many hundreds of women attended those.

The summit gathered women from all departments of the Walt Disney Animation Studios (as it was renamed in 2007). Taking turns sharing their experiences, the participants discussed what it meant to be women and sisters. Some topics were petty, such as fighting over clothes, while others were profound, such as how you helped a sister who was in trouble.

Taking place over several days, the sister summit sparked new inspiration for the writers and story artists. From the themes of exclusion, loneliness, and the resiliency of sisterly bonds, a delicate balance was born between the characters Elsa and Anna. They crafted Anna as the little sister that so many of the women remembered, the one who begs for a playmate, as Anna does in the song "Do You Want to Build a Snowman?" The group had previously cut the song, feeling it was too poignant, but now it allowed them to show the heart of the girls' relationship, as Anna pleads with her sister to tell her why they can't be friends anymore. The piece would also end up having personal significance, as Jennifer's daughter and the Lopezes' daughter each sang part of the song in the final film.

Jennifer also felt strongly about humanizing their female cast — she didn't want to depict unflawed princesses. Whereas typically only male characters benefited from bathroom humor, Jennifer decided to make Princess Anna gassy. In story meetings, they chuckled over her burps. Bigger themes also emerged. With Jennifer's guidance, the central concept of the film moved to the bigger premise of love vanquishing fear.

As the sister summit wound down, Michael Giaimo stepped into the room to listen (men weren't allowed to speak at the summit). He knew he was witnessing a singular moment in the studio's history; "Disney energy at its best," he would later call it. Giaimo had spent decades at the studio and held a multitude of different positions, but his passion for Mary Blair's work had only grown in intensity. For *Frozen,* he was occupying Mary's role, that of art director, and he brought the lessons he had learned from the female pioneer to his styling on the film. He revisited Mary's work on a 1954 animated short called *Once Upon a Wintertime.* In Mary's depictions of ice and snow, Giaimo was particularly struck by her use of color to suggest the varied temperatures of emotion. The icy forms of the film are not a single shade of white but instead reflect the sky, the characters, and the action of each scene.

Michael brought these principles into his color palette, finding a way to infuse color as an emotional subtext to the film. When Elsa stalks angrily around her ice palace, the walls turn a striking cool red. During moments of calm, a frosty blue overtakes the scene. Michael selected bright magentas pooling in the snow to reflect the aurora borealis overhead and found a role for the color yellow. When he first mentioned using that shade, executives were concerned: "Not yellow snow?" they asked. Yet Michael found a way to bend the color to the narrative, using yellow as a warning light that signified the rising tension of the scene before it went red.

Michael's work on *Frozen* is indicative of an earlier age, when concept art was unafraid to be daring. He credits Mary as his muse, saying, "What she did went beyond the project into a pure art form. It became art. It became a statement unto itself."

It wasn't just the story that sparkled in *Frozen* — the effects animation was the most advanced the studio had yet pursued.

The eighty animators on the film created over two thousand unique snowflakes. To produce the copious quantities of snow required for *Frozen,* the group turned to a computer-generated tool called Material Point Method, developed by researchers at the University of Missouri. The simulation-based technique enables scientists to predict how fire and explosions will affect structures, which allows improvement of construction design and building materials. At the Walt Disney Animation Studios, the group took the same algorithm and altered it to determine how snowballs smashed and ice palaces shattered.

Creating Elsa's detailed ice palace was the most technically difficult part of the film. The sequence showing the long steps of the castle's grand foyer, with its exquisite glacial walls and detailed balcony, proved a strain on the four thousand computers — double the number of machines required for 2013's *Monsters University* — rendering the film one frame at a time. A single frame, the one in which Elsa steps onto the balcony of her ice palace, took more than five days for the thousands of computers to render, far longer than other contemporaneous films. For comparison, it took eleven hours to render a single frame of *Cars 2* and twenty-nine hours for a frame in *Monsters University.* It was a testament to the care with which each detail of the scene was conceived, and now the artists finally had enough computing muscle to power through.

During the production of *Frozen,* the studio brought in a live reindeer for the animators to sketch. As the group sat around the majestic animal with its soft, velvety antlers, the scene was reminiscent of the studio more than seventy years earlier, when Walt had brought in two fawns for his artists to sketch for *Bambi.* At that time, only one woman, Retta Scott, sat in the circle drawing the deer. Now a dozen female animators were working on the film.

The beauty in the story and art of *Frozen* would never have been possible without the resurgence of women in the story and animation departments at Walt Disney Animation Studios. These departments, which in the 1970s and 1980s had been practically emptied of female artists, were now bursting with new talent. The new generation, including Claire Keane and Jean Gillmore, both visual-development artists with roles akin to those of Bianca and Sylvia, brought a diversity of experiences to their work.

Prasansook Veerasunthorn, known as Fawn to her friends and colleagues, was also a story artist on the feature. Born and raised in the Chonburi province of Thailand, Fawn watched *Dumbo* repeatedly as a child and cried at the scene, designed by Mary Blair, of the mother elephant cradling her baby with her trunk. Fawn moved to the United States on a student visa at age nineteen and attended art school in Ohio. At first she felt uncomfortable with English. Her conversational grasp of the language was clumsy, so she found the visual medium of film intensely appealing. There, she could communicate without words.

Fawn bounced between animation studios before landing in the story department at the Walt Disney Animation Studios in 2011 to work on *Frozen.* Her hiring was no longer an exceptional event. Fawn was now just one of many women and immigrants brought into the studio.

Fawn began creating beatboards, a type of storyboard that gives a quick pitch of an idea that can fit within existing sequences. Her drawings depicted the mischievous antics of a young Anna and Elsa as they played in the snow and ice-skated with Olaf in the great hall of their palace. Her art captured the childhood wonder of the sisters, mesmerized by Elsa's magic, before it all went awry. In the story room, the group turned the air-conditioning low and put the finishing touches on the "party is over" sequence, in which an adult Elsa finally reveals her powers to both Anna and a ballroom full of guests. It was Fawn who brought emotional nuance to the scene, tingeing Anna's and Elsa's reactions with sadness to illustrate this downturn in their sisterly relationship.

When the film was released in November 2013, no one was prepared for the response from audiences around the world. The reviews, as they so often are for Disney films, were mixed, with *Variety* criticizing the "generic nature of the main characters," the *New York Daily News* declaring that the film lacked "memorable tunes," and *Slate* decrying the soundtrack as "musically thin." Other critics were more complimentary, calling the movie "a second renaissance" for the studio. The box office would have its own story to tell: just 101 days after its release, the movie had made more than one billion dollars and become the highest-grossing animated film of all time.

At the eighty-sixth Academy Awards, Jennifer Lee walked the red carpet with her sister, Amy, as a tribute to the inspiration that their sibling relationship had given the film. When *Frozen* won an Oscar for Best Animated Feature Film, the celluloid ceiling shattered. It marked two dramatic firsts for women at the studio: the first time a female director from Walt Disney animation had received an Academy Award, and the first female director in history whose film earned over one billion dollars at the box office.

Two days later, Fawn cradled the coveted golden statue in her hands in the studio offices. It was a humbling experience to hold the award that she had helped make possible. She was intensely proud to be part of the team. With her name in the credits and the Academy Award (temporarily) in her grasp, she had a kind of recognition that for many decades had been denied female story artists.

New projects presented themselves. Both Jennifer and Fawn worked on *Zootopia* (2016), which features an ambitious female rabbit police officer and tackles larger themes of discrimination and tolerance. The film was well received by reviewers, with *USA Today* praising how the plot "subtly weaves in racial profiling, stereotypes and preconceived notions of others in a creative way." Fawn also worked on the box-office success *Moana* (2016), which tells of a resilient Polynesian heroine chosen by the ocean herself to return balance to the natural world and rescue her people. She does so without the aid of any love interest whatsoever. *Variety* declared that the film "marks a return to the heights of the Disney Renaissance."

No movie can be everything to everybody. Certainly none of the recent films from Walt Disney Animation Studios is perfect in its treatment of gender and race. While some are the subject of warm praise today, twenty years hence, audiences may find them lacking in needed perspective and sensitivity. Yet the new features coming from the studio signify change in the industry, and behind each one are real people committed to transforming the stories of childhood.

In 2018, Fawn was promoted to head of the story department. Standing on the shoulders of the many who came before her, she and her fellow story artists are using their creativity to help usher in a new era in the representation of female and multicultural characters, unhindered by previous stereotypes.

Struggles will persist, and not only in the

technical aspects of three-dimensional animation. Women have long kept quiet about sexual harassment and discrimination in the workplace. Only with the rise of the #MeToo movement in 2017 did the shroud of silence begin lifting, across disciplines, but particularly in entertainment.

When John Lasseter, former chief creative officer of Pixar and Walt Disney Animation Studios, was put on a leave of absence in 2017 for his alleged repeated misconduct toward women, the surprise for those inside the studio was not necessarily what was being said about their boss's behavior but that such a powerful man had finally been called to account. (Lasseter said his behavior was "unquestionably wrong," and he has apologized for his actions.) Other such allegations from within the animation industry may come to light in the future, but every year fewer abuses will go unreported in an industry that seems to be evolving at last.

It is the kind of abuse that generations of women in animation have endured and many still persevere under. For all the creative freedom and influence of the early women of the Walt Disney Studios, the closest they ever came to a sister summit was during the story meetings that Sylvia Holland held for the *Nutcracker* sequence of

Fantasia, when the women gathered to develop story lines that the men spurned as too feminine.

For these pioneering women, the idea that one day story meetings full of confident female artists could dominate the vision for a feature film would have been very welcome indeed. And yet, in the more than eighty years since Bianca Majolie began in the story department, is it enough?

Pete Docter doesn't think so. In 2018, he and Jennifer Lee took over Lasseter's position as chief creative officers of Pixar and Walt Disney Animation Studios, respectively. Both are intent on shifting the culture of the company. Docter also wants to ensure that the female pioneers of the studio are finally acknowledged. He started at Pixar in 1990 the day after he graduated from Cal-Arts. From the beginning, he had a strong sense of how the history of animation influenced the present. In his directorial debut on *Monsters, Inc.* (2001), Docter found inspiration in Mary Blair's color palette. In the much-acclaimed *Up* (2009), which he co-directed, he made the character Ellie, the beloved late wife of the main character, in Blair's image. Ellie's paintings in the film are a direct tribute to the legendary artist's work. Her style would also be reflected in the colorful interiors of a young girl's mind featured in *Inside Out* (2015), also directed by Docter.

Mary Blair's art is the latest to come out of hiding, although few who are inspired by the themes of innocence and joy that run through her work know that it was created under circumstances that were sometimes painful and often abusive. As Mary's art is given new attention and continues influencing new projects, so should the legacies of all the great underestimated women artists of her era be revived.

Their inspiration is needed now more than ever. While the lack of female representation in the sciences is often lamented and organizations strive to bring more women into STEM fields, women have an even smaller presence in filmmaking. Although 60 percent of all students studying animation in art schools across the United States are women, they make up only 23 percent of all animators in Hollywood. Women make up only 10 percent of all writers and 8 percent of all directors working on the top one hundred highest-grossing films. A 2018 research report published by San Diego State University's Center for the Study of Women in Television and Film found that when there is a female director, the effect trickles down to the crew, where more women are employed as writers, editors, cinematographers, and composers. These statistics are similar for movies made across the world, from Canada to France to Japan.

Women are often missing on-screen as well; fewer than 24 percent of protagonists in the top one hundred highest-grossing domestic films are female. In animated features in 2017, this fraction was shockingly low: only 4 percent. The Bechdel test, sometimes called the Bechdel-Wallace test, was conceived in the 1980s by cartoonist Alison Bechdel, and although originally proposed in jest, it has now become a common method of evaluating how women are portrayed in entertainment. To pass the Bechdel test, a work must have three characteristics. First, there must be at least two women in it. Second, the women must speak to each other. Third, they have to talk about something other than men. The films that fail to meet these three simple requirements are surprisingly numerous. Of 1,794 Hollywood films made between 1970 and 2013, only 53 percent passed the test.

For many children, movies represent their first glimpse of their culture and the roles of men and women in that realm. In the impressionable minds of this audience, our future world is being shaped, and it is one that could only benefit from greater equality.

Bianca ran out of the story meeting in terror, leaving the ripped scraps of her work on the floor behind her. As she fled down the hall that fateful afternoon in 1937, she hated being the only woman in the story department. Her isolation was her purest agony. If only the current women of Walt Disney animation could hold out their hands to the artist, crossing the boundaries of time and space, they would surely reassure her that things would eventually get better. "It's okay," they would tell her. "You can slow down now."

EPILOGUE:
HAPPILY EVER AFTER

I stand with my five-year-old daughter in Disneyland's Tomorrowland in front of two massive murals that face each other. "Why are you looking at those paintings, Mama?" my daughter Eleanor asks as throngs of visitors move around us. "Is it because you like space?" I do love images of outer space, especially the planets, as my daughter well knows. But this isn't why I'm staring at the long, curved walls, each one stretching fifty-four feet.

"An artist named Mary Blair made beautiful tile murals of children playing right there," I say to Eleanor, pointing at the walls, "but we can't see them anymore." "They're just hiding, right, Mama?" Eleanor asks, and she looks a little sad now as we stare at the current murals, which, despite the planets and spacecraft, seem bland and lifeless. I nod my head yes, but the answer is only partially true. One was chipped away in 1986, but the other Mary Blair mural, created in 1967, is likely still there, its images hopefully intact and entombed under layers of plaster. The mural, like Mary's rich legacy, remains hidden despite being right in front of us.

To cheer both of us up, I take Eleanor on the It's a Small World ride. The boat rocks along its canal as we enter the cavernous interior, whose brilliance and gaiety soon have us smiling. "Do you see that doll up there by the Eiffel Tower?" I lean in and ask my daughter as she whips her head from side to side, trying to see everything and exclaiming so enthusiastically that at first I'm not sure she heard me. "The one holding the red balloon?" she cries excitedly. "Yes, that one, with the short blond hair," I say. "That's Mary Blair. She made this ride." Eleanor turns her face to me and grins. "I love it."

She is hardly alone. Although Disneyland was designed by Walt to be in a constant state of flux, old attractions making way for new ones, the It's a Small World ride remains popular and has earned a permanent home in the park; it's still here more than forty years after its designer passed away, on July 26, 1978, of a cerebral hemorrhage. The Walt Disney Studio's weekly newsletter announced Mary's passing in a short paragraph buried in the middle of its pages. On the front of the newsletter was a photo and lengthy article memorializing a company tax accountant who had passed away that same month.

In her last years, Mary found peace within her family circle; she delighted in her nieces and frequently painted. Her sense of color, in decline during her last years, returned at the end, and she painted scenes as vibrant and joyful as those that marked the height of her career. Her ashes were scattered at sea after a sparsely attended funeral service at the Episcopalian church in Capitola, California. In 1991, Mary was named a Disney Legend, a high honor. Lee Blair, still jealous of her, said to a friend, "Why are they giving it to Mary? She's dead." He chose not to attend the ceremony.

Mary's dear friend Retta Scott similarly found peace and satisfaction late in life. In the 1980s, Retta Scott made a triumphant return to animation, working on *The Plague Dogs* for a company that would later be bought out by the Pixar Animation Studios and freelancing on animated shorts and other commercial endeavors. She told her son Benjamin, "You can't draw anything if you don't understand it." The words were spoken from the depths of her experience. Retta suffered a stroke in December 1985 that left her weak and unable to communicate. She died on August 26, 1990, at age seventy-four, her passing nearly concurrent with the death of hand-drawn animation itself.

Grace Huntington distinguished herself in aviation, holding numerous speed and altitude records. She passed away from tuberculosis in 1948 at the age of thirty-five, leaving behind her husband and a five-year-old son. Her husband felt that Grace died not only of the bacterial infection, incurable in the 1940s, but also of a broken heart, never having been able to overcome the prejudice that existed against women in aviation. Shortly after she became ill, the military put out a call for woman pilots who were willing to ferry aircraft. It was the opportunity that she had long dreamed of, but it arrived too late.

Sylvia Holland worked for MGM Studios after being laid off from Walt Disney Studios in 1946. She then became a children's book illustrator and, later, a greeting-card designer. She put her long-neglected architectural skills to use in the 1950s, building two houses of her own design, then started picking up new hobbies. Her love of felines, once expressed by feeding and petting the strays of the Walt Disney Studios, inspired her to develop a new breed of Siamese cat, the Balinese, gaining her an international reputation. The breed continues to thrive today, as do the cats that wander about the studio in Burbank. In her old age, arthritis began to take over her limbs, and yet she insisted on drawing despite the debilitating pain. She hoped to write her memoirs one day but, sadly, never had an opportunity to do so. She died of a stroke in 1974.

Bianca Majolie got the last laugh. The first woman to be hired at the story department lived far longer than most of her 1930s contemporaries. After leaving the studio, Bianca married fellow artist Carl Heilborn. The two opened the Heilborn Studio Gallery, where Bianca frequently exhibited her work. The gallery was located on Hyperion Avenue, just down the street from where her career in animation started. In Bianca's declining years, her eyesight worsened and it became difficult for her to sketch and paint. "I don't think that I shall ever be touching paint again," she said, "but if it should happen, I shall place my fingers in a paint pot and work like a child. It might be a wonderful experience to start life all over again, as a child." Bianca passed away at age ninety-seven on September 6, 1997.

As obscured as an entombed mural in Disneyland, the work of these female artists surrounds us, even though many of their names have faded from our consciousness, often replaced by those of the men they worked with. They have shaped the evolution of female characters in film, advanced our technology, and broken down gender barriers in order to give us the empowering story lines we have begun to see in film and animation today. In the shadow of their artistry, millions of childhoods have been shaped, with an untold number yet to come.

ACKNOWLEDGMENTS

A heartfelt thank-you to the readers whose messages and stories have buoyed me at low moments, spurring me to write further. This book would not have been possible without Maggie Richardson, who from the beginning has encouraged me, made available seemingly endless research materials, and strengthened my resolve with her own powerful storytelling ability. I am very grateful to all the current and former Disney employees I spoke with as well as their family and friends, who shared both their memories and archival material: the wonderful Jeanne Chamberlain, Berkeley Brandt, Ben Worcester, Theo Halladay, Ann Tarvin, Steve and Suzi Onopa, Carol Hannaman, Michael Giaimo, Pete Docter, Brenda Chapman, Ellen Woodbury, Rita Hsiao, and many others. I am indebted to the many Disney historians who helped me in my research, in particular John Canemaker.

Without their invaluable collections of photographs, artwork, interviews, story-meeting transcripts, and so much more, this book would not have been written. A special thank-you to the many librarians and archivists, including Katherine Platz, who aided my search and helped me find documents that I didn't even know existed. I am also very grateful to the members of the Hyperion Historical Alliance, who have not only assisted my research but also allowed me to join their rich community.

I would be lost without Laurie Abkemeier, my wonderful agent who supports and inspires me. I have infinite gratitude for my editor, the talented Asya Muchnick, and am so fortunate to benefit from her expertise. Thank you to Jayne Yaffe Kemp and Tracy Roe, who not only improved the manuscript considerably but also made me smile with their witty edits and comments.

For my Met Hill family: Rachael and Gerry Coakley, Susie and Ben Bird, Elizabeth Keane, Sean Cashman, and Sarah Elliott. For my Ventucky crew: Elizabeth Shaw, Emlyn Jones, Jennifer and Payson Thompson, Tim Flanagan, J. A. and Joline MacFarland, Amy Cantor and Scott Ambruster. For my dear friends: my BFF Anna Seltzer, Dorothy and Mariano Deguzman,

Jeremy Bennett, Rebecca Lee and Rich Cegelski, Darcie and Mark Tuite, Lisa and Luther Ward, Deborah Ward, and Megan Furniss. I am so grateful to my little turkeys who have lifted me up during the darkest of days: Kristin Rascon, Ashlee Mikels, Amy McCain, Amanda Webb, Shelly McGill, Kate Brum, Michelle Danley, Lisa Funari, Samantha Wilson, Jessica Sakaske, Erika Hilden, AJ Lund, Andrea Alexander, Stacey Williams, Holly Button, Jenna Wood, Rachael Nelson, Erica Johansen, Jessica Mydland, Callie Slama, Becky Brown, Kimberly Philip, Amanda Schuster, Valerie Halsey, Clare Rice, Rosie Forbes, Karyln Goodman, Kiersti Pilon, and Amy Blackwell. For the teachers: Jennifer O'Reilly, Ms. McCool, Koresha Braxton, Stacey Isles, and Jacqueline Rosario. For my family: Marco Katz, Betsy Boone, Joyce Boone, Rose Grundgeiger, Claire and Jerry McCleery, Shane, Frannie, Ruby, Harrison, and Andrew Vesely, Scott Holt, and Shea Holt. For my sweet Hannah Holt. In memory of a loving father and grandfather: Kenneth Fry Holt.

To the most important people in my life: my husband, Larkin, and the girls who inspire me every day with their curious minds: Eleanor and Philippa.

NOTES

Research for this book relied heavily on family collections from Maggie Richardson, Jeanne Chamberlain, Berkeley Brandt, Theo Halladay, and Benjamin Worcester, and archival material collected by historian John Canemaker. In addition to the excellence of the published work of Canemaker, their vast personal and publicly available collections of interviews, story-meeting transcripts, correspondence, photographs, and artwork offer a wealth of details about the studio and its female employees. Unpublished interviews conducted by John Canemaker and used with his permission formed an essential core of biographical information. Story-meeting transcripts were obtained from personal collections or script libraries and archives. In addition, I conducted interviews with former and current members of the Walt Disney and Pixar Animation Studios as well as their friends and

547

family members.

Unless otherwise credited, biographical material on Bianca Majolie, Sylvia Holland, Retta Scott, Grace Huntington, and Mary Blair was obtained from correspondence, notes, sketches, photographs, journals, and interviews with relatives, friends, and co-workers.

Chapter 1: One Day When We Were Young
Further information on Bianca Majolie, including examples of her work, can be found in John Canemaker, *Before the Animation Begins: The Art and Lives of Disney Inspirational Sketch Artists* (New York: Hyperion, 1996); John Canemaker, *Paper Dreams: The Art and Artists of Disney Storyboards* (New York: Hyperion, 1999); and Didier Ghez, *They Drew As They Pleased,* vol. 1, *The Hidden Art of Disney's Golden Age: The 1930s* (New York: Hyperion, 2015).

Details of the meeting where Bianca presented a concept for *Snow White* and dialogue were obtained from a story-meeting transcript from January 25, 1937, Bianca's letters, and interviews with her friends.

A recollection of Bianca's disastrous story meeting and the quote that starts "This is why we can't use women" can be found in Didier Ghez, ed., *Walt's People,* vol. 9, *Talking Disney with the Artists Who Knew Him* (Bloomington, IN: Theme Park Press, 2011).

Background on Walt Disney's history, including his service in the American Red Cross ambulance corps, is described in Neal Gabler, *Walt Disney: The Triumph of the American Imagination* (New York: Random House, 2006).

Background on the 1929 stock-market crash as perceived by those at the J. C. Penney offices in New York City was obtained in author interviews with former employees and their families.

A description of the first Mickey Mouse cartoon to synchronize sound can be found in Dave Smith, "Steamboat Willie," Film Preservation Board, Library of Congress.

Thomas Edison said, "Americans prefer silent drama," in *Film Daily,* March 4, 1927.

A description of how sound was incorporated into film can be found in Scott Eyman, *The Speed of Sound: Hollywood and the Talkie Revolution, 1926–1930* (New York: Simon and Schuster, 1997), and Tomlinson Holman, *Sound for Film and Television* (Abingdon, UK: Routledge, 2010).

The history and technique of the click

track are described in Mervyn Cooke, ed., *The Hollywood Film Music Reader* (Oxford: Oxford University Press, 2010).

The financial challenges Walt Disney faced in his early years and the sale of his 1926 Moon Roadster are chronicled in Timothy S. Susanin, *Walt Before Mickey: Disney's Early Years, 1919–1928* (Jackson: University Press of Mississippi, 2011). Letters between Bianca Majolie and Walt Disney have been published in Ghez, *They Drew As They Pleased,* vol. 1.

Salary information was obtained from employee records housed at the John Canemaker Animation Collection in the Fales Library and Special Collections at New York University's Elmer Holmes Bobst Library.

The origin of the Disney life-drawing class can be found in Michael Barrier, *The Animated Man: A Life of Walt Disney* (Berkeley: University of California Press, 2007).

Information about the development and production of *Snow White and the Seven Dwarfs* can be found in J. B. Kaufman, *The Fairest One of All: The Making of Walt Disney's "Snow White and the Seven Dwarfs"* (San Francisco: Walt Disney Family Foundation Press, 2012).

The origins of storyboarding can be found

in Chris Pallant and Steven Price, *Storyboarding: A Critical History* (Berlin: Springer, 2015).

A history of how jobs were defined by gender in the 1930s as well as examples of rejection letters sent by the Walt Disney Studios can be found in Sandra Opdycke, *The WPA: Creating Jobs and Hope in the Great Depression* (Abingdon, UK: Routledge, 2016).

Chapter 2: Whistle While You Work

Information about the early days of the studio when it was located at 2719 Hyperion Avenue can be found in Bob Thomas, *Walt Disney: An American Original* (Glendale, CA: Disney Editions, 1994).

The advertisement "Walt Disney Wants Artists" appeared in the April 1936 issue of *Popular Mechanics.* The ad brought in many talented artists, including several members of Walt's Nine Old Men.

Bianca's early research for *Bambi* is documented in her correspondence at the time as well as subsequent interviews. Background can be found in John Canemaker, *Before the Animation Begins: The Art and Lives of Disney Inspirational Sketch Artists* (New York: Hyperion, 1996).

More information on Felix Salten's work

and its significance can be found in Paul Reitter, *Bambi's Jewish Roots and Other Essays on German-Jewish Culture* (New York: Bloomsbury, 2015).

"Will they ever stop persecuting us?" is one translation of Salten's text. It is sometimes translated as "Will they ever stop hunting us?" and follows a discussion of human cruelty and power. The theme of cultural assimilation in *Bambi* is further expounded upon in Paul Reitter, "The Unlikely Kinship of *Bambi* and Kafka's *Metamorphosis*," *The New Yorker*, December 28, 2017.

Hal Horne and his "gag file" is described in Daniel Wickberg, *The Senses of Humor: Self and Laughter in Modern America* (Ithaca, NY: Cornell University Press, 2015).

Dorothy Ann Blank's story can be found in Didier Ghez, *They Drew As They Pleased,* vol. 1, *The Hidden Art of Disney's Golden Age: The 1930s* (New York: Hyperion, 2015), and Chris Pallant and Steven Price, *Storyboarding: A Critical History* (Berlin: Springer, 2015).

A history of the multiplane camera and its development can be found in Whitney Grace, *Lotte Reiniger: Pioneer of Film Animation* (Jefferson, NC: McFarland, 2017).

The remarkable contributions of Ub Iwerks have been documented in Leslie Iwerks and John Kenworthy, *The Hand Behind the Mouse* (Glendale, CA: Disney Editions, 2001).

The glamorous premiere of *Snow White and the Seven Dwarfs* is described in J. B. Kaufman, *The Fairest One of All: The Making of Walt Disney's "Snow White and the Seven Dwarfs"* (San Francisco: Walt Disney Family Foundation Press, 2012).

Chapter 3: When You Wish Upon a Star

Discontent concerning on-screen credit among studio employees is documented in Todd James Pierce, *The Life and Times of Ward Kimball: Maverick of Disney Animation* (Jackson: University Press of Mississippi, 2019), and Tom Sito, *Drawing the Line: The Untold Story of the Animation Unions from Bosko to Bart Simpson* (Lexington: University Press of Kentucky, 2006).

A history of Los Angeles in the 1930s and of its booming 1923 supply of crude oil can be found in the Federal Writers Project of the Works Progress Administration, *Los Angeles in the 1930s: The WPA Guide to the City of Angels* (Berkeley: University of California Press, 2011).

More information about the excavation of King Tutankhamen and subsequent Tutmania can be found in Ronald H. Fritze, *Egyptomania: A History of Fascination, Obsession and Fantasy* (London: Reaktion Books, 2016).

The European illustrators who inspired artists at Walt Disney Studios are detailed in Bruno Girveau, ed., *Once Upon a Time: Walt Disney: The Sources of Inspiration for the Disney Studios* (Munich: Prestel, 2007).

Analysis of the *Pinocchio* text can be found in Clancy Martin, "What the Original *Pinocchio* Says About Lying," *The New Yorker,* February 6, 2015.

Arnold Gillespie's history at MGM is chronicled in A. Arnold Gillespie, *The Wizard of MGM: Memoirs of A. Arnold Gillespie* (Albany, GA: BearManor Media, 2012).

Visual effects for *Pinocchio* are described in J. B. Kaufman, *Pinocchio: The Making of the Disney Epic* (San Francisco: Walt Disney Family Foundation Press, 2015).

Techniques used by the Ink and Paint department for *Pinocchio* are described in Mindy Johnson, *Ink & Paint: The Women of Walt Disney's Animation* (Glendale, CA: Disney Editions, 2017).

A history of Mickey Mouse merchandise can be found in Alan Bryman, *The Disneyization of Society* (London: Sage Publications, 2004).

Walt Disney's down payment on fifty-one acres in Burbank is described in Erin K. Schonauer and Jamie C. Schonauer, *Early Burbank* (Mount Pleasant, SC: Arcadia Publishing, 2014).

A history of penicillin can be found in Eric Lax, *The Mold in Dr. Florey's Coat: The Story of the Penicillin Miracle* (Basingstoke, UK: Macmillan, 2004).

Dialogue for Grace and her colleagues was obtained from the story-meeting transcript of January 19, 1939.

Barbara Wirth Baldwin's role in airbrushing at the studio is documented in Johnson, *Ink & Paint.*

Chapter 4: Waltz of the Flowers
The quote that starts "This is not the cartoon medium" was said by Walt Disney at a story meeting for the concert feature on December 8, 1938, as obtained from the transcript.

Walt Disney's legendary meeting with Leopold Stokowski and their subsequent collaboration to advance Fantasound are documented in Tomlinson Holman, *Sur-*

round Sound: Up and Running (Abingdon, UK: Taylor and Francis, 2008).

A recounting of Stravinsky's history with Walt Disney and his quote "an unresisting imbecility" can be found in Daniel Albright, *Stravinsky: The Music Box and the Nightingale* (Abingdon, UK: Taylor and Francis, 1989).

Collaborations between the composer and choreographer are explored in Charles M. Joseph, *Stravinsky and Balanchine: A Journey of Invention* (New Haven, CT: Yale University Press, 2008).

George Balanchine's early life is described in Robert Gottlieb, *George Balanchine: The Ballet Maker* (New York: HarperCollins, 2010).

The U.S. premiere of the unabridged ballet of *The Nutcracker* took place on December 24, 1944, and was performed by the San Francisco Ballet. A history of the ballet's performances in the United States can be found in Sarah Begley and Julia Lull, "How *The Nutcracker* Colonized American Ballet," *Time,* December 24, 2014.

Details on the development of Fantasound can be found in Mark Kerins, *Beyond Dolby (Stereo): Cinema in the Digital Sound Age* (Bloomington: Indiana University Press, 2010).

Constraints placed by the Hays Code are described in Thomas Doherty, *Hollywood's Censor: Joseph I. Breen and the Production Code Administration* (New York: Columbia University Press, 2009).

Discussion of Sunflower's character in *Fantasia* can be found in Johnson Cheu, *Diversity in Disney Films: Critical Essays on Race, Ethnicity, Gender, Sexuality, and Disability* (Jefferson, NC: McFarland, 2013).

Dialogue for the development of Sunflower's character is from a transcript of a story meeting that took place on October 17, 1938.

Sylvia's concepts for the Pastoral Symphony were obtained from her sketches and notes made during this period.

Information on the negotiations between the NAACP and Hollywood studio executives is from "Better Breaks for Negroes in Hollywood," *Variety,* March 25, 1942.

"The only unsatisfactory part of the picture" quote is from Pare Lorentz, "Review of *Fantasia,*" *McCall's,* February 1941.

The Pastoral Symphony is called *"Fantasia*'s nadir" in John Culhane, *Walt Disney's "Fantasia"* (New York: Abradale Press, 1983).

Hattie Noel's participation in modeling for the "Dance of the Hours" sequence is documented in Mindy Aloff, *Hippo in a Tutu: Dancing in Disney Animation* (Glendale, CA: Disney Editions, 2008). Subsequent comments made at her expense come from Lee Blair's correspondence.

Information on story meetings for *The Nutcracker Suite* was obtained from story-meeting transcripts of 1938.

The quote "It's like something you see with your eyes half closed" is attributed to Walt Disney in Neal Gabler, *Walt Disney: The Triumph of the American Imagination* (New York: Random House, 2006).

Herman Schultheis's images from their trip to the Idyllwild Nature Center, along with the technical specifications of how stop-motion snowflakes and dewdrops were created for *Fantasia,* can be found in John Canemaker, *The Lost Notebook: Herman Schultheis and the Secrets of Walt Disney's Movie Magic* (San Francisco: Walt Disney Family Foundation Press, 2014).

The BLB mask was designed in 1938 and introduced to the medical community in W. I. Card et al., "The B.L.B. Mask for Administering Oxygen," *Lancet* 235, no. 6079 (1940).

Grace's first altitude record was reported in "Woman Flyer Sets Altitude Record," *Los*

Angeles Times, August 1, 1939.

Biographical information for Gyo Fujikawa obtained from interviews conducted by John Canemaker on October 27, 1994, used by permission; Edwin McDowell, "Gyo Fujikawa, Creator of Children's Books," *New York Times,* December 7, 1998; and Elaine Woo, "Children's Author Dared to Depict Multiracial World," *Los Angeles Times,* December 13, 1998.

One hundred feet of animation garnered on-screen credit at the Walt Disney Studio from its early days until the 1980s according to J. B. Kaufman, "Before *Snow White,*" *Film History* 5, no. 2 (1993).

Oskar Fischinger's papers and works are currently held at the Center for Visual Music in Los Angeles. His history is recounted in William Moritz, "Fischinger at Disney," *Millimeter* 5, no. 2 (1977). The incident of a swastika pinned to his door while working at the studio is recounted in William Moritz, *Optical Poetry: The Life and Work of Oskar Fischinger* (Bloomington: Indiana University Press, 2004).

The Soviet-Japanese border conflicts of the late 1930s are further explained in Stuart Goldman, *Nomonhan, 1939: The Red Army's Victory That Shaped World War II*

(Annapolis, MD: Naval Institute Press, 2012).

Elias Disney's conversation with his son about uses for the studio is recounted in Sarah Kimmorley, "Why Walt Disney's Animation Studio Is Nicknamed 'the Hospital,' " *Business Insider,* August 24, 2017.

The popularity of Mickey Mouse across Europe during the 1930s and '40s is described by Richard J. Evans, *The Third Reich in Power* (New York: Penguin, 2006); Carten Laqua, *Mickey Mouse, Hitler, and Nazi Germany: How Disney's Characters Conquered the Third Reich* (New Castle, PA: Hermes Press, 2009); and Robin Allan, *Walt Disney and Europe: European Influences on the Animated Feature Films of Walt Disney* (Bloomington: Indiana University Press, 1999).

Walt Disney's announcement of a million-dollar cut in expenses is recounted in Gabler, *Walt Disney.*

The production budget and returns for *Pinocchio* are reported at boxofficemojo .com and the-numbers.com.

The premiere of *Fantasia* and its subsequent lukewarm reception are reported in Charles Solomon, "It Wasn't Always Magic," *Los Angeles Times,* October 7,

1990, and Neal Gabler, "Disney's *Fantasia* Was Initially a Critical and Box-Office Failure," *Smithsonian,* November 2015.

Chapter 5: Little April Shower
Animators explain that they believed Scott's sketches for *Bambi* were made by a virile man in Ollie Johnston and Frank Thomas, *Walt Disney's "Bambi": The Story and the Film* (New York: Stewart, Tabori, and Chang, 1990).

Descriptions of the Penthouse Club can be found in the 1943 Walt Disney Studios employee handbook and in Don Peri, *Working with Disney: Interviews with Animators, Producers, and Artists* (Jackson: University Press of Mississippi, 2011).

Walt is quoted as saying "I haven't felt that *Bambi* was one of our productions" in Neal Gabler, *Walt Disney: The Triumph of the American Imagination* (New York: Random House, 2006).

The history of Felix Salten's writing and why his books were banned in Germany can be found in Paul Reitter, *"Bambi*'s Jewish Roots," *Jewish Review of Books* (Winter 2014), and Paul Reitter, *Bambi's Jewish Roots and Other Essays on German-Jewish Culture* (New York: Bloomsbury, 2015).

"The Animators had always hoped" quote

is from a 1940 in-house studio newsletter in Retta Scott's private collection and is also cited in Mindy Johnson, *Ink & Paint: The Women of Walt Disney's Animation* (Glendale, CA: Disney Editions, 2017).

A history of Mildred Fulvia di Rossi, also known as Millicent Patrick, can be found in Tom Weaver, David Schecter, and Steve Kronenberg, *The Creature Chronicles: Exploring the Black Lagoon Trilogy* (Abingdon, UK: McFarland, 2017).

Internal memo from Grace Huntington's private collection beginning "It has always been Walt's hope" was circulated on January 17, 1939.

The number of women working in the studio and specifically in the Ink and Paint department is reported in Johnson, *Ink & Paint.*

Tyrus Wong's history was obtained from an oral history interview with Tyrus Wong, January 30, 1965, Archives of American Art, Smithsonian Institution; John Canemaker, *Before the Animation Begins: The Art and Lives of Disney Inspirational Sketch Artists* (New York: Hyperion, 1996); and Pamela Tom, *Tyrus* (PBS, American Masters, 2017). Wong recounts how he was referred to by a racial slur at the studio in all three of these sources.

A comparison of the experiences endured at Ellis Island and Angel Island by immigrants, including the quote about "the conglomeration of ramshackle buildings," can be found in Ronald H. Bayor, *Encountering Ellis Island: How European Immigrants Entered America* (Baltimore: Johns Hopkins University Press, 2014).

A history of the Chinese Exclusion Act can be found in John Soennichsen, *The Chinese Exclusion Act of 1882* (Santa Barbara, CA: ABCCLIO, 2011).

Examples of xenophobia in reaction to immigration from Asia can be found in J. S. Tyler, "Tiny Brown Men Are Pouring Over the Pacific Coast," *Seattle Daily Times,* April 21, 1900, and the editorial entitled "The Yellow Peril: How the Japanese Crowd Out the White Race," *San Francisco Chronicle,* March 6, 1905.

In 1892, handbills were posted in Tacoma, Washington, that read "Shall We Have Chinese? No! No! No!" One is currently held at the Washington State Historical Society in Tacoma.

Some of the poems etched on the walls at Angel Island can be found in Him Lai, Genny Lim, and Judy Yung, eds., *Island: Poetry and History of the Chinese Immigrants on Angel Island, 1910–1940* (Seattle: University of Washington Press, 1991).

The history of Asian American immigrants working at the Walt Disney Studios can be found in Iwao Takamoto with Michael Mallory, *Iwao Takamoto: My Life with a Thousand Characters* (Jackson: University Press of Mississippi, 2009), and Didier Ghez, ed., *Walt's People,* vol. 9, *Talking Disney with the Artists Who Knew Him* (Bloomington, IN: Theme Park Press, 2011).

Development of *Bambi* obtained from story-meeting transcripts between 1937 and 1940.

Walt's quote beginning "And as the stag goes off" appears in a story-meeting transcript from June 20, 1940. The conversation is reported in Johnston and Thomas, *Walt Disney's "Bambi."*

Diane Disney is reported to have said, "Why did you have to kill Bambi's mother?" in Jamie Portman, "Generations Stunned by Death Scene in *Bambi,*" *Boston Globe,* July 15, 1988.

The impact of Tyrus Wong's art on trimming the dialogue in *Bambi* is explained in Johnston and Thomas, *Walt Disney's "Bambi."*

Frank Churchill's techniques for developing the score of *Bambi* are described in

James Bohn, *Music in Disney's Animated Features: "Snow White and the Seven Dwarfs" to "The Jungle Book"* (Jackson: University Press of Mississippi, 2017).

Visual effects for *Bambi* are described in Johnston and Thomas, *Walt Disney's "Bambi";* Chris Pallant, *Demystifying Disney: A History of Disney Feature Animation* (London: A and C Black, 2011); and Janet Martin, "Bringing Bambi to the Screen," *Nature,* August 9, 1942.

Definitions of cellulose acetate, cellulose nitrate, and properties of cel animation can be found in Karen Goulekas, *Visual Effects in a Digital World: A Comprehensive Glossary of Over 7000 Visual Effects Terms* (San Francisco: Morgan Kaufmann, 2001).

Walt's quote beginning "The main thing is the slower pace" is in Johnston and Thomas, *Walt Disney's "Bambi."*

Chapter 6: Baby Mine
Helen Aberson and Harold Pearl, *Dumbo the Flying Elephant* (Syracuse, NY: Roll-a-Book Publishers, 1939).

Original storyboards for *Elmer Elephant* by Bianca Majolie can be found in John Canemaker, *Paper Dreams: The Art and Artists of Disney Storyboards* (New York: Hyperion, 1999).

Materials concerning Mary Goodrich can be found at the Connecticut Women's Hall of Fame in New Haven. Her role in adapting "The Snow Queen" is discussed in Charles Solomon, *The Art of "Frozen"* (San Francisco: Chronicle Books, 2015).

Walt is quoted as saying "Dumbo is an obvious straight cartoon" in Michael Barrier, *The Animated Man: A Life of Walt Disney* (Berkeley: University of California Press, 2007).

Pinocchio cost $2.6 million to make according to multiple sources, including James Bohn, *Music in Disney's Animated Features: "Snow White and the Seven Dwarfs" to "The Jungle Book"* (Jackson: University Press of Mississippi, 2017).

Pinocchio was dubbed in two languages according to Michael Barrier, *Hollywood Cartoons: American Animation in Its Golden Age* (Oxford: Oxford University Press, 2003).

The quote that starts "The most enchanting film" is in Kate Cameron, "Disney's *Pinocchio* a Gem of the Screen," *New York Daily News*, February 8, 1940.

Mary Blair's concept art for *Dumbo* can be seen in John Canemaker, *The Art and*

Flair of Mary Blair: An Appreciation (Glendale, CA: Disney Editions, 2014).

A discussion of Walt Disney's association with Technicolor can be found in Scott Higgins, *Harnessing the Technicolor Rainbow: Color Design in the 1930s* (Austin: University of Texas Press, 2009).

Natalie Kalmus's story can be found in Christine Gledhill and Julia Knight, eds., *Doing Women's Film History: Reframing Cinemas, Past and Future* (Champaign: University of Illinois Press, 2009).

Dorothy's silver slippers were adapted for political interpretation; see Henry M. Littlefield, "*The Wizard of Oz:* Parable on Populism," *American Quarterly* 16, no. 1 (1964), and Ranjit S. Dighe, *The Historian's "Wizard of Oz": Reading L. Frank Baum's Classic as a Political and Monetary Allegory* (Westport, CT: Praeger Publishers, 2002).

David O. Selznick's comments about Natalie Kalmus are in Patrick Keating, *Hollywood Lighting from the Silent Era to Film Noir* (New York: Columbia University Press, 2009).

Descriptions of the Ink and Paint department, including teatime, can be found in Mindy Johnson, *Ink & Paint: The Women of Walt Disney's Animation* (Glendale, CA:

Disney Editions, 2017), and Patricia Kohn, "Coloring the Kingdom," *Vanity Fair,* February 5, 2010.

The problem with color fading and cellulose acetate is described in Richard Hincha, "Crisis in Celluloid: Color Fading and Film Base Deterioration," *Archival Issues* 17, no. 2 (1992).

Walt Disney offered preferred stock to the public beginning in 1940, and it quickly dropped in value from twenty-five dollars to just over three dollars; see Bryan Taylor, "Disney Reminds Us of a Time When Anyone Could Invest Early and Really Make a Lot of Money," *Business Insider,* November 17, 2013.

Walt's salary of two thousand dollars a week in 1940 and the company's move to Burbank are noted in Neal Gabler, *Walt Disney: The Triumph of the American Imagination* (New York: Random House, 2006).

President Roosevelt recounted the story of the note given to him by a young girl in Franklin D. Roosevelt, *The Public Papers and Addresses of the Presidents of the United States,* vol. 5 (New York: Random House, 1938).

More information on the Fair Labor Standards Act can be found in Cass Sunstein, *The Second Bill of Rights: FDR's*

Unfinished Revolution — And Why We Need It More Than Ever (New York: Basic Books, 2009).

Description of the Snow White Special obtained from the studio restaurant menu held in Grace Huntington's private collection.

Salary averages and ranges at the studio in 1940 and the formation of the Screen Cartoonists' Guild reported in Tom Sito, *Drawing the Line: The Untold Story of the Animation Unions from Bosko to Bart Simpson* (Lexington: University Press of Kentucky, 2006).

The bulk and expense of Fantasound are explained in Charles Solomon, "Fantastic *Fantasia:* Disney Channel Takes a Look at Walt's Great Experiment in Animation," *Los Angeles Times,* August 26, 1990.

Negative reviews for *Fantasia* are quoted in Charles Solomon, "It Wasn't Always Magic," *Los Angeles Times,* October 7, 1990.

The studio's $4.5 million debt is detailed in Gabler, *Walt Disney.*

Bianca's concept art for *Cinderella* and *Peter Pan* can be seen in Didier Ghez, *They Drew As They Pleased,* vol. 1, *The Hidden Art of Disney's Golden Age: The 1930s* (New York: Hyperion, 2015).

Chapter 7: Aquarela do Brasil

Information on the women of Toei Doga can be found in Jonathan Clements and Helen McCarthy, *The Anime Encyclopedia: A Century of Japanese Animation,* 3rd ed. (Southbridge, MA: Stone Bridge Press, 2015).

The full transcript of Walt's speech to his employees on February 10, 1941, can be found in Walt Disney, *Walt Disney Conversations* (Jackson: University Press of Mississippi, 2006).

The roles played by Art Babbitt and Herb Sorrell in the 1941 strike can be found in Tom Sito, *Drawing the Line: The Untold Story of the Animation Unions from Bosko to Bart Simpson* (Lexington: University Press of Kentucky, 2006), and Steven Watts, *The Magic Kingdom: Walt Disney and the American Way of Life* (Columbia: University of Missouri Press, 2013).

Walt Disney's South American travels are described in J. B. Kaufman, *South of the Border with Disney: Walt Disney and the Good Neighbor Program, 1941–1948* (Glendale, CA: Disney Editions, 2009), and Allen L. Woll, "Hollywood's Good Neighbor Policy: The Latin Image in American Film, 1939–

1946," *Journal of Popular Film* 4, no. 2 (1974).

Details on the South America trip obtained from Mary and Lee Blair's records, documents, interviews, and correspondence provided by the Blair family estate.

Chapter 8: You're in the Army Now

Memo sent by Roy Disney obtained from Sylvia Holland's records and provided by Theo Halladay.

Concept art and early development for *The Little Mermaid* obtained by permission from Didier Ghez's research.

Employee reactions to the strike can be found in Don Peri, *Working with Disney: Interviews with Animators, Producers, and Artists* (Jackson: University Press of Mississippi, 2011).

Dumbo was called "a fanciful delight" in Bosley Crowther, "Walt Disney's Cartoon *Dumbo,* a Fanciful Delight, Opens at the Broadway," *New York Times,* October 24, 1941.

A history of Pearl Harbor can be found in Craig Nelson, *Pearl Harbor: From Infamy to Greatness* (New York: Simon and Schuster, 2016).

The reaction of Chileans to *Saludos Amigos* is documented in Jason Borge, *Latin*

American Writers and the Rise of Hollywood Cinema (Abingdon, UK: Routledge, 2008).

Background on Boettiger and the development of *Condorito* can be found in H. L'Hoeste and J. Poblete, eds., *Redrawing the Nation: National Identity in Latin/o American Comics* (Berlin: Springer, 2006).

"It isn't exactly like anything the Disney boys have ever done" comes from Bosley Crowther, "The Screen; *Saludos Amigos,* a Musical Fantasy Based on the South American Tour Made by Walt Disney, Arrives at the Globe," *New York Times,* February 13, 1943.

The FBI response to Pearl Harbor and the subsequent Executive Order 9066 are discussed in Matthew Dallek, *Defenseless Under the Night: The Roosevelt Years and the Origins of Homeland Security* (Oxford: Oxford University Press, 2016).

The history of Ub Iwerks's and Walt Disney's use of optical printers can be found in Jeff Foster, *The Green Screen Handbook: Real-World Production Techniques* (Indianapolis, IN: Wiley Publishing, 2010), and Leslie Iwerks and John Kenworthy, *The Hand Behind the Mouse* (Glendale, CA: Disney Editions, 2001).

The quotes "*Bambi* is gem-like in its

reflection of the color and movement of sylvan plant and animal life" and "glow and texture" are from *"Bambi," Variety,* December 31, 1941.

"The most terrifying curs since Cerberus" is from "The New Pictures," *Time,* August 24, 1942.

"The worst insult ever offered in any form to American sportsmen" is from Raymond J. Brown, "*Outdoor Life* Condemns Walt Disney's Film *Bambi* as an Insult to American Sportsmen," *Outdoor Life,* September 1942.

"His painted forest is hardly to be distinguished from the real forest shown by the Technicolor camera in *The Jungle Book*" and "Why have cartoons at all?" are from "*Bambi,* a Musical Cartoon in Technicolor Produced by Walt Disney from the Story by Felix Salten, at the Music Hall," *New York Times,* August 14, 1942.

Bambi lost one hundred thousand dollars in its first theatrical run, as reported in "101 Pix Gross in Millions," *Variety,* January 6, 1943.

Alexander P. de Seversky, *Victory Through Air Power* (New York: Simon and Schuster, 1943).

The role of *Victory Through Air Power* is discussed in John Baxter, *Disney During World War II: How the Walt Disney Studios*

Contributed to Victory in the War (Glendale, CA: Disney Editions, 2014).

Retta Scott's drawings for the gremlins and background on the project can be found in Didier Ghez, *They Drew As They Pleased,* vol. 2, *The Hidden Art of Disney's Musical Years: The 1940s — Part One* (San Francisco: Chronicle Books, 2016).

A history of Roald Dahl's association with Walt Disney is discussed in Rebecca Maksel, "The Roald Dahl Aviation Story That Disney Refused to Film," *Air and Space,* May 22, 2014.

Chester Carlson's history is told in David Owen, *Copies in Seconds: How a Lone Inventor and an Unknown Company Created the Biggest Communication Breakthrough Since Gutenberg — Chester Carlson and the Birth of the Xerox Machine* (New York: Simon and Schuster, 2004).

Chapter 9: Zip-a-Dee-Doo-Dah
Artwork from and background information on the health-related shorts can be found in Didier Ghez, *They Drew As They Pleased,* vol. 2, *The Hidden Art of Disney's Musical Years: The 1940s — Part One* (San Francisco: Chronicle Books, 2016).

The history of tampons is chronicled in

Elissa Stein and Susan Kim, *Flow: The Cultural Story of Menstruation* (New York: St. Martin's Press, 2009).

A history of Disney's adaptation of *Cinderella* is told in Charles Solomon, *A Wish Your Heart Makes: From the Grimm Brothers' Aschenputtel to Disney's "Cinderella"* (Glendale, CA: Disney Editions, 2015).

Joel Chandler Harris, *Uncle Remus: His Songs and His Sayings* (New York: D. Appleton, 1880).

Discussion of *Song of the South* can be found in Gordon B. Arnold, *Animation and the American Imagination: A Brief History* (Santa Barbara, CA: ABC-CLIO, 2017); Jim Korkis, *Who's Afraid of the "Song of the South"? And Other Forbidden Disney Stories* (Bloomington, IN: Theme Park Press, 2012); Jason Sperb, *Disney's Most Notorious Film: Race, Convergence, and the Hidden Histories of "Song of the South"* (Austin: University of Texas Press, 2012).

Maurice Rapf's involvement with *Song of the South* and *Cinderella,* including the quote "That's why I want someone like you . . . ," is detailed in Maurice Rapf, *Back Lot: Growing Up with the Movies* (Lanham, MD: Scarecrow Press, 1999).

Vern Caldwell's memo concerning *Song*

of the South is reproduced in Neal Gabler, *Walt Disney: The Triumph of the American Imagination* (New York: Random House, 2006).

Some of Mary Blair's concept art for *Song of the South* can be seen in John Canemaker, *The Art and Flair of Mary Blair: An Appreciation* (Glendale, CA: Disney Editions, 2014).

A history of Walter White's accomplishments with the NAACP can be found in Kenneth Robert Janken, *Walter White: Mr. NAACP* (Chapel Hill: University of North Carolina Press, 2006); Melvyn Stokes, *D. W. Griffith's "The Birth of a Nation": A History of the Most Controversial Motion Picture of All Time* (Oxford: Oxford University Press, 2008); Jennifer Latson, "The Surprising Story of Walter White and the NAACP," *Time,* July 1, 2015.

Celebrations occurring in the Port of Los Angeles were reported in *Yank, the Army Weekly,* June 1, 1945.

More information on the experience of African Americans returning from World War II can be found in Christopher S. Parker, *Fighting for Democracy: Black Veterans and the Struggle Against White Supremacy in the Postwar South* (Princeton, NJ: Princeton University Press, 2009), and Rawn James Jr., *The Double V: How Wars, Protest, and Harry Truman Desegregated America's Military* (New York: Bloomsbury Press, 2013).

Langston Hughes's poem "Beaumont to Detroit" is in Langston Hughes, *The Collected Poems of Langston Hughes* (New York: Alfred A. Knopf, 1994).

Alice Walker movingly described her reaction to *Song of the South* in a talk at the Atlanta Historical Society in 1981 that was later published as an essay in Alice Walker, *Living by the Word: Essays* (New York: Open Road Media, 2011).

Reaction and protest to *Song of the South* are documented in Sperb, *Disney's Most Notorious Film.*

"The dialect for Uncle Remus" quote is in "Committee for Unity Protests Disney's *Uncle Remus* Cartoon," *California Eagle,* August 24, 1944.

The quote about "lily-white propaganda" is in "Needed: A Negro Legion of Decency," *Ebony,* February 1947.

Bosley Crowther, "Spanking Disney," *New York Times,* December 8, 1946.

Bob Iger's comments about *Song of the South* were made at a shareholders' meeting in San Antonio, Texas, in 2010 as reported by Paul Bond, "Iger Keeps Options Open for ABC," *Adweek,* March 11, 2010.

Whoopi Goldberg's quotes concerning *Song of the South* were obtained from Kevin Polowy, "Whoopi Goldberg Wants Disney to Bring Back 'Song of the South' to Start Conversation About Controversial 1946 Film," Yahoo Entertainment, July 15, 2017.

Walt is quoted and the atmosphere is described in transcripts of story meetings for *Song of the South* from July 20, 1944; August 8, 1944; and August 24, 1944.

Mary Blair's work titled *Sick Call* can be seen in John Canemaker, *Magic Color Flair: The World of Mary Blair* (San Francisco: Walt Disney Family Foundation Press, 2014).

Frank Braxton's history is recounted in Tom Sito, *Drawing the Line: The Untold Story of the Animation Unions from Bosko to Bart Simpson* (Lexington: University Press of Kentucky, 2006).

Chapter 10: So This Is Love
The 1946 layoffs are described in Michael Barrier, *The Animated Man: A Life of Walt Disney* (Berkeley: University of California Press, 2007).

A history of American television can be

found in James Baughman, *Same Time, Same Station: Creating American Television, 1948–1961* (Baltimore: Johns Hopkins University Press, 2007). While the number of television sets in the United States rose to three million in 1950, this still represented a small proportion of total households, likely around 2 percent.

The percentage of women planning to continue work following 1945 was reported by the Department of Labor, Women's Bureau, *Women Workers in Ten War Production Areas and Their Postwar Employment Plans, Bulletin 209* (Washington, DC: U.S. Government Printing Office, 1946).

An overview of midcentury-modern design can be found in Dominic Bradbury, *Mid-Century Modern Complete* (New York: Abrams, 2014).

Mary Blair's concept art for *Cinderella* can be seen in John Canemaker, *The Art and Flair of Mary Blair: An Appreciation* (Glendale, CA: Disney Editions, 2014).

A discussion of Dior's influence on the fashion of *Cinderella* can be found in Kimberly Chrisman-Campbell, "*Cinderella:* The Ultimate (Postwar) Makeover Story," *The Atlantic,* March 9, 2015, and Emanuele Lugli, "Tear That Dress Off: *Cinderella*

(1950) and Disney's Critique of Postwar Fashion," *Bright Lights Film Journal,* February 15, 2018.

For Iwao Takamoto's history, see Iwao Takamoto with Michael Mallory, *Iwao Takamoto: My Life with a Thousand Characters* (Jackson: University Press of Mississippi, 2009), and Susan Stewart, "Iwao Takamoto, 81, the Animation Artist Who Created Scooby-Doo, Dies," *New York Times,* January 10, 2007.

Walt said, "This is it. We're in a bad way," according to "Recollections of Richard Huemer Oral History Transcript," University of California, Los Angeles, Oral History Program (1969).

Thelma Witmer's background is discussed in Mindy Johnson, *Ink & Paint: The Women of Walt Disney's Animation* (Glendale, CA: Disney Editions, 2017).

Marc Davis's history at the studio can be found in Disney Book Group, *Marc Davis: Walt Disney's Renaissance Man* (Glendale, CA: Disney Editions, 2014). Davis described his early employment and being mistaken for a woman in Rick West, "Walt Disney's Pirates of the Caribbean," *Theme Park Adventure Magazine,* 1998.

Chapter 11: In a World of My Own

For a history of *Alice in Wonderland* at the studio, see Mark Salisbury, *Walt Disney's "Alice in Wonderland": An Illustrated Journey Through Time* (Glendale, CA: Disney Editions, 2016).

Aldous Huxley's participation in *Alice in Wonderland* is discussed in Steffie Nelson, "Brave New LA: Aldous Huxley in Los Angeles," *Los Angeles Review of Books,* November 22, 2013.

Reviews of *Cinderella* in Mae Tinee, "Children Find *Cinderella* Is a Dream Film," *Chicago Tribune,* February 24, 1950, and *"Cinderella," Variety,* December 31, 1949.

Cinderella was the sixth-highest-grossing movie of 1950, as reported in "Top-Grosses of 1950," *Variety,* January 8, 1951.

Retta's illustrations for *Cinderella* can be found in Jane Werner Watson and Retta Scott Worcester, *Walt Disney's "Cinderella"* (New York: Golden Books, 1949).

The success of *Cinderella*'s RCA recordings is described in James Bohn, *Music in Disney's Animated Features: "Snow White and the Seven Dwarfs" to "The Jungle Book"* (Jackson: University Press of Mississippi, 2017).

Mary Blair's concept art for *Alice in Won-*

derland can be found in John Canemaker, *The Art and Flair of Mary Blair: An Appreciation* (Glendale, CA: Disney Editions, 2014).

Kathryn Beaumont explained what it was like to film live-action sequences for *Alice in Wonderland* and her excitement about the film's premiere in Susan King, "*Alice in Wonderland:* Sixty Years Later, Former Disney Child Star Looks Back," *Los Angeles Times,* February 18, 2011.

A history of the television series *Disneyland/The Wonderful World of Color* can be found in J. P. Telotte, *Disney TV* (Detroit: Wayne State University Press, 2004).

The development of Disneyland is chronicled in Neal Gabler, *Walt Disney: The Triumph of the American Imagination* (New York: Random House, 2006). Walt Disney's dissatisfaction with *Alice in Wonderland* and his description of the film as a "terrible disappointment" are recorded in Richard Schickel, *The Disney Version: The Life, Times, Art, and Commerce of Walt Disney* (New York: Simon and Schuster, 1985).

Chapter 12: You Can Fly!
Patterns of divorce rates after World War II are discussed in Jessica Weiss, *To Have and to Hold: Marriage, the Baby Boom, and Social*

Change (Chicago: University of Chicago Press, 2000).

Project Whirlwind is described in Kent C. Redmond and Thomas M. Smith, *From Whirlwind to MITRE: The R&D Story of the SAGE Air Defense Computer* (Cambridge, MA: MIT Press, 2000).

Peter Pan was first performed onstage in London in 1904 and later adapted into a book by the author; see J. M. Barrie, *Peter and Wendy* (London: Hodder and Stoughton, 1911). The character Peter Pan was introduced in J. M. Barrie, *The White Bird* (London: Hodder and Stoughton, 1902).

The quote from Dorothy Ann Blank about Tinker Bell being a "surefire sensation" is in Mindy Johnson, *Tinker Bell: An Evolution* (Glendale, CA: Disney Editions, 2013).

Walt's quote that "Bianca has been working" is from a story-meeting transcript from May 20, 1940.

Mary Blair's concept art for *Peter Pan* can be found in John Canemaker, *The Art and Flair of Mary Blair: An Appreciation* (Glendale, CA: Disney Editions, 2014).

Retta Scott's sketches for *On the Trail* can be seen in Didier Ghez, *They Drew As They Pleased,* vol. 2, *The Hidden Art of Disney's Musical Years: The 1940s — Part One* (San

Francisco: Chronicle Books, 2016). The book she used for reference is *Hopi Katcinas Drawn by Native Artists* (Washington, DC: U.S. Bureau of American Ethnology, 1903).

The stereotypes in *Peter Pan* are analyzed in Angel Aleiss, *Making the White Man's Indian: Native Americans and Hollywood Movies* (Westport, CT: Greenwood Publishing, 2005).

Description of racial caricatures in *Peter Pan* can be found in Sarah Laskow, "The Racist History of Peter Pan's Indian Tribe," *Smithsonian,* December 2, 2014.

Eyvind Earle's early experiences at the studio are recounted in Eyvind Earle, *Horizon Bound on a Bicycle* (Los Angeles: Earle and Bane, 1991).

Marc Davis's role in developing Tinker Bell is described in Johnson, *Tinker Bell.*

"But why does she have to be so naughty?" was said in a story meeting on May 20, 1940.

The role of Ginni Mack in posing for *Peter Pan* and Carmen Sanderson's use of Asian ox bile is explained in Mindy Johnson, *Ink & Paint: The Women of Walt Disney's Animation* (Glendale, CA: Disney Editions, 2017).

A portion of Emilio Bianchi's techniques

are documented in Kirsten Thompson, "Colourful Material Histories: The Disney Paint Formulae, the Paint Laboratory, and the Ink and Paint Department," *Animation Practice, Process, and Production* 4, no. 1 (2014).

The early vision for Disneyland was described in story-meeting transcripts and correspondence from 1948 to 1955. The name Disneyland was attached to the project in 1952 according to Neal Gabler, *Walt Disney: The Triumph of the American Imagination* (New York: Random House, 2006).

Chapter 13: Once Upon a Dream

A history of wide-screen cinema can be found in Harper Cossar, *Letter-boxed: The Evolution of Widescreen Cinema* (Lexington: University Press of Kentucky, 2011).

"Imagine Lauren Bacall on a couch" is documented in Charles Barr, "CinemaScope: Before and After," *Film Quarterly* 16, no. 4 (1963).

The colors of *Peter Pan* were praised before the critic called Tinker Bell a "vulgarity"; see Bosley Crowther, "The Screen: Disney's *Peter Pan* Bows," *New York Times,* February 12, 1953.

Thelma Witmer's backgrounds for *Peter*

Pan were specifically praised by Mae Tinee, "Disney's *Peter Pan* Tailored for the Modern Generation," *Chicago Tribune,* February 5, 1953.

Peter Pan's four-million-dollar production budget was reported in boxofficemojo.com and the-numbers.com.

The difference between Disney and United Productions of America styles is explained in Adam Abraham, *When Magoo Flew: The Rise and Fall of Animation Studio UPA* (Middleton, CT: Wesleyan University Press, 2012). Most artists at the Walt Disney Studios, including Mary Blair, were not interested in the UPA style.

"Produce better pictures at a lower cost" is in Neal Gabler, *Walt Disney: The Triumph of the American Imagination* (New York: Random House, 2006).

Historical analysis of the fairy-tale legend can be found in Tim Scholl, *Sleeping Beauty: A Legend in Progress* (New Haven, CT: Yale University Press, 2004).

A description of the 1946 premiere of *Sleeping Beauty* in London can be found in Jennifer Homans, *Apollo's Angels: A History of Ballet* (New York: Random House, 2010), and Anna Kisselgoff, "*Sleeping Beauty* — The Crown Jewel of Ballet," *New York*

Times, June 13, 1976.

The establishment of WED Enterprises and the creation of Disneyland are told in Martin Sklar, *Dream It! Do It! My Half-Century Creating Disney's Magic Kingdoms* (Glendale, CA: Disney Editions, 2013).

The ABC television series is described in J. P. Telotte, *Disney TV* (Detroit: Wayne State University Press, 2004).

Walt's letter to his sister, Ruth, was written on December 2, 1954, and is archived in the John Canemaker Animation Collection in the Fales Library and Special Collections at New York University's Elmer Holmes Bobst Library.

Biographical information for Alice Davis obtained from author interviews, interviews recorded by Maggie Richardson and John Canemaker, and correspondence used with their permission.

Eyvind Earle's influences for *Sleeping Beauty* and the quote starting "On top of all that" are from Eyvind Earle, *Horizon Bound on a Bicycle* (Los Angeles: Earle and Bane, 1991).

Quota systems for the number of required drawings a day are described in John Canemaker, *Walt Disney's Nine Old Men and the Art of Animation* (Glendale, CA: Disney Editions, 2001).

Biographical information for Elizabeth Case Zwicker obtained from interviews with her family, former coworkers, and previously conducted interviews with the artist made available by her estate.

Chapter 14: Dalmatian Plantation

Biographical information for Elizabeth Case Zwicker obtained from interviews with her family, former coworkers, and previously conducted interviews with the artist made available by her estate.

Introduction of Xerox machines in the studio is explained in Michael Barrier, *Hollywood Cartoons: American Animation in Its Golden Age* (Oxford: Oxford University Press, 2003). Changes necessitated by Xerox are described in Floyd Norman, *Animated Life: A Lifetime of Tips, Tricks, Techniques and Stories from a Disney Legend* (Abingdon, UK: Taylor and Francis, 2013).

Ub Iwerks's involvement in bringing Xerox to the studio is recounted in Karen Paik and Leslie Iwerks, *To Infinity and Beyond!: The Story of Pixar Animation* (San Francisco: Chronicle Books, 2007).

The expense and financial loss of *Sleeping Beauty* are reported in Barrier, *Hollywood*

Cartoons.

Roy Disney urging Walt to consider shutting down the animation department is reported in Haleigh Foutch, "How '101 Dalmatians' and a Xerox Machine Saved Disney Animation," *Business Insider,* February 13, 2015.

Sylvia Roemer and Sammie June Lanham are mentioned in Mindy Johnson, *Ink & Paint: The Women of Walt Disney's Animation* (Glendale, CA: Disney Editions, 2017).

Dodie Smith, *The Hundred and One Dalmatians* (London: Heinemann, 1956).

Biographical details concerning Dodie Smith obtained through correspondence between her and Walt Disney archived in the Fales Library and Special Collections at New York University's Elmer Holmes Bobst Library.

Information concerning Bill Peet can be found in Bill Peet, *Bill Peet: An Autobiography* (Boston: Houghton Mifflin, 1989).

Marc Davis's background and work at the studio are documented in Disney Book Group, *Marc Davis: Walt Disney's Renaissance Man* (Glendale, CA: Disney Editions, 2014).

Earle's quote "not Walt Disney" and Walt's quote "Ken's never going to be . . ." in John

Canemaker, *Before the Animation Begins: The Art and Lives of Disney Inspirational Sketch Artists* (New York: Hyperion, 1996).

Biographical information for Gyo Fujikawa obtained from interviews performed by John Canemaker on October 27, 1994, used by permission.

One of Gyo's early illustrated books was Gyo Fujikawa, *A Child's Garden of Verses* (New York: Grosset and Dunlap, 1957).

An appreciation of Gyo's role in expanding diversity in children's literature is presented in Elaine Woo, "Children's Author Dared to Depict Multicultural World," *Los Angeles Times,* December 13, 1998.

Homogeneity of children's libraries is described in Nancy Larrick, "The All-White World of Children's Books," *Saturday Review,* September 11, 1965.

The book containing controversial images of multicultural infants is Gyo Fujikawa, *Babies* (New York: Grosset and Dunlap, 1963).

Reviews of *One Hundred and One Dalmatians* cited are in "Cinema: Pupcorn," *Time,* February 17, 1961, and *"One Hundred and One Dalmatians," Variety,* December 31, 1960.

The economic impact of *One Hundred and*

One Dalmatians is recounted in Neal Gabler, *Walt Disney: The Triumph of the American Imagination* (New York: Random House, 2006).

Chapter 15: It's a Small World

Rolly Crump biographical information obtained from interviews conducted with John Canemaker and Maggie Richardson, and from his autobiography, Rolly Crump, *It's Kind of a Cute Story* (Baltimore: Bamboo Forest Publishing, 2012).

A brief history of audio-animatronics can be found in Matt Blitz, "The A1000 Is Disney's Advanced Animatronic Bringing *Star Wars: Galaxy's Edge* to Life," *Popular Mechanics,* February 28, 2019.

The difficulty Walt Disney faced in obtaining the rights to P. L. Travers's books is recounted in Valerie Lawson, *Mary Poppins, She Wrote: The Life of P. L. Travers* (New York: Simon and Schuster, 2013).

Petro Vlahos's history is remembered in Anita Gates, "Petro Vlahos, Special-Effects Innovator, Dies at 96," *New York Times,* February 19, 2013.

Sodium-vapor lights and green-screen technology are expanded on in Jeff Foster, *The Green Screen Handbook: Real-World Production Techniques* (Indianapolis, IN:

Wiley Publishing, 2010).

The quotes "Dear Walt, Don't be frightened by the size of the enclosed letter . . ." and "I beg, beg, BEG you to give her a more sympathetic, more Edwardian name . . ." are from a 1963 letter from P. L. Travers to Walt Disney housed in the Fales Library and Special Collections at New York University's Elmer Holmes Bobst Library. Background on Julie Andrews can be found in Richard Stirling, *Julie Andrews: An Intimate Biography* (New York: St. Martin's Press, 2008).

Julie Andrews recalls Walt saying, "We'll wait for you," in Andrea Mandell, "Julie Andrews and Emily Blunt were both new moms making *Mary Poppins,*" *USA Today,* November 30, 2018.

Footage from the premiere of *Mary Poppins* and the short film *The CalArts Story* can be seen in the bonus materials in the fiftieth-anniversary edition of *Mary Poppins,* released on December 10, 2013.

Walt is quoted as saying, "CalArts is the principal thing . . ." on the CalArts website, calarts.edu.

"Disney has gone all-out in his dreamworld rendition" appears in *"Mary Poppins,"* *Variety,* December 31, 1963.

Revenue from *Mary Poppins* and comparison to other features' obtained from box officemojo.com and the-numbers.com.

Protests that occurred during the 1964–1965 World's Fair are described in Joseph Tirella, *Tomorrow-Land: The 1964–65 World's Fair and the Transformation of America* (Lanham, MD: Rowman and Littlefield, 2013).

Sketchpad was first described in Ivan Sutherland, "Sketchpad: A Man-Machine Graphical Communication System" (PhD dissertation, MIT, 1963).

A history of Ivan Sutherland and Sketchpad can be found in Tom Sito, *Moving Innovation: A History of Computer Animation* (Cambridge, MA: MIT Press, 2013).

Walt's passing is recounted in Neal Gabler, *Walt Disney: The Triumph of the American Imagination* (New York: Random House, 2006).

Chapter 16: Up, Down, Touch the Ground

Biographical information for Heidi Guedel obtained from interviews with coworkers and her autobiography, Heidi Guedel, *Animatrix — A Female Animator: How Laughter Saved My Life* (Bloomington, IN: iUniverse, 2013).

Biographical information for Edwin

Catmull obtained from Edwin Catmull and Amy Wallace, *Creativity, Inc.: Overcoming the Unseen Forces That Stand in the Way of True Inspiration* (New York: Random House, 2014), and Karen Paik and Leslie Iwerks, *To Infinity and Beyond!: The Story of Pixar Animation* (San Francisco: Chronicle Books, 2007).

The 1972 video "A Computer Animated Hand" can be found online at https://boing boing.net/2015/08/05/watch-breakthrough -computer-an.html.

Women made up 28 percent of computer science graduates in the 1970s, according to data released by the U.S. Department of Education, National Center for Education Statistics, Higher Education General Information Survey (HEGIS), "Degrees and Other Formal Awards Conferred" surveys, 1970–71 through 1985–86.

The number of women enrolled at Cal-Arts in 1975 is reported in Deborah Vankin, "Animation: At CalArts and elsewhere, more women are entering the picture," *Los Angeles Times,* May 25, 2015.

The impact of the Equal Employment Opportunity Commission is discussed in Frank Dobbin, *Inventing Equal Opportunity* (Princeton, NJ: Princeton University Press, 2009).

Biographical information on Michael Giaimo was obtained from author interviews.

Chapter 17: Part of Your World

Brad Bird is quoted as saying "These bunglers tended to play . . ." in Keith Phipps, "Every Brad Bird Movie, Ranked," *Vulture,* June 14, 2018; the "incredibly exacting" quote is from Hugh Hart, "How Brad Bird Went from Disney Apprentice to Oscar-Winner and Architect of *Tomorrowland,*" *Fast Company,* May 29, 2015.

Biographical information for Edwin Catmull obtained from Edwin Catmull and Amy Wallace, *Creativity, Inc.: Overcoming the Unseen Forces That Stand in the Way of True Inspiration* (New York: Random House, 2014).

A history of special effects used in the Star Wars original trilogy can be found in Thomas Graham Smith, *Industrial Light and Magic: The Art of Special Effects* (New York: Ballantine Books, 1986), and J. W. Rinzler, *The Making of Star Wars* (New York: Ballantine Books, 2013).

Background on the formation of Pixar can be found in Catmull and Wallace, *Creativity, Inc.,* and Karen Paik and Leslie Iwerks, *To Infinity and Beyond!: The Story of Pixar Ani-*

mation (San Francisco: Chronicle Books, 2007).

Information on corporate restructuring and the role of Roy E. Disney and Michael Eisner can be found in James B. Stewart, *Disney War* (New York: Simon and Schuster, 2005).

A history of the Pixar Image Computer can be found in David A. Price, *The Pixar Touch* (New York: Alfred A. Knopf, 2008).

Biographical information for Ellen Woodbury obtained from author interviews.

Tina Price's history at the studio is documented in Mindy Johnson, *Ink & Paint: The Women of Walt Disney's Animation* (Glendale, CA: Disney Editions, 2017).

The role of Menken and Ashman at the studio, footage from Ashman's speech in the animation department, and the performer Divine's influence on the creation of the character Ursula is documented in bonus materials to *The Little Mermaid: Walt Disney Signature Collection* released by Walt Disney Home Entertainment on February 26, 2019. Further details on Divine's legendary role in cinema can be found in "Divine, Transvestite Film Actor, Found Dead in Hollywood at 42," *New York Times,* March 8, 1988, and Suzanne Loudermilk, "Divine, in Death as in Life," *Baltimore Sun,*

October 15, 2000.

Background on Ashman can be found in David J. Fox, "Looking at 'Beauty' as Tribute to Lyricist Who Gave 'Beast His Soul,' " *Los Angeles Times,* November 15, 1991, and Joanna Robinson, "Inside the Tragedy and Triumph of Disney Genius Howard Ashman," *Vanity Fair,* April 20, 2018.

Background on Brenda Chapman obtained from Nicole Sperling, "When the Glass Ceiling Crashed on Brenda Chapman," *Los Angeles Times,* May 25, 2011; Adam Vary, "*Brave* Director Brenda Chapman Breaks Silence on Being Taken Off Film," *Entertainment Weekly,* August 15, 2012; Seth Abramovitch, "Female Director of Pixar's *Brave* on Being Replaced by a Man: 'It Was Devastating,' " *Hollywood Reporter,* August 15, 2012; and author interviews.

Jeffrey Katzenberg is quoted as calling *The Little Mermaid* a "girl's film," in bonus materials to *The Little Mermaid: Walt Disney Signature Collection.*

Ursula was called a "visual feast" in the review *"The Little Mermaid," Variety,* December 31, 1989.

Ebert called Ariel's character "fully realized" in his review; see Roger Ebert, *"The*

Little Mermaid," *Chicago Sun-Times,* November 17, 1989.

Box-office performance for *The Little Mermaid* obtained from box officemojo.com and the-numbers.com.

Information on Linda Woolverton obtained from Eliza Berman, "How *Beauty and the Beast*'s Screenwriter Shaped Disney's First Feminist Princess," *Time,* May 23, 2016; Rebecca Keegan, "First Belle, Now Alice: How Screenwriter and Head-banger Linda Woolverton Is Remaking Disney Heroines for a Feminist Age," *Los Angeles Times,* May 29, 2016; Seth Abramovitch, "Original *Lion King* Screenwriter Apprehensive of Remake: 'I Wasn't Thrilled with *Beauty and the Beast,*' " *Hollywood Reporter,* December 3, 2018; and author interviews.

Roy E. Disney is quoted as calling Howard Ashman "another Walt" in bonus materials to *The Little Mermaid: Walt Disney Signature Collection.*

Perspective on the role of AIDS in shaping lyrics in *Beauty and the Beast* can be found in Joanna Robinson, "The Touching Tribute Behind Disney's First Openly Gay Character," *Vanity Fair,* March 1, 2017.

The stigma that individuals living with

HIV in the 1980s experienced is recalled in Natasha Geiling, "The Confusing and At-Times Counterproductive 1980s Response to the AIDS Epidemic," *Smithsonian,* December 4, 2013.

Janet Maslin described Ashman as "an outstandingly nimble lyricist" in her review "Disney's *Beauty and the Beast* Updated in Form and Content," *New York Times,* November 13, 1991.

The number of AIDS-related deaths in the United States in 1991 was 29,850, as reported by the CDC in "Mortality Attributable to HIV Infection/AIDS Among Persons Aged 25–44 Years — United States, 1990, 1991," *MMWR Weekly,* July 2, 1993.

Controversy over lyrics in *Aladdin* was reported in David J. Fox, "Disney Will Alter Song in *Aladdin,*" *Los Angeles Times,* July 10, 1993.

Dialogue for female characters obtained from Karen Eisenhauer, "A Quantitative Analysis of Directives in Disney Princess Films" (master's thesis, North Carolina University, 2017); Jeff Guo, "Researchers Have Found a Major Problem with *The Little Mermaid* and Other Disney Movies," *Washington Post,* January 25, 2016; and Oliver Gettell, "Here's a Gender Breakdown of Dialogue in 30 Disney Movies," *Entertain-*

ment *Weekly,* April 7, 2016.

Chapter 18: I'll Make a Man Out of You

Biographical information for Rita Hsiao obtained from author interview.

Robert San Souci's consulting role in *Mulan* is described in Jeff Kurtti, *The Art of "Mulan"* (Glendale, CA: Disney Editions, 1998).

Early script challenges during the development of *Mulan* are discussed in the bonus materials to *Mulan: Special Edition,* released by Walt Disney Home Entertainment on October 26, 2004.

A few examples of criticism of Jasmine in *Aladdin* can be found in Roger Ebert, *"Aladdin," Chicago Sun-Times,* November 25, 1992, and Janet Maslin, "Disney Puts Its Magic Touch on *Aladdin," New York Times,* November 11, 1992.

The development of *Pocahontas* at the studio is recalled in Patrick Rogers, "A True Legend," *People,* July 10, 1995; Nicole Peradotto, "Indian Summer: How *Pocahontas* Creators Drew on Life and Legend," *Buffalo News,* June 25, 1995; and Michael Mallory, "Pocahontas and the Mouse's Gong Show," *Animation,* February 23, 2012.

The main character of Pocahontas was

criticized as "generic" in Owen Gleiberman, *"Pocahontas," Entertainment Weekly,* June 16, 1995. The character was called "Poca-Barbie" in Peter Travers, *"Pocahontas," Rolling Stone,* June 23, 1995.

A statement criticizing *Pocahontas* was released by the Powhatan Renape Nation on July 1, 1996, and can be viewed on the Manataka Indian Council website: https://www.manataka.org/page8.html.

Further history of Pocahontas can be found in Camilla Townsend, *Pocahontas and the Powhatan Dilemma: The American Portraits Series* (New York: Farrar, Straus, and Giroux, 2005).

The origin of DreamWorks Animation is described in Scott Mendelson, "15 Years of DreamWorks Animation and Its Complicated Legacy," *Forbes,* October 2, 2013. Biographical information for Edwin Catmull obtained from Edwin Catmull and Amy Wallace, *Creativity, Inc.: Overcoming the Unseen Forces That Stand in the Way of True Inspiration* (New York: Random House, 2014).

CAPS at the studio and the making of *Toy Story* are discussed in Chris Pallant, *Demystifying Disney: A History of Disney Feature Animation* (London: A and C Black, 2011), and Karen Paik and Leslie Iwerks, *To Infinity and Beyond!: The Story of Pixar Animation* (San Francisco: Chronicle Books, 2007).

RenderMan's utility is explained in Anthony A. Apodaca, Larry Gritz, and Ronen Barzel, *Advanced RenderMan: Creating CGI for Motion Pictures* (Burlington, MA: Morgan Kaufmann, 2000).

Production of *Toy Story* is described in Burr Snider, "The *Toy Story* Story," *Wired,* December 1, 1995.

It took Lasseter five days to animate twelve and a half seconds, according to David A. Price, *The Pixar Touch* (New York: Alfred A. Knopf, 2008).

John Lasseter's difficulties in creating the *Luxo Jr.* short are described in Brent Schlender, "Pixar's Magic Man," *Fortune,* May 17, 2006.

The quote beginning "Its lure is the image of girls" is in Nadya Labi, "Girl Power," *Time,* June 24, 2001.

Biographical information on Brenda Chapman obtained from author interviews. The quote beginning "At the start of my career" is from a panel organized by the Geena Davis Institute on Gender in Media on October 12, 2006.

The quote beginning "Sometimes women express an idea" is from Brenda Chapman,

"Stand Up for Yourself, and Mentor Others," *New York Times,* August 14, 2012.

The "We finally get a black princess" quote is from Brooks Barnes, "Her Prince Has Come. Critics, Too," *New York Times,* May 29, 2009.

Production budgets and profits obtained from boxofficemojo.com and the-numbers.com.

Brave was predicted to be a "pretty standard princess movie" in Ray Subers, "Forecast: Pixar Aims for 13th-Straight First Place Debut with *Brave,*" boxofficemojo.com, June 21, 2012.

Brenda Chapman thanked her daughter at the Academy Awards according to Dave McNary, "Oscars: *Brave* Wins Tight Animation Race," *Variety,* February 24, 2013.

Chapter 19: For the First Time in Forever

Biographical information for Jennifer Lee obtained from John August and Craig Mazin, "*Frozen* with Jennifer Lee," *Scriptnotes,* iTunes app, January 28, 2014; Jill Stewart, "Jennifer Lee: Disney's New Animation Queen," *L.A. Weekly,* May 15, 2013; Sean Flynn, "Is It Her Time to Shine?," *Newport Daily News,* February 17, 2014; Michael Cousineau, "UNH Degree Played a Part in Oscar-Winning Movie,"

New Hampshire Union Leader, March 29, 2014; Will Payne, "Revealed, the Real-Life *Frozen* Sisters and the Act of Selfless Love That Inspired Hit Film," *Daily Mail,* April 7, 2014; Karen Schwartz, "The New Guard: Jennifer Lee," *Marie Claire,* October 21, 2014; and James Hibberd, "*Frozen* Original Ending Revealed for First Time," *Entertainment Weekly,* March 29, 2017, as well as author interviews.

Development of "The Snow Queen" is described in Charles Solomon, *The Art of "Frozen"* (San Francisco: Chronicle Books, 2015).

The sister summit for *Frozen* is described in Dorian Lynskey, "*Frozen*-Mania: How Elsa, Anna and Olaf Conquered the World," *Guardian,* May 13, 2014, and Kirsten Acuna, "One Huge Change in the *Frozen* Storyline Helped Make It a Billion-Dollar Movie," *Business Insider,* September 3, 2014.

Biographical information on Michael Giaimo was obtained from personal interviews conducted by the author.

The use of Material Point Method to create snow and ice is explained in Zhen Chen et al., "A Particle-Based Multiscale Simulation Procedure Within the MPM Framework," *Computational Particle Mechanics* 1, no. 2 (2014).

Biographical information for Fawn Veerasunthorn obtained from Todd Ruiz, "From Chonburi to the Red Carpet, Academy Award Winner Chased Her Dream," Coconuts.co, March 14, 2014; Bobby Chiu, "Developing Style," *ChiuStream,* Podcast Republic, February 2, 2017, as well as author interviews.

"Generic nature of the main characters" is from Scott Foundas, *"Frozen," Variety,* November 3, 2013.

A lack of "memorable tunes" is from Elizabeth Weitzman, *"Frozen,* Movie Review," *New York Daily News,* November 26, 2013.

"Musically thin" is from Dan Kois, *"Frozen," Slate,* November 26, 2013.

Frozen's financial success is reported in Maane Khatchatourian, "Box Office: *Frozen* Crosses $1 Billion Worldwide," *Variety,* March 3, 2014.

The "subtly weaves in racial profiling" quote is from Brian Truitt, *"Zootopia* Animal World Reflects Human Issues," *USA Today,* March 3, 2016.

"Marks a return to the heights of the Disney Renaissance" is from Peter Debruge, "Film Review: *Moana,* " *Variety,* November 7, 2016.

A discussion of *Moana*'s history can be

found in Doug Herman, "How the Story of *Moana* and Maui Holds Up Against Cultural Truths," *Smithsonian,* December 2, 2016.

Background on the #MeToo movement can be found in Christen A. Johnson and K. T. Hawbaker, "#MeToo: A Timeline of Events," *Chicago Tribune,* March 7, 2019.

Lasseter acknowledged that his actions were "unquestionably wrong" and apologized for his behavior as reported in Anthony D'Alassandro, "John Lasseter Expresses Deep Sorrow and Shame About Past Actions at Emotional Skydance Animation Town Hall," *Deadline,* January 19, 2019.

Biographical information for Pete Docter obtained from author interviews.

Pete Docter and Jennifer Lee taking over Lasseter's position, as reported in Brooks Barnes, "*Frozen* and *Inside Out* Directors to Succeed Lasseter at Disney and Pixar," *New York Times,* June 19, 2018.

Percentage of women studying animation versus those working in the field was reported in Emilio Mayorga, "Annecy: Women in Animation Present Gender Disparity Data," *Variety,* June 17, 2015.

Current statistics on female directors, writers, and on-screen portrayal obtained from Martha M. Lauzen, "It's a Man's (Celluloid) World: Portrayals of Female Characters in the 100 Top Films of 2017," Report from Center for the Study of Women in Television and Film at San Diego State University, 2018; and Stacy L. Smith et al., "Inequality in 1,100 Popular Films: Examining Portrayals of Gender, Race/Ethnicity, LGBT and Disability from 2007 to 2017," Report of the USC Annenberg Inclusion Initiative, 2018.

Information about the Bechdel test obtained from Alison Bechdel, *Fun Home: A Family Tragicomic* (Boston: Houghton Mifflin Harcourt, 2007).

Only 53 percent of films pass the Bechdel test was reported in Walt Hickey, "The Dollars-and-Cents Case Against Hollywood's Exclusion of Women," FiveThirtyEight.com, April 1, 2014.

Epilogue: Happily Ever After
Mary Blair's original murals at Disneyland can be viewed at https://www.yesterland.com/maryblair.html.

ABOUT THE AUTHOR

Nathalia Holt, PhD, is the *New York Times* bestselling author of *Rise of the Rocket Girls: The Women Who Propelled Us, from Missiles to the Moon to Mars* and *Cured: The People Who Defeated HIV.* Her writing has appeared in numerous publications including the *New York Times,* the *Los Angeles Times, The Atlantic, Slate, Popular Science,* and *Time.* She is a fellow at the Ragon Institute of MGH, MIT, and Harvard University. She lives with her husband and their two daughters in Pacific Grove, California.

The employees of Thorndike Press hope you have enjoyed this Large Print book. All our Thorndike, Wheeler, and Kennebec Large Print titles are designed for easy reading, and all our books are made to last. Other Thorndike Press Large Print books are available at your library, through selected bookstores, or directly from us.

For information about titles, please call:
(800) 223-1244

or visit our website at:
gale.com/thorndike

To share your comments, please write:
Publisher
Thorndike Press
10 Water St., Suite 310
Waterville, ME 04901